DATE DUE

THE FEMALE EXPERIENCE
IN EIGHTEENTH- AND
NINETEENTH-CENTURY AMERICA

GARLAND REFERENCE LIBRARY
OF SOCIAL SCIENCE
(VOL. 35)

The Female Experience in Twentieth-Century America: A Guide to the History of American Women by Jill K. Conway is planned for publication in 1983 or 1984. This publication will supplement the present volume with themes that arise in, or are especially pertinent to, the twentieth century.

THE FEMALE EXPERIENCE IN EIGHTEENTH- AND NINETEENTH-CENTURY AMERICA
A Guide to the History of American Women

Jill K. Conway
with the assistance of
Linda Kealey and Janet E. Schulte

GARLAND PUBLISHING, INC. • NEW YORK & LONDON
1982

Library of Congress Cataloging in Publication Data

Conway, Jill K., 1934–
    The female experience in eighteenth-
and nineteenth-century America.

    (Garland reference library of the social science ;
v. 35)
    Includes bibliographies and index.
    1. Women—United States—History—Bibliography.
I. Kealey, Linda, 1947–   II. Schulte, Janet E., 1958–
III. Title. IV. Series.
Z7961.C64 1982 [HQ1410]   016.3054'0973   82-48041
ISBN 0-8240-9936-2

Printed on acid-free, 250-year-life paper
Manufactured in the United States of America

CONTENTS

SECTION II: INDUSTRIALIZATION, WOMEN'S WORK,
AND THE TRANSFORMATION OF THE
HOUSEHOLD, 1810–1910

SECTION III: CULTURAL ROLES OF MIDDLE-CLASS
WOMEN IN INDUSTRIALIZING AMERICA:
SCHOOLS, LITERACY, AND WOMEN'S
INTELLECTUAL WORK 81

INTRODUCTION

This is a bibliography and an interpretive guide to sources on the history of women in America and an extended commentary about the theories and assumptions which have shaped secondary writing on that history. Its purpose is to speed the work of the beginning researcher and to raise theoretical questions which must be addressed if that history is to be more than episodic and antiquarian in nature, questions which must be answered if the narrative is to fit seamlessly into the general canvas of American history.

The bibliography's scope and emphasis are inevitably shaped by the nature of the printed sources which I and scores of patient students have uncovered over the last decade and by the general themes which I think relevant to an examination of the place of women in American culture. This makes the excursion from colonial times to the present something of a fresh voyage through little-charted seas. Travelers who expect to view the towering cliffs of debate on the social character of the Revolution, sweep through the cataracts of prose on the nature of participation in Jacksonian politics, or cast anchor in the ample harbor of dispute about the sources of Progressivism will be disappointed, for these familiar lineaments of American history will lie in the background of the view, discernible but distant. The purpose of the voyage will be to discover the major configurations of the familiar landscape and the nature of the currents of change which shaped women's experience.

Thus a single section takes us from the high point of what Perry Miller called provincial culture to the early national period. Its focus is both the stated and unstated assumptions about female sexuality, marriage, and the family that took shape in the colonial period and were articulated in the new republican culture. It provides a guide to the materials that must be examined if we are to ask what "the pursuit of happiness" meant with respect to man's generative self, rather than his significance as an economic or political animal.

Section II surveys the materials in print and the secondary writing about the impact of industrialization on women's work and the domestic setting which supported their generative functions. These are taken to be the material base on which rested the cultural and religious functions examined in Sections III and IV. Section V surveys women's relationships to power and political institutions from the American Revolution through the completion of the suffrage battle and the politics of the 1920s. It attempts to provide the sources which explain both suffrage and anti-suffrage political activity in consistent terms.

Section VI brings the first volume to a conclusion. It surveys the concerns with female health, sexuality, and sociobiological function that played such a critical role in defining the social territory and identity accorded the educated woman by the early twentieth century. The definition of this territory then allows the student to narrow the focus of attention and to examine in detail the relationship between social territory, role, and consciousness for the women who made up the emerging new service professions. *The Female Experience in Twentieth-Century America: A Guide to the History of American Women* will open with this narrowed focus which in Section VII is directed toward the rich body of primary sources available to document the history of women's lives during the Progressive era. The autobiographical material drawn from the lives of women professionals in this period is so rich that it will clearly reward the attention of future prosopographers and psychohistorians.

Sections VIII and IX lead the reader through the themes of war and postwar reaction as they affect American women and raise questions about the concept of total mobilization and the impact of modern warfare on women. Section X returns to the theme of sociobiology and indicates the literature of the social and natural sciences which laid the groundwork that shaped perception of women and the family in the learned culture of postindustrial America. Section XI examines the same themes in relation to the arrival of mass culture and the mass media. The definition of the place accorded women and the sources which indicate women's perception of their place in mass culture are a logical point of conclusion for the survey since the subsequent history of twentieth-century feminism, the recurrent debates concerning sociobiology, and the shifting patterns of sexual mores are all perturbations within that culture, the lineaments of which are firmly established by the 1930's.

The bibliographical listings began as a guide to graduate students to open up for them the richness and variety of the sources available for studying the history of women and their place in the general fabric of American society. The guide took on a larger scope as I and other researchers struggled with the theoretical questions raised by the documents. If we were not to come up with some Whig interpretation of a century of progress leading to our own time, we needed to know why the antisuffragists cherished "influence" and feared "power," and why their views were persuasive for so long. What was the function of "influence" in a polity with clearly divided social territories which were assumed to be vital for the stability of the political system? What function do separate social territories perform in stratified societies that must maintain an illusion of equality? These are the kinds of questions this guide should stimulate. They take the reader into territory unfamiliar to most American historians and political scientists, but those eager to scale the cliffs and view the landscape will view the familiar Jacksonian or Progressive terrain from a new and enlightening perspective.

THE HISTORY OF AMERICAN WOMEN

Writing about the history of American women suffers from the lack of a general theory of significant variables or causes of change. This deficiency leads to a second conceptual problem which is the lack of a clear organizing principle for periodization, the essential for all historical narratives. We thus find general writing of two kinds. One variety draws on some presently perceived variable affecting women's lives such as access to work, traces that variable to the colonial period, and thereby produces a narrative in which all events are explained consistently as leading up to the present. This we might call a form of Whiggery expressed in the history of gender. The second variety is based on the acceptance of the established categories of periodization in the writing of American history. The authors of this kind of narrative ask questions such as "What happened to women during the Progressive era?" or "How did urbanization affect women?" or "To what extent did women participate in the Revolutionary ideology?" They then analyze the available evidence to produce answers to such questions. Both varieties of writing beg the question of whether or not there are independent variables operating to shape women's experience, variables that conceivably have a different duration than those factors which have defined our concept of periods or epochs in American history. The lack of a general overall scheme of events by which we can orient ourselves as to the direction of change has prevented much incremental growth in knowledge. Thus the historian of the suffrage movement and the historian of the antisuffrage movement has tended to work each in his own vineyard without seeing, for instance, the need to explain the strength and effectiveness of the antisuffrage movement in terms consistent with explanations introduced for the rise of the suffrage agitation. The treatment of the history of the 1920s is another excellent example of this problem. Much has been written about the changes in manners and mores with the appearance of the flapper, but no one has asked whether a shift in the focus of erotic attention from the bosom to the legs means much in terms of any trend or change in the way women experienced their sexuality.

The governing assumptions of writing about the history of women during the colonial period have been that the disruption of the ratio of females to males in the seventeenth-century migration led to an improvement in women's status as did the Puritan notion of marriage with its open recognition of both female and male sexual appetites. The stress on literacy for all church members is said to have aided the rise of women's status since women became literate for this purpose. Less has been written about the status of women in the southern colonies, though again the disruption in the ratio of males to females in the migration is said to have improved the position of women. Thereafter women's status is assumed to have been rising for unstated reasons until the Revolutionary period. This gender group, like the proverbial middle class during modernization, is assumed to have been permanently improving its position. Little attention has been paid to the anomalies which do not fit this picture. Women in Puritan societies were forbidden to publish—surely a bar to communication or to the life of the mind, whatever the rise in women's literacy meant. Women reached the southern colonies mainly as indentured servants, persons of unfree status whose services were auctioned off to the highest bidder. This fact along with the development of chattel slavery is more significant than the relative scarcity of white women in shaping their social position.

We know little about women's position in the emerging cities of the increasingly secularized provincial society of the eighteenth century. Courtship patterns were changing, not necessarily an indication of a change in the status of women, unless we can determine what changed in the union that was the outcome of the courtship. Women, especially widows, participated in the mercantile life of the growing cities. Like their European counterparts they inherited trades from spouses, whether as printers and publishers of newspapers, as silversmiths, or as traders in softgoods. There were more and older spinsters in the population as arable land became scarcer in New England. The dame school and the finishing school for young ladies appeared in this period as a new form of occupation for respectable women, and as we approach the 1780s and '90s paid work in the sailcloth and textile industries began to draw on the pool of female labor. We know what women read from the *Ladies Miscellanies* printed for their edification, from the religious tracts, and the conduct books that circulated. We know a little about the practice of midwifery and folk medicine from the almanacs available, but in general these sources have not been much mined. Historical enquiry has tended to be of two kinds. Late nineteenth-century writers have written collections of lives of colonial dames and worthies and recent writers have made quick forays into the period to document a current concern. Thus the work of historical demographers now tells us a great deal about fertility rates and family size in colonial New England. Historians outraged by women's exclusion from medical education have studied the decline of midwifery and the rise of male medical practitioners along with the use of surgical forceps. There are isolated versions of other historical genres which describe women's life and work in colonial times, but these tell us little about trends or directions of change.

Accounts of female participation in the political and military actions of the Revolutionary period tend also to be episodic. They focus on standard types of protest such as women's collective action against grain and bread profiteers, on the social life surrounding the military headquarters of royal and patriot forces, and on the isolated examples of women who served as scouts or dressed as men and gave military service. Political historians have noted in passing the disenfranchisement of women during the drafting and adoption of the various state constitutions, but little attention has been given to women's political life apart from their participation in the crowd activities of urban centers. The long debates about the social consequences of the Revolution and the significance of the movement from Confederation to Constitution pay no attention to the direction of change as it affected women except to assume for no good reason that the abandonment of hereditary ranks and primogeniture must have been to their benefit.

As we move into the interpretation of the early national period and of the rise of Jacksonian democracy, we see that the attention of historians has been focused on three main themes: the relationship of genteel culture and the ideal of true womanhood to religious and social-reform movements, the development of a female working class, and the rise of women's writing as a potent force in American popular culture. Some general attempts to interpret the interaction of these three variables have raised the question of whether there was emerging a separate sphere of competence for women in American society and whether this was a positive or negative force in the developing national culture. Much of this discussion has revolved around the question of whether women could experience a rise in status within a small but clearly defined domestic sphere of competence, or whether the cult of true womanhood was an ideology developed to mask their increasing subordination within a society in which reality was defined by capitalist economics. While much attention has been paid to these issues, less has been devoted to the radical communities of the early national and Jacksonian periods that attempted to blend male and female spheres of competence and to question capitalist economics. Indeed, the female religious experience has received little attention except where it gave rise to abolitionism although we see in these years the rise of communities of women religious and the origins of the world's most significant female-led religion, Christian Science.

Accounts of women's participaton in the national life during the Civil War era tend to be concerned with one aspect or another of voluntarism. Thus the emergence of the Red Cross, the beginnings of the nursing profession, the fundraising associated with the work of the United States Sanitary Commission, the beginnings of the organized charitable impulse, and the participation of New England women teachers in the schools established by the Freedmen's Aid Society have all been the subject of detailed studies, though none has been undertaken in terms which would enable the linking of these activities to the social forces treated in the analysis of the antislavery impulse. The existence of some notable women diarists in both North and South has also contributed significantly to the historical record. Although much time has now been given to the analysis of women's access to higher education, the social forces that led to the foundation of women's colleges in the South and the middle states in the 1860s have not been studied, nor do we have any comparative analysis of them in relation to those operating in the Gilded Age in the North. With respect to the rise of women's voluntarism, which is the outstand- ing theme of the period, we have no analysis of its relationship to the strong tradition of male voluntary associations, which was so striking to Tocqueville when he wrote about the American de- mocracy of the 1820s and '30s.

Narratives of the Gilded Age tend to deal briefly with the suffragists' reactions to their failure to win the vote along with the freed male slave and to concentrate on the politics of the spoils system and the depredations of the robber barons. An occasional biography attests to the development of female heroines of con- spicuous consumption as a social type in the Gilded Age, but we have seen no systematic treatment of such women's relationship to patronage in the fine and decorative arts, their roles as collec- tors, and their influence in shaping American taste. Alongside the belief in technology and progress that men of financial and industrial talent took to justify the accumulation of great fortunes went a commitment to education. It is notable that before there was a Stanford or a University of Chicago, there was a series of Northern women's colleges founded on the profits of railroads, breweries, and land speculation. There is as yet no historical work which makes clear why these were the earliest objects of educa- tional philanthropy for industrial wealth or what relationships such institutional developments bore to the earlier religious foun- dations of the 1830s and '40s, the female seminaries which would become collegiate institutions.

Women are seen as participants in the search for order of the Progressive era, as founders of settlements, pioneers in the new female professions, interpreters of technology to the housewife, leaders in the attempt to organize the consumer, propagandists for mental hygiene, protectors of immigrants, and leaders in the use of the big government to regulate society in the interests of women, children, and the family. Historians have differed over whether the enlarged participation of women in the Progressive era represented an enlargement of their separate sphere of com- petence or a genuine search for equality. There are differences of interpretation as to the motives and tactics that finally won the suffrage amendment, but little attention has been paid to the motives, tactics, and social base of the powerful and extraordinarily successful antisuffrage movement.

So far as the intellectual life of women is concerned there is now a considerable body of biographical writing treating the ideas and influence of the leading women reformers of the Progressive era. This biographical writing touches briefly on the women's college as an intellectual milieu but generally focuses on failures of sexual adjustment and neurosis as sources of intellectual energy. The current generation of writers on the history of American education has begun to study the intellectual life of the women's colleges on its own terms and to delineate what the feminine style of scholarly life was before the integrity of college intellectual environments was undermined by male-led national professional associations. Women radicals have likewise received the attention of biographers, though no theory of the process by which women are radicalized has emerged from such narratives. Thus, while we have clear accounts of women's participation in the trades-union movement, the anarchist movement, the socialist movement, and of their leadership in the birth-control movement, we have no general understanding of the social process which produces an Emma Goldman or a Mother Jones. It is assumed either that the determinants of female consciousness are identical with those of men or that sexuality and sexual adjustment alone determine what women think and the feelings of which they are conscious.*

When we arrive at the study of the impact of the First World War and the cultural changes which followed it in the decade of the 1920s, we find an embarrassment of riches in sources and a confusing set of contradictory interpretations of the direction of change as it related to women and their place in the social structure. In the economic sphere the war opened up new opportunities for women, but only in the service areas of the economy,

---

*The woman scientist and the woman social scientist have received relatively little attention though research is now under way on a collective biography of successive generations of women scientists in America, so that the process by which their inquiries were moved from the center to the margins of their fields should shortly be documented.

since the black migration north supplied the labor pool for heavy industry. Thus there was an increased opportunity for women to work accompanied by continuity in the sense that a pattern of occupational segregation was continued and service activities were seen as consistent with domestic functions. Historians of the war and the twenties have tended to note the increased female participation in the work force and the change in social mores which accepted work outside the home for the married woman, thereby emphasizing change rather than continuity. Social and cultural change has been given undue prominence by the attention given to the changed manners of the small proportion of the female age cohort who attended college in the twenties. Although these changes have been taken to imply radical changes of attitude concerning sexuality and female identity, intellectual historians at the same time note the debunking of feminism, the quick acceptance of Freudian ideas, and the popular concern with "normality" and sexual adjustment. These trends have not been linked together in any complex model of the interacting social, economic, and intellectual trends of the period, though such a model is obviously essential if we are to understand the history of women in this critical era of twentieth-century America. Historians of politics and political participation have noted with puzzlement that women's political participation seems to have declined after the achievement of the suffrage and that membership in women's reform organizations such as the Consumer's League fell off during the twenties. This change is hard to fit with the development of sexual radicalism and the attempt to assert women's right to sexual fulfillment that was part of the avant-garde culture of literary and artistic circles. Sexual and economic exploitation were linked together in radical debates, but in the developing mass media other continuities may be found. Popular-opinion surveys found that the public did not like the sound of women's voices discussing or reporting on current events, politics, or nondomestic subjects, and silent films treated the lives of poor girls who triumphed through virtue linked to sexual power. These were themes which reached back to the cult of true womanhood so that historians who concentrated attention on radical circles or the college generation missed the significance of the declining political participation,

the denigration of women who achieved alone, and the strength
of the conservatism in the emerging mass culture.

How then might we construct a general theory of significant
variables which interact to shape the lives of women? If we could
do this, what chronology would it suggest for significant periods
or eras in the history of women in America? What documents and
secondary sources are available to the individual who wants to
understand any of those particular periods and fit them into a
larger chronology of events in the total society? In any study of
women's lives we must start with the basic information about
generativity for this, except for the very recent past, has shaped
women's lives. Thus one baseline for such a study must be
demography. Information about rates of fertility, age at marriage,
percentages of an age cohort never married, ratios of males to
females in the population will give us clear indicators about
change and continuity in women's experience. If we look at the
twenties, for instance, we discover that in this era the age at
marriage was declining for women and that the proportion of the
cohort of marriageable age actually married was the highest in the
history accessible to us from recorded data. Knowing this, we
have some perspective from which to view the radical critique of
marriage. Once we have our demographic data, we must move on
to the cultural factors which shape the way generativity is perceived, the cluster of ideas and beliefs which determine what may
be thought and felt at any given period about this baseline of the
female experience. The key indicators of this cultural matrix are
medical writings on the ailments of the female and conduct books
that set our social norms and explain why they must be upheld.
They thus tell us about socially sanctioned sexuality and about
illicit sex. Students of such materials will be startled to discover
the extent of variation over time of ideas about the nature of
female sexual appetites. Seventeenth-century writers thought of
the female appetites as stronger than the male and virtually
insatiable. By the nineteenth century that male appetite had
become the stronger, and genteel females were thought to experience no sexual sensations except those associated with maternity.
A change so remarkable prompts us to speculate whether social
systems function by other forms of expropriation beside that of
the product of man's labor under capitalism. Were there such
changes in female consciousness that these feelings were gen-

uinely repressed for the nineteenth-century woman? Even if this was not the case, why was it necessary to hold such beliefs? What function did they serve for the polity viewed not merely as the formal institutions of power and subordination but the informal and unstated ones as well?

Once we have some concept of the way in which sexuality was experienced, we must turn to the institution within which generativity was controlled and supported, the family. The nature of the marriage union, the pattern of child-rearing practices, and the relations between family members together constitute the emotional climate of the household whether or not it contains other members who are not biological kin. In pre-industrial societies the household economy and the division of labor within it must be understood. Thus historians have tended to see women's access to the labor market associated with industrialization as a significant factor producing a rise in status. We can only tell whether that is the case if we can judge what proportion of the household's goods and services she provided through her work in the domestic economy and what proportion she could provide for through her wages for work outside the home. Letters, advertisements, account books, diaries, wills, court records, and travel accounts provide sources which document this economic baseline of our model.

Having established our generative and economic baselines, we must then turn to the relationships which hold between the family and society's institutions of public authority, both secular and sacred. We must know the law that regulates the family in the interests of the state and the religious rules defining it as an institution related to the salvation of its members. Once we have established the framework of law regulating the family, we can then try to establish what part women played in the life of the institutions that define that law, and what the nature of that participation was. For instance, much has been been made of the extent to which women participated in revival culture as preachers. Participate they did, but if we examine what they preached, they do not appear as agents of change but supporters of extreme orthodoxy. The sources here are the familiar ones of legal documents, legislative records, sermons, tracts, and religious publications.

Since Puritan culture was so hostile to women's intellectual life, we can find few sources for women's participation in the life of the mind and the creations of the imagination until the mid- to late eighteenth century. This side of their life comes to light only through diaries and letters until the Revolutionary period. On the other hand, from the early eighteenth-century we see developing as a by-product of the American Enlightenment a lively literature of discussion on the nature of marriage and the purpose of the marriage union. In the early national period we see women as historians chronicling the great upheavals of their time, as journalists, and as writers of fiction and religious tracts.

These sources suggest that the seventeenth-century colonial family was not unlike that of its northern European counterpart, varying only by the American experience of plenty and the absence of recurring famine. Somewhere between about 1710 and 1740 the lineaments of a new provincial society began emerging. The indicators are changes in courtship patterns, changes in the rate of illegitimate births, and the numbers of pregnant brides. Speculation about the nature of the marriage union, its permanence, and its functions beyond the basic one of procreation began to appear in the press, and the notion of marriage as a romantic union fundamental to the pursuit of happiness entered the arena of public discussion. Decreasing numbers of parents arranged the marriages of their children in the northern and middle colonies, and a discernible change became evident in the proportions of parental estates bequeathed to daughters as compared to sons. Taking all these indicators together, we are entitled to conclude that people were behaving differently with respect to their generative selves and to speculate about what the changes might mean. We must wait for the Revolutionary period to hear women's voices on the subject, but we can deduce from pamphlets such as the one attributed to Benjamin Franklin, "Reflections on Courtship and Marriage," that the idea that man was entitled to life, liberty, and the pursuit of happiness raised some problems when applied to the basic unit of society, for many marriage unions were notably unhappy. The notion that happiness was a goal of marriage beyond that of procreation and economic alliances placed a new emphasis on courtship, and the notion that a young man searched for the woman who would make him happy made it less necessary to make daughters an object of desire by bequeathing them substantial shares of the

family property. We may logically take mid-century for the starting point of this romantic notion of marriage noting that the
pursuit of happiness was still a male activity and that subordination of the female within marriage was a subject firmly resolved in
favor of male authority well before the formal change in political
allegiance. We could note the conclusion of this era in the 1840s
when a disturbance in the demographic balance in the ratio of
females to males prompted the rise of speculation about women's
rights and the possibility that their lives might have other mean-
ings beside those of family life.

Looking at the economic baseline we see a period from the
1790s through 1900 during which women's work inside and outside the household was transformed by the forces of industrialization and technological change. The close of the period may be
dated by the emergence of the woman as consumer rather than
producer in the domestic setting, and by the waning of the
cultural role assumed by middle-class women during the era of
industrial change and the urbanization of America.

In the religious sphere a distinctive period can be defined
from 1790 to the 1860s in which the religious participation of
women took the form of questioning established institutions,
either slavery or, in the more radical religious communities, the
nature of Christian marriage. In the political sphere the dynamics
of feminism and antifeminism were played out from 1776 through
the deflation of the feminist movement in the 1920s. After 1860
the main area of debate about women's social function became
not theology but sociology as the advent of Darwinism and the
rise of the university gave rise to a learned and scientific culture.
From 1890 to 1910 the modern service professions for women
were established and an adjustment in the professional structure
of society effectively disposed of the potential force for change
unleashed by women's access to higher education. No transformation in the lives of women has been so consistently documented by female autobiography as the change brought about by
the establishment of the service professions. This provides the
opportunity for a study of the relationship between role and
consciousness not easily carried out in earlier eras.

The period from 1910 through the twenties allows us to study
the relationship between feminism and pacifism in American
culture, and the arrival of mass culture in the twenties enables us

to view the components of the stereotype of women as it was formed in the popular mind. It was a stereotype which incorporated the major themes about female sexuality, marriage, and the family which are to be found in the early national period but which expressed them in terms which enshrined the values which had made the antisuffrage movement so long successful. There were adjustments for the work outside the home, often an economic necessity, but work was certainly subordinate to woman as generative being and consumer. Thereafter feminism might be nurtured in the learned culture in universities and professional associations but only major upheavals in the society would give it mass appeal.

THE FEMALE EXPERIENCE
IN EIGHTEENTH- AND
NINETEENTH-CENTURY AMERICA

SECTION I

AMERICAN CULTURE AND SOCIETY, 1750-1840

A. General Works

Writing about the place of women in colonial culture has been
prompted by the early rise of the social sciences, by the
child-study movement, by the interests of isolated women historians representative of no particular movement in American
intellectual history, and by the rise of interest in social
history which since the late 1950s has directed increasing
attention toward the study of the family, sex roles, and
ideas about the family and its functions.

Arthur W. Calhoun's *Social History of the American Family*
(1917-19) represents the early American social-science
interest in folkways or popular culture, and because of this
interest Calhoun reports as much hearsay as well-documented
fact. He did not check vital statistics to validate his
assumptions about the earliness of marriage in colonial times
or to substantiate his ideas about fertility and family size.
His massive three-volume study was in part propagandist in
motive designed to demonstrate that, while the strength of
American society had been built on early marriage and a high
birthrate, this bourgeois form of the family would eventually
give way to a smaller unit based on eugenics, the liberation
of women from exclusively domestic concerns and socialization
of the means of production. Despite Calhoun's missionary
zeal for the coming socialist utopia, his work is valuable
because it represents the only systematic effort to trace the
contours of family life in America from colonial times to the
early twentieth century. As an apostle of the eugenics movement, Calhoun shared the racial bigotry of his day, and his
treatment of the southern family, black and white, reveals
this bias. The student should be wary of accepting his facts
and figures, but his survey leads us to a compendium of
sources which can be used to far greater effect with the
quantifying techniques of the contemporary historian.

Carl Holliday's *Women's Life in Colonial Days* (1922) is
an example of the typical genre of writing about colonial

3

women. Written without much research into or understanding
of women's participation in economic and social life in
eighteenth-century Europe, these descriptive accounts use the
evidence of women's participation in merchandising, printing,
and other skilled trades to suggest an improvement in their
status in colonial America. The same may be said of Elizabeth
W. Dexter's *Colonial Women of Affairs: A Study of Women in
Business and the Professions in America Before 1776* (1924).
The information contained in these basically descriptive accounts will be useful for students, and Dexter's work provides bibliographic information including a careful documentation of newspaper and periodical materials from which her
conclusions are drawn. These sources can be usefully tapped
once the user has a clearer comparative grasp of women's
economic role in seventeenth- and eighteenth-century England.
     This comparative context is now easily available. Alice
Clark's *Working Life of Women in the Seventeenth Century*
(1919) is the trail-blazing work written from a neo-Marxist
point of view charting the impact of a capitalist labor market on women's status. Roger Thompson's *Women in Stuart
England and America: A Comparative Study* (1974) provides a
clear summary of the available evidence and documents the few
directions in which he sees variation in women's role between
seventeenth-century England and North America.
     Sidney H. Ditzion's *Marriage, Morals and Sex in America:
A History of Ideas* (1953) and Mary S. Benson's *Women in
Eighteenth Century America: A Study of Opinion and Social
Usage* (1935) are first attempts to write about the history of
attitudes and customs shaping sexual behavior in the colonial
and early national period. Written without the knowledge of
birthrates, rates of illegitimacy, and numbers of pregnant
brides that have been provided by historical demography, the
work tells us more about prescriptive literature than behavior. It can now be supplemented and corrected by the information provided in Philip Greven's *Four Generations: Population, Land and Family in Colonial Andover, Massachusetts*
(1970), and its references to the transplanted tradition of
misogyny in America can be placed in context by Katharine
Rogers' *The Troublesome Helpmate: A History of Misogyny in
Literature* (1966).
     By far the most scholarly work describing the position of
the colonial woman is Julia Cherry Spruill's *Women's Life and
Work in the Southern Colonies* (1938). This work is truly
that of a pioneer feminist historian who took ten years to
carry out her research in colonial records to document the
contours of the daily life of the southern woman. She treats
accurately and unflinchingly the crudity and barbarousness of
the Carolina frontier and the wretched status of the woman

settler. Women's participation in economic life and in popular political protest is noted but not overemphasized. Customs of courtship and child rearing are meticulously described.
Spruill's bibliographic notes are painstaking and serve as an
excellent introduction to southern archival materials.
Readers will find Spruill's work packed with information but
devoid of an overview which would place the social reality
described within in the general context of change and evolution in American society.

This context of evolution and change is sketched sugges-
tively in Winthrop Jordan's *White Over Black* (1968), which
treats the evolution of attitudes toward race in the southern
colonies and in antebellum society and draws conclusions about
the impact of a multiracial society and the practice of black
concubinage on male and female attitudes toward family and
sexuality. The literary evidence on attitudes to family is
analyzed with great insight in William R. Taylor's *Cavalier
and Yankee* (1961). Taylor's study charts the evolution of
differing regional attitudes and values about family life and
draws attention to the increasing participation of women
writers in shaping northern attitudes in post-revolutionary
America. The writing of Jordan and Taylor is indicative of
the increased attention paid by social and cultural historians
to the history of attitudes and behavior with respect to the
family and sexuality. This interest has now produced the
multitude of specialized studies listed in Part C of this
section. Although we have seen two decades of sustained interest in this area of research, it can be said with confidence that we still await its synthesis and its incorporation
in a general overview of the direction of change in family
life in the colonial and early national period and the interaction of the family as a social variable with economic and
political forces. We do know that the integrity of family
life and the purity of domestic morals had great political
significance for the Founding Fathers and took on important
significance as a guarantor of order for a society that had
with trepidation and foreboding disposed of the cement of
hereditary monarchy and established church in binding together
the component parts of the polity, but we have as yet no clear
history of the institution on which so much political and
social weight was laid at the time of the Revolution.

About one of its functions we do have some general writing.
Bernard Wishy's *The Child and the Republic: The Dawn of Modern
American Child Nurture* (1967) is an attempt at a general account of the way in which the concept of the child and the
family's role in its nurture developed in nineteenth-century
America. Wishy researched the material before the upsurge of
writing about the history of the family and child-rearing

practices that followed the publication of Philippe Aries'
Centuries of Childhood (1962), Wishy's work has links to the
child-study movement and the interest in early childhood education which spawned many of the institutes for child study
associated with faculties of education or departments of psychology in the 1950s. His work draws attention to the importance placed on the family as the center for the inculcation
of republican values and its enhanced political significance,
but, drawn as it is from conduct manuals and prescriptive
writing, the work tells us little about actual child-rearing
practices. Anne L. Kuhn's *The Mother's Role in Childhood
Education: New England Concepts, 1830-1860* (1947) is a work
in the same genre, using the same kinds of sources. Kuhn
draws attention to the increased responsibility assigned to
women for the education of small children in the early
national period and points to the cluster of social forces in
early American society which encouraged the definition of the
home as a valued agency for conservatism and social stability.
Kuhn correctly identifies feminism as in opposition to these
forces and writes from the standpoint of the 1940s and the
glorification of old-fashioned motherhood and home life. Because her work lacks a comparative dimension, she is unable
to distinguish clearly what is distinctively American in the
elevation of motherhood from the general forces that sentimentalized the home in response to industrialism in England
and Europe as well as in North America.

At this point it will be clear to the reader that general
works covering the period 1750-1840 are few in number. No
cumulative historical effort has built on the work of succeeding generations of historians concerned with the social
institutions of this period and the way they shaped the lives
of women. The dates of the works cited indicate that syn-
thetic works which supply a general chronology and long-term
view of trends affecting the family have until recently
appeared episodically, and that the work done has been provincial in character and has not seen the emerging American
society in its transatlantic perspective. There is no lack
of such a perspective in the new school of social historians
at work on the history of the family, so we may look to the
future with a justified expectation that these shortcomings
will soon be remedied.

BIBLIOGRAPHY

Aries, Philippe. *Centuries of Childhood: A Social History of
    Family Life*. Translated by Robert Baldick. New York:
    Alfred A. Knopf, 1962.

Benson, Mary S. *Women in Eighteenth Century America: A Study of Opinion and Social Usage.* New York: Columbia University Press, 1935.

Calhoun, Arthur W. *A Social History of the American Family from Colonial Times to the Present.* 3 vols. Cleveland: Arthur H. Clark, 1917-19.

Clark, Alice. *Working Life of Women in the Seventeenth Century.* New York: E.P. Dutton & Co., 1919.

Dexter, Elizabeth W. *Colonial Women of Affairs: A Study of Women in Business and the Professions in American Before 1776.* Boston: Houghton Mifflin Co., 1924.

Ditzion, Sidney H. *Marriage, Morals and Sex in America: A History of Ideas.* New York: Bookman Associates, 1953.

Greven, Philip. *Four Generations: Population, Land, and Family in Colonial Andover, Massachusetts.* Ithaca, New York: Cornell University Press, 1970.

Holliday, Carl. *Women's Life in Colonial Days.* Boston: Cornhill Publishing Co., 1922.

James, Edward T., ed. *Notable American Women, 1607-1950: A Biographical Dictionary.* Cambridge, Mass.: Harvard University Press, Belknap Press, 1971.

Jordan, Winthrop. *White Over Black: American Attitudes Toward the Negro, 1550-1812.* Chapel Hill: University of North Carolina Press, 1968.

Kuhn, Anne L. *The Mother's Role in Childhood Education: New England Concepts 1830-60.* New Haven: Yale University Press, 1947.

Rogers, Katharine M. *The Troublesome Helpmate; A History of Misogyny in Literature.* Seattle: University of Washington Press, 1966.

Spruill, Julia Cherry. *Women's Life and Work in the Southern Colonies.* Chapel Hill: University of North Carolina Press, 1938.

Taylor, William R. *Cavalier and Yankee: The Old South and American National Character.* New York: George Braziller, 1961.

Thompson, Roger. *Women in Stuart England and America: A Com-
    parative Study*. London, Boston: Routledge and Kegan Paul,
    1974.

Wishy, Bernard. *The Child and the Republic : The Dawn of Mod-
    ern American Child Nurture*. Philadelphia: University of
    Pennsylvania Press, 1967.

B. Medical Literature of the
Eighteenth and Early Nineteenth Centuries

    Even though we may demonstrate that biology has not deter-
mined women's destiny, Western society has believed until
very recently that women's biological functions governed all
other aspects of their personality and history. This means
that we must understand the prevailing medical view of the
female generative system if we want to understand how women
were perceived by themselves and by men and what aspects of
women's biology different sets of social arrangements sought
to support or control. The eighteenth-century view of female
sexuality was down to earth. Women's sexual appetites were
seen as much greater and more difficult to discipline than
those of men. Women's physical strength was not questioned,
and the process of conception and giving birth was treated as
relatively uncomplicated. Some concern is evident in medical
writing on the subject of female masturbation but little is
expressed about homosexuality. As we enter the nineteenth
century, we see growing attention paid to sexual "disorders,"
the difficulties of childbirth and the frailty and delicate
nervous balance of women. This medical view is the opinion
of the emerging male medical profession of whom Dr. Charles
D. Meigs, Professor of Obstetrics at the Jefferson Medical
College in Philadelphia, was the most influential. By 1850
the study of ·obstetrics had taken large strides with the
practice of postmortem examinations of patients whose medical
problems during pregnancy or labor resulted in death. The
use of surgical forceps had become widespread, and the prevailing view was of pregnancy as a difficult process and
delivery as fraught with danger. Observation of postpartum
mania or melancholy resulted in the view that the pregnant
female was peculiarly subject to mental illness and could be
unbalanced by shock or any unusual stimuli.
    John Brown's *The Elements of Medicine* (1788) shows some
traces of this change in attitude which is fully elaborated
in Charles D. Meigs' *Females and Their Diseases; A Series of
Letters to His Class* (1848). We may trace the development
of an American science of obstetrics from the publication of

Samuel Bard's *A Compendium of the Theory and Practice of Mid-Wifery* (1807). Bard's work was read alongside influential works by British writers such as William Buchan's *Domestic Medicine* (1771, first American edition) which went through 22 English and 29 American editions. John Wesley's *Primitive Physic* (1747) was also a much used general text as was Scotsman Alexander Hamilton's *A Treatise on the Management of Female Complaints, and of Children in Early Infancy* (1795). By the 1820s the emerging medical profession was beginning to separate the diseases of women from those of children, a change marked by the publication of William P. De Wees' *A Treatise on the Physical and Medical Treatment of Children* (1825) and *A Treatise on the Diseases of Females* (1826).

There was a special literature critical of the perception of the delicate and easily unhinged procreative woman. Rooted in the tradition of midwifery and maintained by both male and female writers, this literature is summarized in Irving S. Cutter's *Historical Sketch of the Development of Midwifery and Gynecology* (1933). The concern with female mental hygiene and the critique of the dominant trend in official medicine found expression in the extremely popular genre of writing on phrenology of which George Combe's *A System of Phrenology* (1825) and Johann G. Spurzheim's *Outlines of Phrenology* (1832) were the most widely read examples.

While the stereotype of the delicate female was being formed, a companion development occurred which redefined the male temperament. Thus theological works like the anonymous *Onania, or the Heinous Sin of Self-Pollution, and All Its Frightful Consequences in Both Sexes Considered* (1725), still widely read in the 1790s, came to be replaced by Sylvester Graham's *A Lecture to Young Men on Chastity* (1834). Graham's view of mental hygiene also linked mental and sexual function in males. Masturbation was the main cause of mental and emotional problems in the male, and the loss of energy associated with the expenditure of sperm, whether in masturbation or copulation, was the main cause of undue fatigue in men. Thus we see a general tendency to link sexual function and mental health in both males and females. The female sexual appetite was no longer viewed as strong, while the male appetite, though powerful, could be subject to rational discipline.

A subgenre which circulated alongside the critics of official medicine was the literature of birth control which was made available to Americans in the writings of Charles Knowlton, Richard Carlile, and Robert Dale Owen. Owen's *Moral Physiology* (1836) was the first American work to appear. Written for the benefit of the aspiring artisan or young married clerk, it was roundly rejected as immoral by the public for which it had been designed. However, its reasoned

arguments for the use of coitus interruptus were widely read
by middle-class Americans. Richard Carlile's *Every Woman's
Book*, published first in London in 1826, was circulating
widely in the United States by 1829. It represented the
first frank discussion in English of the economic, social,
and medical aspects of the control of conception. Charles
Knowlton's *Fruits of Philosophy* (1832) was written with fuller
reference to female sexual appetites and provided for the
first time information about methods of preventing conception
that might be used by the female. All three works circulated
widely. Students should pay careful attention to these documents illustrating the history of nineteenth-century contraceptive knowledge because many later accounts of the birth-
control movement misrepresent or directly suppress the nature
and extent of knowledge of contraceptive techniques in nineteenth-century America. We know that these techniques were
in use from about 1790 because of the evidence of historical
demographers about patterns of birth intervals.

No matter how carefully we study this medical literature,
we find ourselves confronted with a series of contradictions.
On the one hand the female was gaining more knowledge of the
ways in which to regulate her reproductive capacity. On
the other she was being depicted by a male medical profes--
sion as governed intellectually and emotionally by her sexual
functions and increasingly as physically weak and frail. We
in the twentieth century automatically equate control of conception with increased libido and pleasure in sexual activity.
Yet the nineteenth-century evidence suggests the possibility
of another direction of change, toward lost consciousness of
sexuality and inhibited physical energies. When we ask why
this might be the case, we are brought immediately to the
question of the possible interrelationships between the world
of reproduction and the world of work, between political
power and maternal and paternal authority, between science
and religion as shapers of world views. The direction of
change in this fundamental aspect of women's consciousness
cannot be understood without reference to the other spheres
of human activity which shape identity and perceptions of
reality.

BIBLIOGRAPHY

Primary Sources

Alexander, William. *The History of Women from the Earliest
    Antiquity to the Present Times*. Dublin: printed by J.A.
    Husband, 1779.

American Spectator or Matrimonial Preceptor. *A Collection of Essays, Epistles, Precepts and Examples, Relating to the Married State, from the Most Celebrated Writers, Ancient and Modern.* Boston: D. West, 1797.

Bard, Samuel. *A Compendium of the Theory and Practice of Midwifery, Containing Practical Instructions for the Management of Women during Pregnancy, in Labor, and in Childbed.* New York: Collins & Perkins, 1807.

Brown, John. *The Elements of Medicine: or, a Translation of Elementa Medicinae Brunonis.* 2 vols. in 1. London: J. Johnson, 1788.

Buchan, William. *Domestic Medicine.* Philadelphia: printed for and sold by R. Aitken, at his bookstore, 1771.

Carlile, Richard (supposed author). *Every Woman's Book; or, What is Love?* 4th ed. London, 1826.

Combe, George. *A System of Phrenology.* 2nd ed. Edinburgh: J. Anderson, 1825.

DeWees, William P. *A Treatise on the Physical and Medical Treatment of Children.* Philadelphia: H.C. Carey & I. Lea, 1825.

DeWees, William P. *A Treatise on the Diseases of Females.* Philadelphia: H.C. Carey & I. Lea, 1826.

Graham, Sylvester. *A Lecture to Young Men [on Chastity].* Providence: Weeden & Cory, 1834.

Hamilton, Alexander. *A Treatise on the Management of Female Complaints, and of Children in Early Infancy.* New York: printed & sold by Samuel Campbell, 1795.

Knowlton, Charles. *The Fruits of Philosophy, or, the Private Companion of Young Married People.* 2nd ed., with additions. Boston: 1833.

Mather, Cotton. *The Pure Nazarite.* *Advice to a young man concerning an impiety and impurity ... which many young men are ... drawn into.* Boston: printed by T. Fleet for John Phillips, 1723.

Meigs, Charles D. *Females and Their Diseases; A series of Letters to His Class.* Philadelphia: Lea & Blanchard, 1848.

Onania: or the Heinous Sin of Self-Pollution, and All Its Frightful Consequences in both Sexes Considered. London: Crouch, 1723.

Owen, Robert Dale. *Moral Physiology; or, a Brief and Plain Treatise on the Population Question.* 2nd ed. New York: Wright & Owen, 1831.

Place, Francis. *Illustrations and Proofs of the Principles of Population.* London: Longman, Hurst, Rees, Orme & Brown, 1822.

Sanger, William W. *History of Prostitution: Its Extent, Causes, and Effects throughout the World.* London: Sampson, Low, 1858.

Spurzheim, Johann G. *Outlines of Phrenology.* Boston: Marsh, Capen & Lyon, 1832.

Wadsworth, Benjamin. *Unchaste Practices Procure Divine Judgment.* c. 1716.

Weems, Mason. *God's Revenge Against Adultery.* 2nd ed. Philadelphia: Printed for the author, 1816.

Wesley, John. *Primitive Physic; or, an Easy and Natural Method of Curing Most Diseases.* London: Thomas Trye, 1747.

Woodward, Samuel B. *Hints for the Young in Relation to the Health of Body and Mind.* 2nd ed., Boston: W.D. Ticknor, 1838.

Secondary Sources

Beall, Otho T. "Aristotle's Masterpiece in America: A Landmark in the Folklore of Medicine." *William and Mary Quarterly* 20 (1963):207-222.

Blake, John B. "Women and Medicine in Antebellum America." *Bulletin of the History of Medicine* 39 (1965):99-123.

Curtis, Arthur Hale, ed. *Obstetrics and Gynecology* with 1644 illustrations. 4 vols. Philadelphia: Saunders Co., 1933.

Cutter, Irving S. *Historical Sketch of the Development of Midwifery and Gynecology.* Philadelphia: Saunders Co., 1933.

Duffy, John. *Epidemics in Colonial America.* Baton Rouge: Louisiana State University Press, 1953.

Ehrenreich, Barbara, and English, Deirdre. *Complaints and Disorders: The Sexual Politics of Sickness.* Westbury, N.Y.: Glass Mountain Pamphlet No. 2, 1973.

Heaton, Claude. "Obstetrics in Colonial America." *The American Journal of Surgery* 45 (1939):606-610.

Himes, Norman Edwin. *Medical History of Contraception.* Baltimore: Williams & Wilkins Company, 1936.

Marks, Geoffrey, and Beatty, William K. *The Story of Medicine in America.* New York: Charles Scribner's Sons, 1973.

Mead, Kate Campbell (Hurd). *Medical Women of America: A Short History of the Pioneer Medical Women of America and a Few of Their Colleagues in England.* New York: Froben Press, 1933.

Mead, Kate Campbell (Hurd). *A History of Women in Medicine.* Haddam, Conn.: The Haddam Press, 1938-.

Packard, Francis Randolph. *History of Medicine in the United States.* New York: P.B. Hoeber, 1931.

Rosen, George. *A History of Public Health.* New York: M.D. Publications, 1958.

Rothstein, William G. *American Physicians in the Nineteenth Century: From Sects to Science.* Baltimore: Johns Hopkins University Press, 1972.

Shryock, Richard H. *Medicine and Society in America, 1660-1860.* New York: New York University Press, 1960.

Shryock, Richard H. *Medicine in America: Historical Essays.* Baltimore: Johns Hopkins University Press, 1966.

Shryock, Richard H. *Medical Licensing in America, 1650-1965.* Baltimore: Johns Hopkins University Press, 1967.

Sigerist, Henry E. *American Medicine.* Translated by Hildegard Nagel. New York: W.W. Norton & Co., 1934.

Thomas, Herbert. *Chapters in American Obstetrics.* Springfield, Ill. and Baltimore: C.C. Thomas, 1933.

C. Demography and Family Life

The work of historical demographers published since the
early 1960s has changed our view of the family in past times.
Until demographers began to make use of census data, parish
and church records, wills, and documents establishing land
titles to reconstitute families and households, our view of
the seventeenth- and eighteenth-century family was shaped more
by the theories of sociologists than by actual traces of the
past. The family became a subject of study for the sociologist in the closing decades of the nineteenth century as
social scientists tried to understand the impact of the industrial revolution and urban growth on society. Concurrently
anthropologists were studying family and kinship in non-Western
societies and producing theories about the stages through
which the family had evolved. These converging efforts at
theory building produced the picture that shaped most writing
on the history of domestic life before the 1960s. This picture was of the preindustrial extended family with many generations and many varieties of kin all residing under one roof.
This family system was presumed to have been disrupted by the
forces of the capitalist labor market and the necessity to
concentrate the industrial labor force near sources of power
and raw materials. This theoretical construct has now been
replaced by a more complex and historically grounded understanding of the family as a social and economic unit, and in
particular of its changes during modernization.

A valuable collection of recent studies of the American
family is *The American Family in Social-Historical Perspective*
(1973), edited by Michael Gordon. The collected essays are
demographic in method and are unified by their treatment of
the theme of modernization and its impact on the family. For
comparative insight the collection contains essays touching
relevant points on the history of the family in Britain and
Europe, and a long review essay summarizes past and current
formulations of the impact of industrialization on family
life. The general reader would do well to begin with Peter
Laslett's essay in order to grasp the distinction between
household and family now held to be crucial by historical
demographers. Past students of the family confused household
size with family size and thus arrived at mistaken conclusions
about the impact of industrialization on the family, for
though we may find many large preindustrial households, these
differ from the sociologist's notion of the extended family,
very few samples of which can be found in preindustrial
England. Philip Greven's study of Andover, Massachusetts,
Four Generations (1970), shows by contrast a more extended

kin situation in the American colonies. Thus we find that
there are differing estimates for household size in the colonies and Great Britain at the close of the eighteenth century.
Laslett's estimate for Great Britain is 4.75, compared with
5.8 for the colonies.

Greven's analysis of four generations of reconstituted
families in Andover introduces the reader to another important concept in family history, the concept of family life
cycle. Greven found significant relationships between landholding patterns and demographic trends. Landholding patterns
might lead to the development of what he calls a modified
extended family in which, while all members of a family are
not gathered into one household, all remain in close prox-
imity with a significant degree of economic dependency on
parents. Thus while earlier historians using literary evidence had seen the rapid erosion of paternal authority in
the colonial situation, Greven found four-fifths of the
second generation of his families residing close to the
paternally controlled family farm. By extending his study
through several generations, he also established that there
was greater mobility for offspring of later generations of
his families. Thus we should recognize that it is important
to build our picture of the family in multigenerational terms
which allows us to see the cycles through which it moves.

Two essays by historical demographers aid in sharpening
this concept of family life cycle. Paul Glick and Robert
Park, Jr. point out in "New Approaches in Studying the Life
Cycle of the Family" (1965) that the concept of family life
cycle was first developed by rural sociologists though it
can have universal applicability. Using twentieth-century
census data, Glick and Park have analyzed the family life
cycle of cohorts of women born between 1880 and 1939. By
establishing age at first marriage, age at birth of first
child, age at birth of last child, and survivorship rates,
they are able to add a social and economic dimension to the
concept of family life cycle. They show that peaks in income
vary by class. Income reaches its peak earlier for working-
class families. Ethnicity also has an impact on family life
cycle. Nonwhite families in this period had more younger
children home at a later life stage than did white families.
Tamara K. Hareven, in "The Family Process: The Historical
Study of the Family Life Cycle" (1974), broadens the concept
of family life cycle through her use of nineteenth-century
evidence. She guides the student of family life toward
undertaking longitudinal studies of individual families as
opposed to inferring that a single point in time revealed
through particular census and tax records supplies us with
an accurate picture of family patterns. Through her evidence

she establishes that the same families exhibited very different household patterns at different points in time. Boarders
and lodgers were common at some stages in a family cycle and
absent at others. She thus leads us to see that the patterns
of a family life cycle are not simple expressions of biological time affecting such things as fertility and aging. They
are also expressions of social patterns that vary according
to a logic of their own. Historians of the individual life
cycle have made us see that life stages such as childhood and
adolescence are socially rather than simply biologically
defined, and Hareven suggests that this is true also for the
family life cycle.

Writing before the 1960s should therefore be studied with
care, since the distinctions between family and household and
the concept of family life cycle will be lacking, and estimates about the strength or weakness of the nuclear family
will be built upon contemporary mood or impression rather
than solid demographic data. We see the importance of using
such information when we turn to histories of the rise of the
city and its effect on family life. Contemporary publicists
and diarists saw the rise of the practice of boarding in the
industrial city as evidence of the breakdown of the family
and as a threat to the supposed sexual innocence of the
young. Thus historians who lacked the techniques of the historical demographer have tended to see the rise of the city
as a negative force affecting the stability of family life.
More recent historical analysis based on the techniques of
the historical demographer makes us view the process of
urbanization differently. Tamara Hareven and John Modell, in
"Urbanization and the Malleable Household: An Examination of
Boarding and Lodging in American Families" (1973), have shown
that the institution of boarding, on the rise in the nineteenth-
century American industrial city, began as a form of poor re-
lief but quickly became an adaptive mechanism for the working-
class family. Boarding houses offered a family surrogate for
young working-class people, and the lodging within another
household was a valued form of social control. Thus what one
generation of historians saw as a sign of family breakdown, a
current generation sees as a sign of flexibility and adaptive
strength in the face of social change. Certainly Hareven and
Modell remind us that there has never been a time in modern
history when some person of conservative temperament did not
see change as decline and located the cause of the unaccept-
able direction of social change as the supposed decline of
the family. We must thus use our literary sources very carefully and interpret them in the context of our quantitative
information. It makes a startling difference to our view of
the experience of women in the industrial city if we assume

that they were struggling to maintain a threatened family, or creatively supporting family life through the development of a different type of household.

Demographic studies have also changed the picture of the attitudes and knowledge brought to bear on family limitation in the eighteenth and early nineteenth centuries. Thus, while the reader will find paeans to the fertility of the native born in the early national period, the work of J. Potter published in "The Growth of Population in America, 1700-1860," (in D.V. Glaass and D.E.C. Eversley, eds., *Population in History, Essays in Historical Demography [1965]*) and of Yasukichi Yasuba in *Birth Rates of the White Population of the U.S., 1800-1860* (1962) indicates otherwise. Though demographers can only make estimates for the rate of natural increase of the population until the mid-nineteenth century where fuller records are available, these estimates suggest that for the period 1700 to 1790 the rate of natural increase was between 26 percent and 30 percent. For the period 1790-1850 the estimate is 34.6 percent, declining to 26 percent by the 1860s. These estimates mean that much of the native population must have been limiting conception from the closing years of the eighteenth century and that the rapid population growth of the nineteenth century was the result of immigration, not high birthrates among the native born, for whom the birth rate was actually declining. Thus the student must be alert to the larger questions raised by this new information. If the means for limiting conception were few, we nonetheless see in the early nineteenth century clear evidence that the native born were limiting family size and doing so even as they participated in the great upsurges of religious revivalism which seem at first glance not to fit well into this pattern of modern behavior. The family we see evolving is certainly a planned one for one segment of the population, and what this meant for women's sense of self we have yet to understand. It certainly did not mean that the native born were converts to the feminist view of marriage and women's rights which began to be articulated in the 1840s. We need to understand the practice of family limitation for other social goals and to avoid the tendency of previous historians to equate the practice, as opposed to the advocacy, of birth control with progressive ideas.

BIBLIOGRAPHY

Bloomberg, Susan E., et al. "A Census Probe into Nineteenth Century Family History: Southern Michigan 1850-1880." *Journal of Social History* 5 (1971):25-46.

Bridges, William E. "Family Patterns and Social Values in
    America, 1825-1875." *American Quarterly* 17 (1965):3-11.

Coale, Ansley J., and Zelnick, Melvin. *New Estimates of Fer-
    tility and Population in the United States.* Princeton,
    N.J.: Princeton University Press, 1963.

Davis, K., and Blake, J. "Social Structure and Fertility: An
    Analytic Framework." *Economic Development and Cultural
    Change* 4 (1956):211-236.

Demos, John. "Families in Colonial Bristol, Rhode Island, an
    Exercise in Historical Demography." *William and Mary
    Quarterly* 25 (1968):40-57.

Demos, John. "Notes on Life in Plymouth Colony." *William and
    Mary Quarterly* 22 (1965):264-286.

Demos, John. *A Little Commonwealth: Family Life in Plymouth
    Colony.* New York: Oxford University Press, 1970.

Eblen, Jack E. "An Analysis of Nineteenth Century Frontier
    Populations." *Demography* 2 (1965):399-413.

Farber, Bernard. *Guardians of Virtue: Salem Families in 1800.*
    New York: Basic Books, 1972.

Farber, Bernard. *Family and Kinship in Modern Society.*
    Glenview, Ill.: Scott, Foresman, 1973.

Flaherty, David H. *Privacy in Colonial New England, 1630-1776.*
    Charlottesville: University Press of Virginia, 1972.

Forster, Colin, and Tucker, G.S.L. *Economic Opportunity and
    White American Fertility Ratios, 1800-1860.* New Haven:
    Yale University Press, 1972.

Furstenberg, F.F. "Industrialization and the American Family:
    A Look Backward." *American Sociological Review* 3 (1966):
    326-337.

Glick, Paul, and Parke, Robert, Jr. "New Approaches in
    Studying the Life Cycle of the Family." *Demography* 2
    (1965):187-202.

Goode, William J. "The Process of Role Bargaining in the
    Impact of Urbanization and Industrialization on Family
    Systems." *Current Sociology* 12 (1963-1964):1-13.

Goode, William J. "Family Systems and Social Mobility." In
    Families in East and West, edited by R. Hill and R. Konig,
    pp. 120-131. The Hague, 1970.

Gordon, Michael, ed. *The American Family in Social-Historical
    Perspective*. New York: St. Martin's Press, 1973.

Greenfield, Sidney. "Industrialization and the Family in
    Sociological Theory." *American Journal of Sociology* 67
    (1961):312-322.

Greven, Philip. "Historical Demography and Colonial America."
    William and Mary Quarterly 24 (1967):438-454.

Greven, Philip J. *Four Generations: Population, Land and
    Family in Andover, Massachusetts*. Ithaca, N.Y.: Cornell
    University Press, 1970.

Hareven, Tamara K. "The Family Process: The Historical Study
    of the Family Life Cycle." *Journal of Social History* 7
    (1973-1974):322-329.

Henretta, James A. "The Morphology of New England Society in
    the Colonial Period." *Journal of Interdisciplinary His-
    tory* 2 (1971):379-398.

Higgs, Robert, and Stettler, H. Louis, III. "Colonial New
    England Demography: A Sampling Approach." *William and
    Mary Quarterly* 27 (1970):282-293.

Hill, R., and Konig, R., eds. *Families East and West*. The
    Hague, 1970.

"Historical Population Studies." *Daedalus* 97 (1968).

Jacobson, Paul H. "Cohort Survival for Generations since
    1840." *Milbank Memorial Fund Quarterly* 42 (1964):36-51.

Kasarda, J.D. "Economic Structure and Fertility: A Compara-
    tive Analysis." *Demography* 8 (1971):301-317.

Lammermeier, Paul J. "The Urban Black Family in the Nine-
    teenth Century: A Study of Black Family Structure in the
    Ohio Valley, 1850-1880." *Journal of Marriage and the
    Family* 35 (1973):440-456.

Lansing, John B., and Kish, Leslie. "Family Life Cycle as an
    Independent Variable." *American Sociological Review* 22
    (1957):512-519.

Laslett, Barbara. "The Family as a Public and Private Insti-
    tution: An Historical Perspective." *Journal of Marriage
    and the Family* 35 (1973):480-492.

Laslett, Peter. "The Comparative History of the Household
    and the Family." *Journal of Social History* 4 (1970):75-87.

Laslett, Peter, ed. *Household and Family in Past Time*. Cam-
    bridge, Eng.: Cambridge University Press, 1972.

Lautz, Herman R., et al. "Pre-industrial Patterns in the
    Colonial Family in America: A Content Analysis of Colonial
    Magazines." *American Sociological Review* 33 (1968):413-426.

Lautz, Herman R., Schmitt, Raymond L., and Herman, Richard.
    "The Preindustrial Family in America: A Further Examina-
    tion of Early Magazines." *American Journal of Sociology*
    79 (1973):566-588.

Lévi-Strauss, Claude. "The Family." In *Man, Culture and
    Society*, edited by H.L. Shapiro, pp. 261-285. New York:
    Oxford University Press, 1956.

Levy, Marion, et al. *Aspects of the Analysis of Family Struc-
    ture*. Princeton, N.J.: Princeton University Press, 1965.

Litwak, Eugene. "Technological Innovation and Ideal Forms of
    Family Structure in an Industrial Democratic Society."
    In *Families in East and West*, edited by R. Hill and R.
    Konig, pp. 349-392. The Hague, 1970.

Lockridge, Kenneth. *A New England Town: The First Hundred
    Years, Dedham, Massachusetts 1636-1736*. New York: W.W.
    Norton & Co., 1970.

Markle, Gerald E. "Sex Ratio at Birth: Values, Variance and
    Some Determinants." *Demography* 11 (1974):131-142.

Markle, Gerald E., and Nam, Charles B. "Sex Predetermination:
    Its Impact on Fertility." *Social Biology* 18 (1971):73-82.

Modell, John. "The Peopling of a Working Class Ward: Reading,
    Pennsylvania 1850." *Journal of Social History* 5 (1971):
    71-95.

Modell, John. "Fertility on the Indiana Frontier, 1820."
    American Quarterly 23 (1974):615-634.

Modell, John, and Hareven, Tamara K. "Urbanization and the
    Malleable Household: An Examination of Boarding and
    Lodging in American Families." *Journal of Marriage and
    the Family* 35 (1973):467-479.

Morgan, Edmund S. *Virginians at Home: Family Life in the
    Eighteenth Century.* Williamsburg, Va.: Colonial Williams-
    burg, 1952.

Norton, Susan L. "Population Growth in Colonial America: A
    Study of Ipswich, Massachusetts." *Population Studies* 25
    (1971):433-452.

Norton, Susan L. "Marital Migration in Essex County, Massa-
    chusetts in the Colonial and Early Federal Periods."
    Journal of Marriage and the Family 35 (1973):406-418.

Pleck, Elizabeth. "The Two Parent Household: Black Family
    Structure in Late Nineteenth Century Boston." *Journal of
    Social History* 6 (1972):3-32.

Potter, J. "The Growth of the Population in America, 1700-
    1860." In *Population in History, Essays in Historical
    Demography*, edited by D.V. Glass and D.E.C. Eversley.
    London: E. Arnold, 1965.

Rabb, Theodore K., and Rotberg, Robert I., eds. *The Family in
    History: Interdisciplinary Essays.* New York: Harper &
    Row, 1973.

Rao, S.L.N. "On Long Term Mortality Trends in the U.S. 1850-
    1968." *Demography* 10 (1973):405-419.

Rapson, Richard L. "The American Child as Seen by British
    Travellers, 1845-1935." *American Quarterly* 17 (1965):
    520-534.

Rothman, David J. "A Note on the Study of the Colonial
    Family." *William and Mary Quarterly* 23 (1966):627-634.

Ryder, Norman R. "The Cohort as a Concept in the Study of
    Social Change." *American Sociological Review* 30 (1965):
    843-861.

Saveth, Edward N. "The Problem of American Family History."
    American Quarterly 21 (1969):311-329.

Sennett, Richard. *Families Against the City: Middle Class Homes of Industrial Chicago, 1872-1890.* Cambridge, Mass.: Harvard University Press, 1970.

Seward, Rudy Ray. "The Colonial Family in America: Toward a Socio-Historical Restoration of Its Structure." *Journal of Marriage and the Family* 35 (1973):58-70.

Shanas, Ethel, and Streib, Gordon F., eds. *Symposium on the Family, Intergenerational Relations and Social Structure, Duke University, 1963.* Englewood Cliffs, N.J.: Prentice-Hall, 1965.

Smith, Daniel Scott. "The Demographic History of Colonial New England." *Journal of Economic History* 32 (1972):165-184.

Smith, Daniel Scott. "Parental Power and Marriage Patterns: An Analysis of Historical Trends in Hingham, Massachusetts." *Journal of Marriage and the Family* 35 (1973):419-428.

Shapiro, H.L., ed. *Man, Culture and Society.* New York: Oxford University Press, 1956.

Strong, Floyd Bryan. "Toward a History of the Experiential Family: Sex and Incest in the Nineteenth Century Family." *Journal of Marriage and the Family* 35 (1973):457-466.

Sweezey, A.R. "Economic Explanations of Fertility Changes in the United States." *Population Studies* 25 (1971):255-267.

Thernstrom, Stephan, and Knights, Peter. "Men in Motion and Speculations About Urban Population Mobility in Nineteenth Century America." *Journal of Interdisciplinary History* 1 (1970):7-36.

Uddenberg, N., Almgren, P.E., and Nilsson, A. "Preference for Sex of the Child Among Pregnant Women." *Journal of Bio-Social Science* 3 (1971):267-280.

Uhlenberg, Peter R. "A Study of Cohort Life Cycles: Cohorts of Native Born Massachusetts Women, 1830-1920." *Population Studies* 23 (1969):407-420.

Vinovskis, Maris A. "Mortality Rates and Trends in Massachusetts before 1860." *Journal of Economic History* 22 (1972):184-213.

Vinovskis, Maris A. "Socio-economic Determinants of Interstate Fertility Differentials in the U.S. in 1850 and 1860." Paper 73-15, Center for Demography and Ecology, University of Wisconsin, Madison. Mimeographed.

Wells, Robert V. "Demographic Change and the Life Cycle of American Families." *Journal of Interdisciplinary History* 2 (1971):273-282.

Wells, Robert V. "Family Size and Fertility Control in Eighteenth Century America: A Study of Quaker Families." *Population Studies* 25 (1971):73-82.

Wells, Robert V. "Quaker Marriage Patterns in Colonial Perspective." *William and Mary Quarterly* 29 (1972):415-442.

Wrigley, E.A. "Family Limitation in Pre-Industrial England." *Economic History Review* 19 (1966):82-109.

Yasuba, Yasukichi. *Birth Rates of the White Population of the United States, 1800-1860, an Economic Study.* Baltimore: Johns Hopkins Press, 1962.

Zelnik, Melvin, and Coale, Ansley J. *New Estimates of Fertility and Population in the United States.* Princeton, N.J.: Princeton University Press, 1963.

D. Contemporary Printed Sources on
Marriage and the Family

There are three principal varieties of contemporary writing on marriage and the family in the late eighteenth and early nineteenth century. The first, and by far the most important for the shaping of attitude, is that by moralists commenting on the nature of marriage and the purpose of the family as a social institution. The most significant work in this genre is attributed to Benjamin Franklin and bears the somewhat misleading title of *Reflections on Courtship and Marriage: In Two Letters to a Friend* (1746). This long essay, reprinted frequently in the American colonies and Canada during the eighteenth century, was still in circulation and being referred to by later writers in the 1830s and '40s. The essay sums up the usual misogynist view of marriage as an institution in which man is trapped by scheming women and draws extensively on eighteenth-century writing critical of slatternly wives or of women who are spendthrifts and poor managers. The remedy proposed by the author begins a section of the essay that departs from the use of derivative language and moves into easy colloquial prose. A young man may avoid the ills so frequently dwelt upon by misogynist writers if he pursues a systematic pattern of educating his bride during courtship. Her mind is seen as a *tabula rasa* upon which the

suitor may write what he pleases, and the author recommends a
stiff program of useful reading to teach the intending bride
sound principles of household management and the appropriate
virtues of thrift and industry. The goal of the exercise
should be to teach her the behavior which will be a source of
happiness to her spouse and to find her own happiness in a
harmonious and well-regulated household. In the concluding
section, the author draws on the European Enlightenment
debate on the purpose of marriage as an institution and the
preaching of such figures as William Wollaston to define what
he sees as the purpose of the institution. It is, he concludes, a natural institution created by God to serve two
purposes, procreation and the pursuit of happiness. Here the
author is driven to reflect on who must rule if one partner
has different views of happiness from the other. The male
should rule, because he has a wider experience of the world,
and because any association must have a single head. However,
the best marriages are those in which a women has been educated to find her happiness in making her husband happy.
Here is a theme which is to be found in most subsequent discussions of the education of women in America. In reflecting
on the fact that it is self-evident that the male must rule
but that one of the purposes of the union of marriage is
happiness, the author of the *Reflections* concludes that some
legitimate pretense may be necessary to maintain the illusion
that the marriage union is to serve the happiness of both
partners. In public a man should always treat his wife as
though she were his equal, even though in private he would
necessarily assert his authority. It is interesting to see
the same notion of public role playing and private patriarchy
being repeated in the writings of the Freudian popularizers
of the 1920s. This text then orients the reader for continuities in the development of American thought about marriage
and about women's education.

    There are many other contemporary comments on the themes
treated in *Reflections on Courtship and Marriage*, but it is
the most comprehensive and useful discussion. A variant of
the Franklin theme comes in the writing of Hannah More.
More's writing in England was directed to the men and women
of the rising middle class and inveighed against the sexual
license of both the aristocracy and the working class. In
the United States her readers equated the sexual license of
the aristocracy with corrupt Europe and the loose mores of
the workers with the social anarchy of the frontier. Thus
More had a relevance far beyond the social setting for which
she wrote, and the popularity of her work in the United
States is a testimony to the degree to which her strictures
against aristocratic and working-class attitudes could

transcend geographic and social setting. Indeed, the work of More and Franklin represents a consistent pattern in American ideas about marriage. Borrowing from the conservative chapel and Low-Church Anglican tradition supplied the basic popular view of marriage, though an American borrower would link those moral attitudes to the startling idea of the pursuit of happiness. The political borrowings supplied the context for a change in formal public authority. No such break occurred in the social fabric or in moral attitude. Hannah More's essays were as popular after the Revolution as before, and Franklin's idiosyncratic definition of the pursuit of happiness as a male prerogative in marriage was not questioned.

There was a minor genre of writing on marriage derived from the eighteenth-century Enlightenment and English radical critique of social institutions. It was not well received in the colonies or the new nation. Thomas Paine's essay on marriage, written from the point of view of a pagan critic of Christian culture, appeared in 1776 and evoked shocked criticism or silent rejection from the same population which was to applaud *Common Sense*. We can see in the anonymous piece *An Essay on Marriage; or, The Lawfulness of Divorce in Certain Cases Considered--Addressed to the Feelings of Mankind* (1788) the influence of Mary Wollstonecraft and her *Vindication of the Rights of Women* (1792). Wollstonecraft's ideas are also hinted at in Hannah W. Foster's *The Coquette; or the History of Eliza Wharton* (1797). This, one of the first pieces of American fiction, copies the standard eighteenth-century English novel of seduction and betrayal but gives an American twist to the action. The heroine delays a suitable marriage and rejects a courtship conducted on Franklin's improving lines because she thinks the standard version of American marriage too dull and confining. Eliza Wharton is interested in politics and the theater, and her search for adventure carries her right into the embraces of the typical eighteenth-century romantic seducer. Eliza is an attractive heroine who secures all the reader's sympathy, and the plot of the novel is ambiguous. When she is consigned to perdition, her fate does not seem well merited, and her criticisms of marriage remain uppermost in the mind. Charles Brockden Brown's fiction is similarly inspired and similarly ambiguous in plot and characterization. Strong heroines question the conventions of contemporary marriage and male-female relationships, but no convincing picture of a new morality and a new set of social institutions is produced by the author. This minor genre evoked a strong and overwhelmingly negative reaction. George Bourne's *Marriage Indissoluble: And Divorce Unscriptural* (1813) was the most widely read clerical response to Thomas Paine, while Hannah M. Crocker's *Observations on the*

Real Rights of Women, with Their Appropriate Duties, Agreeable to Scripture, Reason and Common Sense (1818) was the most popular rebuttal of Paine written by a woman. Along with such serious works went a popular literature boosting marriage and the importance of fertility for the new nation. Mason Locke Weems' *Hymen's Recruiting-Serjeant: Or the New Matrimonial Tatoo, for the Old Bachelors* (1816, 6th ed.) was an early example of this type of commentary, while Lorenzo Dow's "Reflections on Matrimony" was the most widely circulated.

While the commentaries on marriage and male-female relationships all drew on European sources, there was a third stream of writing on the institution of the family and its importance in the new Republic that was distinctively American. Its principal source was Benjamin Rush, possibly the most original social theorist of the Revolutionary era. Rush attempted to scrutinize all existing social institutions to determine what would be their appropriate form in a fully developed republican society. He was not concerned with male-female relationships so much as the relationship between family, social order, and political stability. Rush was the first of a long line of American commentators to conclude that, in the absence of an established church to inculcate morals or a hereditary monarchy to ensure allegiance to the state, the family, functioning in the socialization of the young, was an institution of critical political importance. Thus while there is continuity in the standard religious and moral commentary on marriage as an institution of the pre- and post-Revolutionary period, a new perspective emerges in Rush's writing on the family and by implication on the role of women. While there is no change in social or economic territory suggested for women in Rush's writing, the importance he assigned to family life as the psychological setting in which the correct republican motivations must be produced amounts to an increase in women's status, but only within the moral economy of society and only within their allotted social territory.

BIBLIOGRAPHY

Adams, Abigail. *Letters of Mrs. Adams, the Wife of John Adams*. Boston: Little & Brown, 1840.

Adams, Abigail. *New Letters of Abigail Adams, 1788-1801*. Edited by Stewart Mitchell. Boston: Houghton Mifflin Co., 1947.

Adams, John. *Letters of John Adams, Addressed to His Wife*. Edited by his grandson, Charles F. Adams. Boston: Little & Brown, 1841.

Bourne, George. *Marriage Indissoluble: and Divorce Unscriptural.* Harrisonburg, Va.: Davidson & Bourne, 1813.

Brown, Charles Brockden. *Alcuin.* New York: T. & J. Swords, 1798.

Brown, Charles Brockden. *Arthur Mervyn.* Philadelphia: H. Maxwell, 1799.

Brown, Charles Brockden. *Ormond; or, the Secret Witness.* New York: G. Forman, for H. Cantat, 1799.

Brown, Charles Brockden. *Jane Talbot.* Philadelphia: John Conrad & Co.; Baltimore: M. & J. Conrad & Co., 1801.

Crocker, Hannah. *Observations on the Real Rights of Women, with Their Appropriate Duties, Agreeable to Scripture, Reason and Common Sense.* Boston: printed for the author, 1818.

Dow, Lorenzo. *All the Polemical Works of Lorenzo.* "Reflections on Matrimony." New York: J.C. Totten, 1814.

Dwight, Timothy. *Sermons.* 2 vols. New Haven: H. Howe, Durrie & Peck, 1828.

An Essay on Marriage; or the Lawfulness of Divorce, in Certain Cases Considered--Addressed to the Feelings of Mankind. Philadelphia: Printed by Z. Poulson, Jr., 1788.

Foster, Hannah W. *The Coquette; or the History of Eliza Wharton: a Novel, Founded on Fact.* Boston: Samuel Etheridge, for E. Larkin, 1797.

Franklin, Benjamin. *Reflections on Courtship and Marriage: In Two Letters to a Friend.* Philadelphia: B. Franklin, 1746.

Hitchcock, Enos. *Memoirs of the Bloomsgrove Family.* Boston: Thomas & Andrews, 1790.

More, Hannah. *The Works of Hannah More, Including Several Pieces Never Before Published.* 8 vols. Philadelphia: Earle; New York: Eastburn Kirk, 1813-1814.

Paine, Thomas. *The Complete Writings of Thomas Paine.* Collected and edited by Philip S. Foner. New York: The Citadel Press, 1945.

Rush, Benjamin. *Thoughts upon Female Education, Accommodated to the Present State of Society, Manners and Government, in the United States of America.* Boston: Samuel Hall, 1787.

Rush, Benjamin. *The Selected Writings of Benjamin Rush.* Edited by Dagobert D. Runeo. New York: Philosophical Library, 1947.

Rush, Benjamin. *Letters.* Edited by Lyman Butterfield. Princeton, N.J.: Princeton University Press (for American Philosophical Society), 1951.

Weems, Mason Locke. *Hymen's Recruiting-Serjeant: or the New Matrimonial Tatoo, for the Old Bachelors.* Philadelphia: printed for the author, 1816.

Winslow, Hubbard. *Woman as She Should Be.* Boston: Otis, Broaders & Co., 1838.

Wollstonecraft, Mary. *A Vindication of the Rights of Women: With Strictures on Political and Moral Subjects.* Boston: printed by Peter Edes for Thomas & Andrews, 1792.

E. Male and Female Autobiographies, Diaries,
and Letters Commenting on Family Life

The decade of the 1740s marks the birth of the first generation of women whose autobiographical writing manifests the emergence of a new female voice and sense of self in colonial society. Puritan orthodoxy forbade the publication of writing by women, and it was believed in the seventeenth-century colonies that too much thought addled the female brain. Abigail Bailey (1746-1815) produced a memoir of her marriage, its disastrous breakdown, and her divorce, which moves with a fast pace. Her voice is one of inner religious reflection, and her entire sense of self is otherworldly. Nonetheless, she chronicles life with a brutal husband and his incestuous relationship with their daughter in a flat, matter-of-fact manner which makes her eventual self-assertion and decision to divorce entirely credible. Her view of marriage has nothing to do with the pursuit of happiness, but instead assumes that its purpose is to aid in the salvation of both partners. The memoir has been edited somewhat freely for publication as a religious tract, but it is notable for its unsentimental and unblinking scrutiny of human depravity. Susan Mansfield Huntington (1791-1823) represents a later

variety of the same type of inner religious reflection. Her
journal was written as a means to religious discipline and
destroyed as she knew her death was approaching. Her published memoir, compiled after her death, consists of letters
and scraps of her journal which found their way into other
hands. The letters reveal a powerful evangelical mind
focused on the salvation of her three children and the religious progress of friends. She differs from Abigail Bailey
in one clear respect. Bailey was unblushingly frank about
the sins of the flesh and the unredeemed nature of children.
Huntington was widowed before her third child was born and
thereafter directed her will to conforming herself to the
will of God. She is a sustainer of others in a similar
situation, and she shows signs of romanticism about the innocence and defenselessness of childhood. Both products of
stern New England piety, Bailey and Huntington used their
religious reflections to develop a strong sense of self and
as a result assumed great moral authority within their communities.

We see another side of the female temperament and an entirely different climate of family life in the letters of
women born or educated in urban centers in the decades immediately preceding the Revolution. These show young women
assuming considerable freedom outside the family through
travel away to school or under the protection of family
friends. They illustrate the growing sense that marriage is
to be a union for earthly happiness, and they lack the fierce-
ly inturned piety of women raised within the setting of church
and family in a small New England town. They focus attention
on fashion, travel and study, enjoyment of life, and flutters
of the heart for attractive young men. They also illustrate
the emerging style of feminine friendship which has been the
subject of analysis by Carroll Smith-Rosenberg and Nancy Cott.
Smith-Rosenberg, in "The Female World of Love and Ritual"
(1975), draws attention to the close female bonding of young
girlhood and the intense female friendships which competed
with romantic ties with men in early nineteenth-century
American culture. Cott, in *The Bonds of Womanhood: "Woman's
Sphere" in New England, 1780-1835* (1977), argues that this
emerging world of shared experience between women was a pre-
condition for the emergence of feminist rebellion and critical analysis of women's subordination. Students of women's
autobiographical writing will find Cott's careful listing of
unpublished diaries and letters invaluable. Major questions
remain to be resolved about this extensive body of printed
and unpublished writing by women. Sally Wister (1761-1804)
shows a youthful sense of adventure and high spirits in her
journal of life as a young woman in a household that

frequently served as quarters for officers of the Continental
Army in 1777-78. Eliza Southgate Bowne (1783-1809), the
daughter of a prosperous Maine doctor and judge, shows a sense
of humor and a delight in society and human folly which does
not suggest a latent feminist consciousness, but rather the
witty woman commentator on society and manners.

What is clear is the increasing authority with which the
woman diarist or letter writer wrote and the divergence
between urban and rural attitudes. These differences may be
traced in all the autobiographical writing of the period and
notably in women's correspondence.

BIBLIOGRAPHY

Primary Sources

Bailey, Mrs. Abigail (Abbot). *Memoirs of Mrs. Abigail Bailey,*
    Who Had Been the Wife of Major Asa Bailey. Edited by
    Ethan Smith. Boston: Samuel T. Armstrong, 1815.

Biddle, Henry, ed. *Extracts from the Journal of Elizabeth*
    Drinker from 1759-1807. Philadelphia: J.B. Lippincott
    Company, 1889.

Bowers, Benjamin. *A Narrative, or Youth's Mirrors for the*
    dissolute and dissemblers; containing the trials and suf-
    fering that flowed from inconstant and false-hearted
    women; and the author's imprisonment and arrainments
    before the courts and jurors. Swanton, Vt.: printed for
    the author, 1847.

Bowne, Eliza Southgate. *A Girl's Life Eighty Years Ago;*
    Selections from the letters of Eliza Southgate Bowne.
    With an introduction by Clarence Cook. New York:
    C. Scribner's sons, 1887.

Brown, Kate Montrose Eldon. *Kate Montrose; An Autobiography.*
    Sacramento: printed by Russell and Winterburn, 1866.

Dow, George Francis, ed. *The Holyoke Diaries, 1709-1856.*
    Salem, Mass.: The Essex Institute, 1911.

"Extracts from the diary of Miss Mary Fleet, Boston, 1755-
    1803," Communicated by Henry Elliot, Esq. *New England*
    Historical and Genealogical Register 19:59-61.

Livingston, Nancy. *Nancy Shippen, Her Journal Books.* Edited
    by Ethel Armes. Philadelphia: J.B. Lippincott, Co., 1935.

Marshall, Mary. "The Life and Sufferings of the Author." In *The Rise and Progress of the Serpent from the Garden of Eden, to the Present Day with a Disclosure of Shakerism.* Concord, N.H.: printed for the author, 1847.

Myers, Albert C., ed. *Sally Wister's Journal, a True Narrative; Being a Quaker Maiden's Account of Her Experiences with Officers of the Continental Army 1777-78.* Philadelphia: Ferris and Leach, 1902.

Roe, Mrs. Elizabeth A. *Recollections of Frontier Life.* Rockford, Ill.: Gazette Publishing House, 1885.

Stewart, Mrs. Ellen Brown. *Life of Mrs. Ellen Stewart, Together with Biographical Sketches of Other Individuals.* Akron, Ohio: Beebe and Elkins, 1858.

Willett, Edward. *The Matrimonial Life of Edward Willett; with a variable style.* New York: Thomson, 1812.

Wisner, Benjamin B. *Memoirs of the Late Mrs. Susan Huntington, of Boston, Mass.* Boston: Crocker and Brewster, 1829.

Secondary Sources

Cott, Nancy F. *In the Bonds of Womanhood: "Woman's Sphere" in New England, 1780-1835.* New Haven: Yale University Press, 1977.

Smith-Rosenberg, Carroll. "The Female World of Love and Ritual." *Signs: A Journal of Women in Culture and Society* 1 (1975):1-29.

F. Child Rearing

The field of historical demography and the field of psychohistory intersect in the study of childhood and child-rearing practices. The same demographic techniques that have enabled the reconstruction of families and the study of fertility have stimulated intense interest in the study of childhood. Since the 1960s, a simple and reductive Freudianism has been replaced by an interest in life stages and developmental crises in response to the theoretical and historical writing of Erik Erikson.* General debate in this

*Erik H. Erikson. *Young Man Luther; a Study in Psychoanalysis and History.* New York: Norton, 1958. and *Ghandi's Truth on the Origins of Militant Nonviolence.* New York: Norton, 1969.

field has centered on patterns of change in what we now see
to be socially defined lifestages, attitudes of parents to
children, the psychosocial consequences of such customs as
swaddling, trends of change in the awareness of infantile
sexuality, and variations in institutional arrangements for
the socializing of the young, such as the transfer of educational functions from family to school.

All of these concepts are germane to the study of child
rearing in colonial and early nineteenth-century America.
The student may become quickly acquainted with the secondary
writing on the subject by consulting Lloyd De Mause's *History
of Childhood* (1974), a collection of recent essays on the
subject introduced by a long interpretive study by De Mause.
De Mause has constructed a linear evolutionary schema for
interpreting child-rearing practices in which parental emotional involvement in children and levels of child care
regress through recorded time. In this scheme he identifies
six modes of parent-child relations: the Infanticidal mode
dates from antiquity to the fourth century A.D., the Abandonment mode from the fourth century to the thirteenth, the
Ambivalent mode from the thirteenth to the seventeenth, the
Intrusive mode appearing in the eighteenth century, and the
Socialization mode which emerges in the nineteenth and takes
full form in the twentieth-century helping style of parent-
hood. The crucial transition which can be documented is the
transition to the Intrusive mode in the eighteenth century
and the emergence of new concepts of childhood in the nineteenth century. The remainder of the interpretive framework
is based on a psychogenic theory of personality change for
which De Mause introduces only fragmentary evidence. De
Mause contradicts the view expounded earlier by Aries in
Centuries of Childhood (1962) which locates the beginnings
of a new concept of childhood in seventeenth-century Europe.
The most provocative essay in *History of Childhood* touching
on colonial America is by John Walzer, based on the reading
of child-care manuals, family papers, and almanacs. Walzer
interprets this evidence to suggest deep ambivalence on the
part of adults about children. They are seen on the one
hand as malleable and educable, but on the other as possessing
unbridled appetites and passions. The reader may put such
evidence in context by consulting Philip Greven's *Childrearing
Concepts, 1628-1861: Historical Sources* (1973). Greven has
here assembled sources illustrative of the governing concepts
of child-rearing from the Puritans through such eighteenth-
century theorists as Locke to the emerging sense of the child
as the future citizen in the writing of Benjamin Rush, and

the sentimental religious reformers of the evangelical era such as Horace Bushnell.

The linkages between such views of the child and other broader-gauged reform movements in American society is treated in Bernard Wishy's *The Child and the Republic* (1967). Wishy sees Locke and Rousseau as secular intellectual sources for the early nineteenth-century notion of the child as redeemable, and the work of such religious reformers as Horace Bushnell as an adaptation of standard Protestant culture to these ideas. Bushnell made popular the notion that proper Christian nurture of the child could counteract infant depravity, and thereby made salvation dependent on child rearing rather than the adult experience of conversion. Such views had important social consequences for the position of women and for household development, since the need to control the home environment conditioned attitudes to servants and nonfamily members.

Joseph Kett's work draws attention to the new emphasis on adolescence as a life-stage which becomes part of American writing on child care during the late eighteenth and early nineteenth centuries. The notion of the arrival of puberty as a difficult life-stage evoked a flood of books of conduct and advice addressed to youth. In part these were inspired by the concept of youth as a period of psychological as well as chronological change. With this focus on the psyche came differing treatment of males and females at puberty. The medical literature introduces the concept of the onset of menstruation as debilitating and suggests particular emotional delicacy in the female at the onset of puberty.

Despite the discovery that concepts such as adolescence or of infantile sexuality are socially determined, we can nonetheless regard the study of the history of childhood as relatively undeveloped, and note that the field is one in which theoretical constructs derived from psychiatry have as yet been brought into little more than episodic relationship with the available primary sources.

William P. DeWees' *The Physical and Medical Treatment of Children* (1825) is a useful compendium of early nineteenth-century child care and indicates the emerging interest in childhood as a life-stage in which physical and moral care were needed to support physical and psychological health. John S.C. Abbott's *The Mother at Home; or, the Principles of Maternal Duty Familiarly Illustrated* (1833) indicates the persistence and popularity of the concept of infant depravity. The work sold more than 125,000 copies, and its instructions on the "breaking" of the child's dangerously unredeemed will were widely quoted.

The forces of theological reform adjusting this view to
contemporary philosophy are best exemplified in Horace
Bushnell's *Christian Nurture* (1861), which became a staple of
every well-educated home. In the 1847 edition and in a larger
revision of 1861, Bushnell denied the importance of an adult
conversion experience and insisted on the importance of en-
vironmental factors in the early years of childhood in mas-
tering infant depravity. Bushnell is a key transitional
figure, since with only minor adjustments his ideas on
Christian nurture could be adapted to Darwinian thought and
the environmentalism of the later nineteenth century.

While Bushnell's work may be seen as representative of
the adjustment of traditional Calvinism to nineteenth-century
Romanticism, it is important to remember that there were
strong strands of popular utopianism in American popular culture derived from eighteenth- and early nineteenth-century
millenarianism. These forces of Christian perfectionism drew
on a long medieval and early modern tradition of perfectionism
which anticipated the second coming and the arrival of the
perfected kingdom at any moment. These forces were strong in
the varieties of Methodist enthusiasm transferred to the colonies in the later stages of the Great Awakening, and they
lingered on in the evangelical culture of the early national
period. In Bronson Alcott these ideas found formal expression
in the learned culture of New England expressed in terms of
Romanticism and German idealist philosophy. Alcott rejected
the concept that infants were tainted by original sin and saw
the child as a being worthy of reverence and respect who
carried the seeds of perfection within him if only correctly
reared. These views were tested in the utopian Transcendentalist community of Fruitlands, in Alcott's careful observation of the infancy of his daughters, and in the Temple
School, an experiment in pedagogy which is reported in
Peabody's *Record of a School* (1835). The creation of Utopia
via the coming generation and perfected methods of child care
thus became an important component of American culture in the
early national period, both as Christian nurture and as
secular experiment. It would give rise to successive waves
of educational reform and would fuel both conservative and
radical impulses toward feminism.

Since the nurture of the child had both physical and moral
components, we see an interest in child rearing emerging
among health reformers, notably among leading phrenologists
who insisted that phrenological analysis would enable parents
to identify the pattern of education best suited to the
child's inherited character. Orson Fowler's *Love and Parentage, Applied to the Improvement of Offspring* (1844) and
Andrew Combe's *A Treatise on the Physiological and Moral*

Management of Infancy (1840) are the most useful introductions to this popular medical literature, more widely read and more influential than Alcott's writings.

The importance of these sources for the study of wider social movements and institutional developments in the United States cannot be overemphasized. Students unfamiliar with the literature on Christian nurture will not be aware of the power of the religious and emotional forces that tied the mother to her sphere and prohibited the assistance of others in child rearing and in other household tasks. The amalgam of strong belief in the perfectibility of American society, the need to educate women, and the absolute necessity of keeping her within her sphere is most visible in the child-rearing literature of the early national period, as are its consequences in the autobiographical writing listed in Section E. It is only when the spectrum of religious and secular beliefs on the nature of childhood and nurture are understood that we can understand the contradictory forces juxtaposed in the movement for the higher education of women and the pro- and anti-suffrage movement to which that movement gave birth. Further, to return to the psychohistorical issues raised at the opening of this section, we can only begin to speculate about the psychological consequences of the mother-child relationship in which maternal nurture bore the responsibility for salvation.

BIBLIOGRAPHY

Primary Sources

Abbott, John S.C. *The Mother at Home; or, the Principles of Maternal Duty Familiarly Illustrated.* Boston: Crocker & Brewster, 1833.

Alcott, Bronson. *Observations on the Principles and Methods of Infant Instruction.* Boston: Carter & Hendee, 1830.

Alcott, William A. *The Young Mother, or Management of Children in Regard to Health.* 2nd ed. Boston: Light & Stearns, 1836.

An American Matron. *The Maternal Physician; a treatise on the nurture and management of infants from birth until 2 years old. Being the result of 16 years experience in the nursery.* New York: Isaac Riley, 1818.

Barwell, Mrs. Louise Mary. *Advice to Mothers on the Treat-
    ment of Infants: With Directions for Self-Management
    Before, During and After Pregnancy.* Philadelphia: J. &
    J.L. Gihon, 1850.

Beck, John Brodhead. *An Inaugural Dissertation on Infanti-
    cide.* New York: Printed by J. Seymour, 1817.

Blackwell, Elizabeth. *Counsel to Parents on the Moral Edu-
    cation of their Children.* London: Hyrst Smyth & Son,
    1878.

Brownson, Orestes A. *The Convert: or, Leaves From My Experi-
    ence.* New York: E. Dunigan and Brother, 1857.

Bushnell, Horace. *Christian Nurture.* New York: C. Scribner,
    1861.

Child, Lydia Maria. *The Mother's Book.* Boston: Carter,
    Hendee & Babcock, 1831.

Combe, Andrew. *A Treatise on the Physiological and Moral
    Management of Infancy.* Edinburgh: Moclachlan, Stewart, 1840.

Crispus, (Anon.). "On the Education of Children." *The
    Panoplist and Missionary Magazine* 10: 393-403.

DeWees, William Potts. *A Treatise on the Physical and Medical
    Treatment of Children.* Philadelphia: Carey and Lea, 1825.

Dwight, Theodore. *The Father's Book or, Suggestions for the
    Government and Instruction of Young Children, on Princi-
    ples Appropriate to a Christian Country.* Springfield,
    Mass: G. & C. Merriam, 1834.

Earle, Alice M. *Child Life in Colonial Days.* New York: The
    Macmillan Co., 1899.

Ewell, James. *Letter to Ladies Detailing Important Informa-
    tion Concerning Themselves and Infants.* c. 1817.

Ford, W.C., ed. *Diary of Cotton Mather 1681-1724.* 2 vols.
    "On the Education of His Children," pp. 534-537, vol. 1.
    Collections of the Massachusetts Historical Society,
    1911-12.

Fowler, Orson Squire. *Love and Parentage, Applied to the
    Improvement of Offspring.* 40th ed. New York: Fowler &
    Wells, 1844.

Fowler, Orson Squire. *Perfect Men, Women and Children in Happy Families.* c. 1878.

Goodrich, Samuel G. *Recollections of a Lifetime, or, Men and Things I Have Seen.* 2 vols. New York: Miller, Orton, and Mulligan, 1856.

Hopkins, Samuel. *The Life and Character of the Late Reverend, Learned and Pious Mr. Jonathan Edwards, President of the College of New Jersey Together with Extracts from his Private Writings and Diary. And also 17 select sermons on various important subjects.* Northampton: Printed by Andrew Wright for S. & E. Butler and sold at their bookstore, 1804.

Jennings, Samuel Kennedy. *The Married Lady's Companion: or, Poor Man's Friend.* 2nd ed. New York: L. Dow, 1808.

Locke, John. "Some Thoughts Concerning Education," in *The Works of John Locke.* 10 vols. London: printed for Thomas Tegg, W. Sharpe and Son, 1823.

Moody, Eleazar. *The School of Good Manners. Composed for the Help of Parents in Teaching Their Children How to Carry It in Their Places During Their Minority.* Boston: Reprinted and sold by T. & J. Fleet, 1772.

Moss, William. *An Essay on the Management and Feeding of Infants.* Philadelphia: Published by Benjamin Johnson, Printed by Joseph Rakestraw, 1808.

Peabody, Elizabeth. *Record of a School, Exemplifying the General Principles of Spiritual Culture.* Boston: James Munroe & Co., 1835.

Sigourney, Lydia. *Letters to Mothers.* Hartford: Hudson & Skinner, 1838.

Underwood, Michael. *A Treatise on the Diseases of Children, with General Directions for the Management of Infants from the Birth.* 2 vols. London: Printed for J. Mathews, 1789.

Wadsworth, Benjamin. *The Well-Ordered Family: or, Relative Duties.* Boston: Printed by B. Green for Nicholas Buttolph at his shop in Corn Hill, 1712.

Secondary Sources

Aries, Philippe. *Centuries of Childhood: A Social History of
    Family Life.* Translated by Robert Baldick. New York:
    Alfred A. Knopf, 1962.

De Charms, Richard, and Moeller, Gerald H. "Values Expressed
    in American Children's Readers, 1800-1950." *Journal of
    Abnormal and Social Psychology* 64 (1962):136-142.

De Mause, Lloyd, ed. *The History of Childhood.* New York:
    Psychohistory Press, 1974.

Demos, John, and Demos, Virginia. "Adolescence in Historical
    Perspective." *Journal of Marriage and the Family* 31:
    632-638.

Fleming, Sandford. *Children and Puritanism: The Place of
    Children in the Life and Thought of New England Churches,
    1620-1847.* New Haven: Yale University Press, 1933.

Fox, Claire E. "Pregnancy, Childbirth and Early Infancy in
    Anglo-American Culture, 1675-1830." Ph.D. Dissertation,
    University of Pennsylvania, 1966.

Graff, Harvey J. "Patterns of Adolescence and Child Depen-
    dency in the Mid-Nineteenth Century City: A Sample from
    Boston, 1860." *History of Education Quarterly* 13:129-143.

Greven, Philip J. comp. *Childrearing Concepts, 1628-1861:
    Historical Sources.* Itasca, Ill.: F.E. Peacock Publishers,
    1973.

Handlin, Oscar, and Handlin, Mary F. *Facing Life: Youth and
    the Family in American History.* Boston: Little, Brown,
    1971.

Hareven, Tamara K., ed. *Anonymous Americans: Explorations in
    Nineteenth Century Social History.* Englewood Cliffs,
    N.J.: Prentice-Hall, 1971.

Kelly, Robert Gordon. "Mother was a Lady: Strategy and Order
    in Selected American Children's Periodicals, 1865-1890."
    Ph.D. Dissertation, University of Iowa, 1970.

Kett, Joseph F. "Adolescence and Youth in Nineteenth Century
    America." *Journal of Interdisciplinary History* 2 (1971):
    283-298.

Kiefer, Monica. "Early American Childhood in the Middle Atlantic Area." *Pennsylvania Magazine of History and Biography* 68 (1944):3-37.

Kiefer, Monica. *American Children Through Their Books, 1700-1835*. Philadelphia: University of Pennsylvania Press, 1948.

Kuhn, Anne L. *The Mother's Role in Childhood Education: New England Concepts, 1830-1860*. New Haven: Yale University Press, 1947.

Lopez, Manuel D. "A Guide to the Interdisciplinary Literature of the History of Childhood." *History of Childhood Quarterly* 1 (1974):463-494.

Mead, Margaret and Wolfenstein, Martha, eds. *Childhood in Contemporary Cultures*. Chicago: University of Chicago Press, 1963.

Schnaiberg, Allan. "The Concept and Measurement of Child Dependency: An Approach to Family Formation Analysis." *Population Studies* 27 (1973):69-84.

Slater, Peter Gregg. "Views of Children and Child Rearing During the Early Period. A Study in the New England Intellect." Ph.D. Dissertation, University of California, Berkeley, 1970.

Strickland, Charles. "A Transcendentalist Father: The Child-Rearing Practices of Bronson Alcott." *Perspectives in American History* 3 (1969):5-73.

Wishy, Bernard. *The Child and the Republic; The Dawn of Modern American Child Nurture*. Philadelphia: University of Pennsylvania Press, 1967.

G. Legal Status of Women

The study of the legal status of women in America has until fairly recently focused on one or two aspects of women's legal position and assumed that the direction of change to be found, say, with respect to women's ability to sue for divorce, represented the general pattern of development with respect to women's rights. The tendency has also been to assume a simple linear development from colonial times to the present rather than to see fluctuations in law and custom. In fact,

the pattern of development has been by no means linear.
Seventeenth- and eighteenth-century women could and did sue
for divorce within the context of Puritan religious attitudes,
which were tolerant of ending the marriage contract. As the
home and family began to accumulate new social and political
significance and to support important new emotional functions
in nineteenth-century America, this access to divorce was
greatly reduced, to be reacquired in the latter half of the
century on secular terms.

Secularization, customarily thought of as a force for
widening the legal competence of women, was in the nineteenth
century also consistent with reducing their ability to make
contracts and defining them as particularly at risk in certain kinds of moral climates, as we can see with the development of the protective legislation of the closing decades of
the nineteenth century. This contraction of competence in
one area, while there is apparent progress in another, has
been missed by the historians of particular rights--the suffrage, married women's property, divorce--who thus fail to
make us aware of the complex pattern of legislation and custom regulating family life, women's access to work, her
property rights, her political rights, and her reproductive
rights.

Another important question which must be analyzed if we
are to interpret the direction of legal change is the nature
of the arguments that proved persuasive in justifying legal
change. Historians of the suffrage have pointed out that the
movement to extend the suffrage to women was not successful
until the granting of the suffrage was urged on grounds of
expediency to enable the white woman's vote to counteract
that of blacks and undesirable immigrant males. We may thus
see legal change which is expedient in terms of larger social
issues but not necessarily a sign of a fundamental shift of
opinion on women's rights. The same point cannot be overemphasized with respect to women's reproductive rights and
the battle to make the dissemination of birth-control information legal. This struggle was not successful until arguments about the use of birth-control techniques to limit the
population growth of lesser races were adopted, and until the
use of birth control was given medical approval as necessary
to maternal and child health. Such a change could be introduced without any alteration in social attitudes on the fundamental question of female sensual liberation. Thus the
social context of legal change and the arguments used in its
successful advocacy must be clearly understood before we can
interpret legal change.

Unfortunately we have no comprehensive treatment dealing
with legal change and its social context sensitive to the

shifts of direction in one area of women's competence that
may accompany changes in status in another. Two nineteenth-
century works are helpful in elucidating legal forms and the
attitudes that undergirded them. Edward D. Mansfield's *Legal
Rights, Liabilities and Duties of Women* (1845) is a helpful
guide to the status quo at the time of the onset of the movement for women's rights. The proceedings of the Boston
Women's Rights Convention of 1855 contain a lengthy *Reports
on the Laws of New England, presented to the New England
Meeting* (1855), which is a painstaking documentation of the
status quo from the point of view of the early feminist movement. Caroline H. Dall's *The College, the Market and the
Court; or Woman's Relation to Education, Labor and Law* (1867)
contains a useful summary of women's access to education and
employment and the legal barriers to increased access in the
first half of the nineteenth century. Dall's earlier *Women's
Rights Under the Law* (1861) is a shorter and more polemical
piece summarizing women's legal and political rights and the
law of the family from Roman times to the nineteenth century.
    Colonial historians have documented the legal underpin-
nings of the family. By far the most useful discussion of
women's legal status in colonial society is found in Richard B.
Morris' *Studies in the History of American Law* (1930). Charles
Rothenberg's "Marriage, Morals and the Law in Colonial America"
(1940) provides useful insights into the practice that guided
the courts in marital disputes, as does Noel C. Stevenson's
"Marital Rights in the Colonial Period" (1955). Edmund S. Morgan's *The Puritan Family* (1944) provides a sensitive and vivid
account of law and custom regulating family life, stressing
women's rights within marriage.
    Social workers, concerned with family instability and
with the rights of the state or private agencies to intervene
within the pattern of family relationships for the good of
child or spouse, were obliged to write extensive general
texts on family law. Edited by Sophonisba P. Breckinridge,
The Family and the State: Select Documents (1934) is a text
written from the famous lectures of one of the founders of
the profession of Social Work at the University of Chicago
School of Social Welfare. Helen I. Clarke's *Social Legislation: American Laws Dealing with the Family, Child, and
Dependent* (1940) represents one of the first standard under-
graduate texts in the history of family law, while Fowler V.
Harper and Jerome H. Slocknick's *Problems of the Family* (1962)
represents a later variant of the same kind of history.
    Since the 1960s two trends have shaped writing on the
subject of family law and women's legal rights. Social
workers and lawyers have collaborated in the teaching of

family law so that the psychological dimensions of family
systems may be understood by the lawyers, judges, and social
workers who deal as professionals with the state's efforts to
ensure family function. Typical of this effort is Joseph
Goldstein and Jay Katz, *The Family and the Law* (1965). This
text endeavors to provide a comprehensive analysis of all
current laws regulating family life and to summarize the
history of the law and changing family functions to which the
law responds. In so doing the authors use excerpts from legal
decisions going back to the seventeenth century and provide
copious bibliographic references. The second major influence
on writing on the subject of women's legal status has been the
resurgence of feminism in the 1960s and the effort to use the
courts to ensure that women were protected from bias in employment, in access to education, and in access to reproductive freedom. Leo Kanowitz's *Women and the Law: The Unfinished
Revolution* (1969) was prompted by this movement and provides
an invaluable summary of the forms of legal bias affecting
women in the 1960s together with a brief summary of their historical origins. Kanowitz's work is the first to recognize
that women or persons defined as dependent in legal terms are
enmeshed in a complex web of legal relationships, all of which
interact to constrain freedom of action, none of which are
much modified by change in a single area such as the suffrage
or access to birth control information. As such his work
represents a new consciousness of the pervasiveness of bias,
the complexity of social systems and their resistance to
change.

BIBLIOGRAPHY

Bradway, John S. "Progress in Family Law." *Annals of the
    American Academy of Political and Social Science* 383
    (1969):1-158.

Breckinridge, Sophonisba P., ed. *The Family and the State:
    Select Documents.* Chicago: University of Chicago Press,
    1934.

Brooks, Carol F. "The Early History of the Anticontraception
    Laws in Massachusetts and Connecticut." *American Quar-
    terly* 18 (1966):3-23.

Clarke, Helen I. *Social Legislation: American Laws Dealing
    with the Family, Child, and Dependent.* New York: D.
    Appleton-Century Co., 1940.

Dall, Caroline Wells (Healey). *The College, the Market, and the Court; or Women's Relation to Education, Labor and Law.* 1867. Reprint. New York: Arno Press, 1972.

Dall, Caroline Wells (Healey). *Women's Rights Under the Law: in Three Lectures Delivered in Boston.* Boston: Walker, Wise & Co., 1861.

De Pauw, Linda Grant. "Land of the Unfree: Legal Limitations on Liberty in Pre-Revolutionary America." *Maryland Historical Magazine* 68 (Winter 1973), 355-368.

Farber, Bernard. "Historical Trends in American Family Law." Paper read at the National Conference on Family Social Structure and Social Change, April 27-29, Clark University, Worcester, Mass., 1972.

Goldstein, Joseph, and Katz, Jay. *The Family and the Law: Problems for Decision in the Family Law Process.* New York: Free Press, 1965.

Harper, Fowler V. and Slocknick, Jerome H. *Problems of the Family.* Rev. ed. Indianapolis: Bobbs-Merrill, 1962.

Kanowitz, Leo. *Women and the Law: the Unfinished Revolution.* 1st ed. Albuquerque: University of New Mexico Press, 1969.

Mansfield, Edward D. *Legal Rights, Liabilities and Duties of Women with an Introductory History of Their Legal Condition in the Hebrew, Roman, and Feudal Civil Systems.* Salem, Mass.: J.P. Jewett & Co; Cincinnati: W.H. Moore & Co., 1845.

Morgan, Edmund S. *The Puritan Family: Essays on Religion and Domestic Relations in Seventeenth Century New England.* Boston: Trustees of the Public Library, 1944.

Morris, Richard B. *Studies in the History of American Law, with Special Reference to the Seventeenth and Eighteenth Centuries.* New York: Columbia University Press, 1930.

Morris, Richard B. *Studies in the History of American Law, with Special Reference to the Seventeenth and Eighteenth Centuries.* 2nd ed. New York: Octagon Books, 1963.

Rothenberg, Charles. "Marriage, Morals and the Law in Colonial America." *New York Law Review* 74 (1940):393-398.

Stevenson, Noel C. "Marital Rights in the Colonial Period."
    New England Historical and Genealogical Record 109 (1955):
    84-90.

Vernier, Chester Garfield. *American Family Laws, a Compara-
    tive Study of the Family Law of the 48 American States,
    Alaska, the District of Columbia, and Hawaii.* Stanford,
    Calif.: Stanford University Press, 1931-1938.

Woman's Rights Convention. *Reports on the Laws of New Eng-
    land, Presented to the New England Meeting.* Boston, 1855.

H. Travel Accounts and Memoirs Commenting
on the Place of Women in American Society

One of the more valuable sources of information about the
emerging provincial society of the colonies and the social
institutions of the new republic are the travel diaries and
comments of foreign visitors or American journalists reporting on the character of the new nation.
The reports of foreign visitors are of three types. The
initial stimulus to such writing and for curiosity about the
nature of American society came from the presence of the
French army in the United States during the Revolutionary
War. The most outstanding narratives come from the pens of
two such visitors, the Marquis de Chastellux and Ferdinand M.
Bayard. Their comments provide us with a snapshot of American institutions as seen by informed, sympathetic, and curious visitors just at the point of the establishment of the
new nation. The diaries of the Marquis de Chastellux were
published as *Travels in North America in the Years 1780-1781-
1782* (1827). Bayard's travel notes appeared as *Travels of a
Frenchman in Maryland and Virginia, with a Description of
Philadelphia and Baltimore in 1791* (1950). Similar views may
be found in Jacques Pierre Brissot de Warville's *New Travels
in the United States in America. Performed in 1788* (1792)
and Michel Chevalier's *Society, Manners and Politics in the
United States* (1839).
The French commentators, used to a society of aristocratic
manners, dalliance, conquest, and tolerance of extramarital
liaisons, were uniformly struck by the freedom of young unwed
American women and puzzled by the society's marital customs.
The institution of marriage seemed to constrain both partners
equally, and the heritage of Puritanism made for plain manners and a conspicuous lack of gallantry in the north and
middle states. Travelers in the south found a society whose
lineaments seemed more familiar. The presence of slave

concubines and the tradition of protecting white women had a
notable effect on women's position. Visitors observed the
codes of coquettishness and exaggerated male deference to
white women of high status, the brutality of the slave system,
and the miserable situation of the southern poor white women.
In general the commentary is sympathetic and optimistic, but
the reader must be aware of the difficulty visitors steeped
in a Latin tradition of the relationship between the sexes
had in interpreting what they saw of male-female relationships.

In sharp contrast to this early French commentary is the
view of American society expressed by visiting British writers
and journalists. The most blistering of these accounts came
from Charles Dickens whose *American Notes for General Circulation* (1842) blasted American manners, satirized the sentimentality and what Dickens saw as the vacuity of American
marriage relationships, and contrasted the feminine pursuit
of religion with the male obsession for making money. Frances
M. Trollope's *Domestic Manners of the Americans* (1832) is in
the same vein. Trollope focuses her attention on the crudity
of manners, the absence of servants, the decline of the domestic arts, and the vapidity of women's lives. Trollope and
Dickens clearly came with the intent of validating their
assumptions of British superiority, and their accounts of
American manners indicate what they see as a society falling
away from accepted British notions of decorum and behavior.

By the 1820s and '30s a different genre of travel writing
was being produced by visiting Europeans who viewed American
society from the standpoint of European radicalism or from
the perspective of the revolutions of 1789 and 1830. Frances
Wright and Harriet Martineau were particularly keen observers
of the position of women in America, so that their comments
are wide ranging about feminine life and their speculation on
the direction of change an important source of contemporary
comment. The finest piece of such commentary is, of course,
Alexis de Tocqueville's *Democracy in America* (1835). It is
interesting that de Tocqueville, Wright, and Martineau, writing
from very different political perspectives, come to the same
puzzled conclusion that American society tolerates considerable freedom for American women before marriage, a freedom
consistent with improved status and European radical views
about women's position, but that this freedom vanished once
women entered the married state.

A fourth type of travel writing was produced by native
Americans to describe the character and nature of American
society. Anne Grant's *Memoirs of an American Lady: With
Sketches of Manners and Scenery in America, as they Existed
Before the Revolution* (1808) is an invaluable account of

domestic life and manners in colonial New York written by the
daughter of a Loyalist whose childhood memories were of Albany
society and the gracious style of life of the Schuyler family.
Anne Royall's *Sketches of History Life and Manners in the
United States* (1826) is the work of an early American woman
journalist forced by widowhood to support herself by her pen.
Her descriptions of travel throughout the colonies are vivid
and constitute one of the earliest attempts at systematic
descriptions of life and manners by a native American. Royall
is a booster of the new Republic and negative observations
are firmly excluded from her commentaries.

All four genres of comment are useful for the researcher
since the points of agreement in observation let us know we
are on firm ground and help to provide a context within which
to interpret literary evidence, especially the autobiographical writing of women.

BIBLIOGRAPHY

Bayard, Ferdinand M. *Travels of a Frenchman in Maryland and
    Virginia, with a Description of Philadelphia and Baltimore
    in 1791*. Translated and edited with introduction, notes,
    and index, by Ben C. McCrary. Ann Arbor, Mich.: Edwards
    Brothers, 1950.

Bell, Margaret Van Horn (Dwight). *A Journey to Ohio in 1810*.
    Edited by Max Farrand. New Haven: Yale University Press,
    1913.

Birkbeck, Morris. *Letters from Illinois*. London: Taylor &
    Hessey, 1818.

Birney, Catherine. *The Grimke Sisters. Sarah and Angelika
    Grimke, the First American Women Advocates of Abortion
    and Woman's Rights*. "Private Diary, 1755-1803," pp. 55-
    123. Boston: Lee & Shepard, 1885.

Brissot de Warville, Jacques Pierre. *New Travels in the
    United States of America. Performed in 1788*. Translated
    from the French. Dublin: printed by W. Corbet, for P.
    Byrne, A. Gueber, etc., 1792.

Chastellux, Francois Jean, Marquis de. *Travels in North
    America, in the Years 1780-1781-1782*. New York: Gallaher
    & White, 1827.

Chevalier, Michel. *Society, Manners and Politics in the
    United States*. c. 1839.

Dickens, Charles. *American Notes for General Circulation.*
London: Chapman & Hall, 1842.

Grant, Anne. *Memoirs of an American Lady: With Sketches of
Manners and Scenery in America, as They Existed Previous
to the Revolution.* London: Lougman, Hurst, Rees & Orme,
etc., 1808.

Kalm, Pehr. *Travels in North America: The English Version
of 1770.* Revised from the Original Swedish and edited
by Adolph B. Benson. With a translation of new material
from Kalm's diary notes. New York: Wilson-Erickson, 1937.

Kemble, Frances Anne. *Journal of a Residence on a Georgian
Plantation in 1838-1839.* New York: Harper & Brothers,
1863.

Lieber, Francis. *The Stranger in America.* Philadelphia:
Carey, Lea & Blanchard, 1834.

Martineau, Harriet. *Society in America.* London: Saunders &
Otley, 1837.

Royall, Anne. *Sketches of History, Life and Manners in the
United States.* New Haven: printed for the author, 1826.

Tocqueville, Alexis de. *Democracy in America.* Translated by
Henry Reeve. London: Saunders & Otley, 1835.

Trollope, Frances (M. Hon.). *Domestic Manners of the Americans.* 4th ed. Paris: Baudry's Foreign Library, 1832.

Wright, Frances D'Arusmont. *Views of Society and Manners in
America; in a Series of Letters from that Country to a
Friend in England, During the Years 1818, 1819, and 1820.*
London: Longman, Hurst, Rees, Orme & Brown, 1821.

I. Histories by Women of the Revolutionary
and Early National Periods

Women historians were among the first chroniclers of the
Revolution. Hannah Adams' *A Summary History of New England,
from the First Settlement at Plymouth, to the Acceptance of
the Federal Constitution* (1799) is written with apologies
that a woman should undertake such an historical narrative
and with the excuse that much of her wording is an adaptation
from the documents produced by the major actors in the

narrative, all of whom are male. The work is a standard historical narrative for the time, chronicling the rise of
colonial society, the oppression of the British, and the
growth of the colleges and universities in the efflorescence
of American culture in the 1790s. Adams wrote because of the
need to support herself by her pen, and as she explains in
her autobiography, she thought her work would be justified to
the extent that it might have been written by a man. Mercy
Otis Warren's *History of the Rise, Progress and Termination
of the American Revolution* (1805) is written as a work of
patriotism by a learned woman close to the central figures of
the Revolutionary generation in Massachusetts. She, too,
takes her task to be chronicling the actions of major political figures, and her excuse for writing is that she has the
time and the knowledge to create the record. Elizabeth Ellet
(1818–1877) represents a second generation of chroniclers of
the Revolution, and she takes the domestic life of the country
at the time of the Revolution as her theme, and sets as her
goal recording the contributions of American women to the
victorious outcome of the conflict. Ellet's writing is
piously hagiographical, unctuous in the extreme when writing
about the women of the Washington, Adams, and Jefferson families. However, she takes time to report the achievements of
women guides and messengers, women who spied on the British.
Her work is based on anecdote, and her reconstruction of
events is of the novelistic kind describing scenes, action,
and feelings about which she could not possibly have clear
evidence. She is of the conservative feminist school in
wanting to record and praise women's achievement in the Revolutionary period while reserving her most unqualified praise
for the woman whose sole contribution to the Revolution was
to give birth to George Washington. Lydia Maria Child's *The
History of the Condition of Women, in Various Ages and Nations*
(1835) is an unambiguously radical feminist work clothed in
discreet language. Child deliberately uses the analysis of
women's position in classical times to comment on her own
time and to draw attention to the need for access to education
and improved poverty rights for American women. Adams, Ellet,
and Child are all examples of a new development in the early
national period, that of the woman writer living by the sale
of her work and turning her attention to the condition of
women. They are clearly part of an emerging set of secular
cultural activities becoming open to the educated woman for
the first time.

BIBLIOGRAPHY

Adams, Hannah. *A Memoir of Miss Hannah Adams, Written by Herself.* Boston: Gray & Bowen, 1832.

Adams, Hannah. *A Summary History of New England, from the First Settlement at Plymouth, to the Acceptance of the Federal Constitution.* Dedham, Mass.: printed by H. Mann & J.H. Adams for the author, 1799.

Child, Lydia Maria. *The History of the Condition of Women, in Various Ages and Nations.* Boston: J. Allen & Co., 1835.

Ellet, Elizabeth Fries (Lummis). *The Women of the American Revolution.* New York: Baker & Scribner, 1848-50.

Ellet, Elizabeth Fries (Lummis). *Domestic History of the American Revolution.* New York: Baker & Scribner, 1850.

Warren, Mercy Otis. *History of the Rise, Progress and Termination of the American Revolution.* Boston: printed by Manning & Loring, for E. Larken, 1805.

J. Women Missionaries, Religious, and
Evangelists of the Early National Period

While women were finding a voice as secular writers in the late eighteenth and early nineteenth century, it is clear that religious culture provided the most striking opportunities for new roles and new authority for women of talent as preachers and popular leaders. The popular millennial culture of late eighteenth-century England described in J.F.C. Harrison's *The Second Coming: Popular Millenarianism 1780-1850* (1979) found fertile soil in the simple agricultural communities of colonial New England. Harrison sees millenarian beliefs as a form of popular rejection of the ideas of the Enlightenment which grew out of evangelical protestantism, hence its strength in the culture of rural New England. In the 1770s Mother Ann Lee (1736-1784) brought her small band of followers to New York and began to recruit converts to Shakerism, while Jemimah Wilkinson founded the first sectarian group led by a native-born American woman, assuming the title of Universal Friend. Lee and Wilkinson both taught that celibacy was the only pure state in which to prepare for the second coming, and both attracted a high proportion of women converts. Edited by Rufus Bishop and Seth Wells, *Testimonies of the Life, Character, Revelations and Doctrines of Our*

Blessed Mother Ann Lee (1888, second ed.) is a primary source
which gives a vivid sense of the mentality and emotional life
of the first Shaker converts. Benjamin Seth Young's *The
Testimony of Christ's Second Appearing* (1808) summarizes the
doctrine which declared that Mother Ann Lee represented the
risen Christ. Jemima Wilkinson was popularly attributed
the same distinction in folklore though she herself merely
claimed to speak by divine inspiration. Herbert A. Wisbey,
Jr. has written a well-balanced biography of Wilkinson,
*Pioneer Prophetess: Jemima Wilkinson, the Publick Universal
Friend* (1964). The account is based on the Wilkinson Papers
extant only in microfilm form in the Collection of Regional
History of Cornell University. The collection has particular
value for the psychohistorian because of the practice of
recording dreams in great detail followed by the Universal
Friend and her fellow believers. We can see in these millenarian movements a powerful drive toward improving women's
status, a drive present in varying forms in all varieties of
Christian perfectionism. All were directed toward the perfection of society, either through the Second Coming or
through the establishment of the perfected community freed
from the sin of Eve. Millenarian culture provided the opportunity for strong women religious leaders to assume authority
and to redress the pattern of male domination in Protestant
culture by claiming that the risen lord had assumed a female
form. Since human generativity was of no importance to those
expecting the world's end in their lifetime, sexuality and
the governance of the family could be ignored in millenarian
thinking. Edward D. Andrews' *The People Called Shakers*
(1953) provides a vivid picture of Shaker social life and
religious practice, though the author is less interested in
the general context of millennial culture than J.F.C. Harrison,
and thus does not relate Shakerism very effectively to the
general Protestant culture of colonial New England.

The Great Awakening released powerful religious emotions
focused on the perfection of humanity through the correct
brand of faith. So much attention has been focused on the
psychological dimensions of the sense of sin that permeated
revival culture that historians have tended to underestimate
the social forces released by the idea that the truly repen-
tant could be brought into the right relationship to Christ.
These were consistent with enhancing the role of women in
Protestant religious life. We see in Almond H. Davis' *The
Female Preacher; or, Memoir of Salome Lincoln* (1843) a clear
record of how this enhancement came about. Once the path to
Christian truth became inspiration rather than learning and
the study of doctrine, most arguments against women preaching
vanished, since the scriptural grounds for women's capacity

to prophecy could easily override St. Paul's prohibition against women speaking in church. Phoebe Worrel Palmer's *Faith and Its Effects* (1849) demonstrates the woman preacher's concern with family relationships and her sense of the family as the main setting for the drama of salvation.

While the role of preacher and religious leader was emerging for women in millennial and revival culture, the role of Christian missionary and teacher was taking both traditional Catholic and new Protestant forms. The traditional Catholic form found expression in the pioneer ventures of the Sisters of the Sacred Heart and the Sisters of Charity in Christian education and missionary work on the frontier of Kentucky and Missouri in the years following the War of 1812. Women religious endured the hardships of the frontier and experienced the independence which went with self-directing communities of women. Philippine Duchesne's letters are liberally quoted in Louise Callan's *Philippine Duchesne: Frontier Missionary of the Sacred Heart 1769-1852* (1957). The hundredth-anniversary history of the Society of Sisters of Charity of Nazareth, Anna B. McGill's *The Sisters of Charity of Nazareth, Kentucky* (1917), draws on extensive primary sources from the founding years of the Society but displays all the faults of pious writing about Catholic religious. It is important to tap these bodies of information about the pioneer communities of Catholic women on the frontier because they provide a perspective on the new literature produced by the Protestant woman missionaries of the 1820s and '30s. We can see also in the growth of these religious communities the strength of traditional Catholic culture in a century when the women teachers and reformers who have attracted historians have been almost exclusively Protestant.

A distinctly new path for Protestant women opened with the establishment of the American Foreign Mission Society and with the first missionary efforts directed to the West Coast Indians. Mission societies did not permit single women to take up foreign missionary work so that women who were called to missionary endeavors had to agree to arranged marriages with suitable spouses prior to departure. The diaries, letters, and historical accounts of missionary work produced by the first generation of Protestant women missionaries illustrate how thoroughly travel and encounters with non-Western cultures freed nineteenth-century women from the romantic sentimentality which was to become the staple of American domestic culture. Clifford M. Drury has collected the writing of the first women missionaries to travel to the West Coast. His meticulously edited *First White Women Over the Rockies* (1963-1966) is an invaluable record of the changes in consciousness experienced by the woman missionary.

A healthy life out of doors and freedom from the crippling
codes of fashionable dress for women enabled the new travelers
to discover a sense of health and strength not otherwise
available to women, and familiarity with Indian cultures provided a new perspective on the world back "home." The three
wives of the Reverend Adoniram Judson--Sarah, Emily, and Ann
--likewise found arranged marriage and travel to Burma productive of a strong sense of self and freedom from many forms
of culturally required feminine weaknesses. A shared call to
missionary work produced a sense of common purpose in marriage
not part of the contemporary pattern of courtship in the early
national period, while the interdependence produced by life
in an alien culture removed all signs of the subordinate relationship assigned the wife in a conventional marriage.
Each of Judson's three wives had a gift for pungent prose,
and their letters formed the basis for eulogistic memoirs.
Despite the pieties of evangelical biographers, the women
speak through their letters, and their writing deserves scrutiny for their strength and vigor of mind.

The writing of the women of the Newell and Bridgman
families provides a similar record of the first American
missions to China and a similar indication of the effect of
travel and cross-cultural perspective on women's consciousness. *The Life and Writings of Mrs. Harriet Newell* (1831)
and Eliza Jane Bridgman's *Daughters of China; or, Sketches of
Domestic Life in the Celestial Empire* (1853) were widely read,
as were the accounts of the Burma missions by the Judsons,
and their popularity suggests that the missionary experience
may have provided important role models for the early nineteenth-century American woman. While genteel culture required
the cult of delicate and self-effacing "true womanhood," the
lives of the missionaries showed women moving out of their
assigned sphere, sharing the labors and hazards of men, and
working as equals. If we look for the counterpart of the
frontier for the Protestant woman of the northeast, we see it
in the foreign missions where adventure, danger, and excitement could all be part of women's lot. Catholic culture
allowed this adventure to the woman religious, safe within
the discipline of her order and the guidance of her male con-
fessor. Protestant culture permitted it initially only to
spouses, but in so doing unintentionally provided a model of
equal partnership. Thus when we assess the significance of
the popularity of the mission literature with American women,
we must allow for the possibility that part of its attraction
was the new set of roles for women and men and the dashing
image of "true womanhood" which it contained.

In general we see in the social and intellectual patterns of
colonial and early nineteenth-century America a situation
paradoxical in the terms in which standard historical narratives are written. The forces of the secular culture assign
a clear social territory to women, excluding them from political life and insisting on their subordination within the
family. The new forces of nationalism unleashed by the Revolution place a new importance on that family structure and on
women's containment within it. By contrast, within the religious culture of the period we see a ferment of ideas tending
toward change in women's position. The abandonment of the
notion of infant depravity gave new meaning to motherhood and
child rearing, the intellectual climate of Christian perfectionism prompted fresh speculation about the place of women
freed from Eve's sin, and the new role of missionary or
preacher gave women a social territory as large as the heathen
world. The new male medical profession was evolving a picture
of the female as physically weak and psychologically unstable,
and the only counter-literature with wide readership came
from the redoubtable female missionaries whose health and
mental balance stood in marked contrast to the advancing body
of medical opinion. We are not used to seeing the rise of
professions as a negative social force or evangelical religious culture as a source of consciousness raising for women,
but in fact in the early nineteenth century the main "progressive forces," if we equate progress with the opportunity
to assume new roles and cross social boundaries, were to be
found not in secular but in religious culture.

BIBLIOGRAPHY

Allinson, William J., comp. *Memorials of Rebecca Jones*.
     Philadelphia: H. Longstreth, 1849.

Andrews, Edward Demira. *The People Called Shakers: A Search
     for the Perfect Society*. New York: Oxford University
     Press, 1953.

Barnard, Hannah. *An Appeal to the Society of Friends, on
     the Primitive Simplicity of Their Christian Principles
     and Discipline*. c. 1801.

Bishop, Rufus, and Wells, Seth, eds. *Testimonies of the Life,
     Character, Revelations and Doctrines of Our Blessed Mother
     Ann Lee*. 2nd edition. Albany, N.Y.: Weed, Parsons & Co.,
     printers, 1888.

Bridgman, E.C. *The Life and Labors of Elijah Coleman Bridgman*.
     c. 1863.

Bridgman, Eliza Jane (Gillett). *Daughters of China; or,
    Sketches of Domestic Life in the Celestial Empire.*
    New York: R. Carter & Brothers, 1853.

Brumberg, Joan J. *Mission for Life: The Story of the Family
    of Adoniram Judson.* New York: Free Press, 1980.

Callan, Louise. *The Society of the Sacred Heart in North
    America.* London: Longmans, Green & Co., 1937.

Callan, Louise. *Philippine Duchesne, Frontier Missionary of
    the Sacred Heart, 1769-1852.* With an introduction by
    Joseph E. Ritter. Westminster, Md.: Newman Press, 1957.

Davis, Almond H. *The Female Preacher; or, Memoir of Salome
    Lincoln.* 1843. Reprint. New York: Arno Press, 1972.

Drury, Clifford Merrill, ed. *First White Women over the
    Rockies: Diaries, Letters, and Biographical Sketches of
    the Six Women of the Oregon Mission Who Made the Overland
    Journey in 1836 and 1838.* Glendale, Calif.: A.H. Clark
    Co., 1963-66.

Forester, Fanny, [pseud.] *Memoir of Sarah B. Judson, a
    Member of the American Mission to Burmah.* New York:
    L. Colby & Co., 1848.

Harrison, John Fletcher Clews. *The Second Coming: Popular
    Millenarianism, 1780-1850.* New Brunswick, N.J.: Rutgers
    University Press, 1979.

Kendrick, Asahel C. *The Life and Letters of Emily C. Judson.*
    New York: Sheldon & Co.; Boston: Gould & Lincoln, 1860.

Knowles, James D. *Life of Mrs. Ann H. Judson, late Mission-
    ary to Burmah; including an Account of the American Bap-
    tist Mission to that Empire.* Philadelphia: American
    Sunday School Union, 1830.

McGill, Anna B. *The Sisters of Charity of Nazareth, Kentucky.*
    New York: Encyclopedia Press, 1917.

Newell, Harriet (Atwood). *The Life and Writings of Mrs.
    Harriet Newell.* Rev. ed. Philadelphia: American Sunday
    School Union, 1831.

Palmer, Phoebe W. *Faith and Its Effects; or, Fragments from
    My Portfolio.* New York: The author, 1849.

Richardson, Marvin M. *The Whitman Mission, the Third Station on the Old Oregon Trail*. Walla Walla, Wash.: Whitman Publishing Co., 1940.

Wayland, Francis. *A Memoir of the Life and Labors of the Rev. Adoniram Judson, D.D.* Boston: Phillips, Sampson and Company, 1853.

Wisbey, Herbert A., Jr. *Pioneer Prophetess: Jemima Wilkinson, the Publick Universal Friend*. Ithaca, N.Y.: Cornell University Press, 1964.

Young, Benjamin Seth. *The Testimony of Christ's Second Appearing*. c. 1808.

SECTION II

INDUSTRIALIZATION, WOMEN'S WORK, AND THE TRANSFORMATION OF THE HOUSEHOLD, 1810-1910

A. General Works

Industrialization and its impact on the participation of women in waged labor has engendered lively discussion among historians. While most historians like Robert Smuts in *Women and Work in America* (1959) have accepted the view that industrial society expanded the options open to women, they have also accepted the notion that the participation of women in the work force has had serious repercussions on family life. Smuts also assumes that women worked for "pin money," and, while recognizing the disparities between women's work and men's work, he maintains that the overall effect has been positive. Women scholars have questioned these assumptions as they have also stressed the importance of women's unpaid work.

Edith Abbott's important study, *Women in Industry* (1910), surveys the specific conditions of women's work in textiles, printing, cigar making, and other industries and concludes that the position of women in these industries was undermined as mechanization and the needs of industry changed the nature of the work. Pointing to the increasing disparities between men's and women's wages, her conclusion questions the optimistic view of the effect of industrialization on women, a conclusion shared by Alice Clark in *Working Life of Women in the Seventeenth Century* (1919) (see p. 4).

BIBLIOGRAPHY

Abbott, Edith. *Women in Industry; a Study in American Economic History*. New York: D. Appleton & Co., 1910.

Bancroft, Gertrude. *The American Labor Force: Its Growth and Changing Composition*. New York: John Wiley & Sons, 1958.

Calhoun, Arthur W. *A Social History of the American Family
From Colonial Times to the Present.* 3 vols. Cleveland:
Arthur H. Clark Co., 1917-1919.

Lerner, Gerda. "The Lady and the Mill Girl: Changes in the
Status of Women in the Age of Jackson." *Midcontinent,
American Studies Journal* 10 (1969):5-15.

Meyer, Annie N., ed. *Woman's Work in America.* New York:
H. Holt & Co., 1891.

Smuts, Robert W. *Women and Work in America.* New York:
Columbia University Press, 1959.

B. Early Industrialization

As background to the discussion of early industrialization, David Montgomery's 1968 article, "The Working Classes
of the Pre-Industrial American City, 1780-1830," delineates
the process by which artisanal skills were undermined and
transformed. Women were recruited into the early textile
mills partly because their labor would not challenge the
established crafts. The westward migration of males produced
a surplus of young single women who were forced to provide
for themselves. These early mills provided single women with
an alternative to domestic labor on family farms, but the
majority of the operatives used their jobs as a temporary
means to earn enough money to pay off the family debts or to
send their siblings to school. Lucy Larcom's classic autobiography, *A New England Girlhood* (1889), recounts her experiences as a factory hand at Lowell, Massachusetts. This
important firsthand account also describes in detail the
boarding-house system, the attempts to organize the operatives, and the creation of a female culture centered around
The Lowell Offering. *The Golden Threads* (1949) by Hannah
Josephson represents the best secondary study to date of the
New England textile mills.

BIBLIOGRAPHY

Bartlett, Elisha. *A Vindication of the Character and Condition of the Females Employed in the Lowell Mills,
Against Charges Contained in the Boston Times and the
Boston Quarterly Review.* Lowell: L. Huntress, printer,
1841.

Josephson, Hannah. *The Golden Threads: New England's Mill Girls and Magnates.* New York: Duell, Sloan & Pearce, 1949.

Larcom, Lucy. *A New England Girlhood, Outlined From Memory.* Boston: Houghton Mifflin Co., 1889.

The Lowell Offering. *Mind Amongst the Spindles: a Selection from the Lowell Offering, A Miscellany Wholly Compiled by the Factory Girls of an American City.* Edited by Charles Knight. London: C. Knight & Co., 1844.

Montgomery, David. "The Working Classes of the Pre-Industrial American City, 1780-1830." *Labor History* 9 (1968):3-22.

Robinson, Harriet J. *Loom and Spindle: or Life Among the Early Mill Girls.* New York: T.Y. Crowell & Co., 1898.

C. Domestic Service

Factory labor competed with more traditional forms of women's work in the nineteenth century. Lucy Salmon's important early survey, *Domestic Service* (1897), explored the position of the domestic in the late nineteenth century. Her study documented the increasing preference for factory work over domestic service. Women preferred the independence of waged work to the restrictions of the live-in domestic. Salmon urged that domestic service be drawn "into the general current of industrial development" by removing most chores from the individual household and turning these tasks over to catering, cleaning, and laundry services. Cooperative housework was unthinkable to Salmon because of the power of the American ideal of individual family and domestic units.

BIBLIOGRAPHY

Beecher, Catharine. *Letters to Persons Who Are Engaged in Domestic Service.* New York: Leavitt & Trow, 1842.

Salmon, Lucy M. *Domestic Service.* New York: Macmillan Co., 1897.

Stigler, George Joseph. *Domestic Servants in the U.S., 1900-1940.* New York: National Bureau of Economic Research, 1946.

D. Prostitution

A much neglected form of women's paid work, prostitution, provided another alternative to factory work. Mid-nineteenth-century reformers worried about the connection between domestic service, factory work, and prostitution, but they failed to perceive prostitution as a rational alternative to the long hours and low pay of other types of work. The prevailing view of writers like William Sanger in *History of Prostitution* (1858) attributed prostitution, despite evidence to the contrary, to individual moral failure and the influence of immigration and urbanization. Sanger's survey of prostitution in New York City represents a valuable source of information. David Pivar's *Purity Crusade: Sexual Morality and Social Control, 1868-1900* (1973) analyzes the need for increased moral reform in an era of anxiety about rapid social change. He demonstrates that the emphasis on individual reformation through religious means was replaced by the need for social control of the "dangerous classes" in an age of rapid industrial growth.

Sanger's 1858 study of New York prostitutes stood alone in importance until the 1911 Chicago Vice Commission's survey appeared. *The Social Evil in Chicago* (1911) remains the single most important study of prostitution of the Progressive period. Initiated by reformers like Jane Addams, the study sought to investigate allegations of widespread "white slave" traffic in young women. This document provides the historian with invaluable information on the structure of the prostitute's world and insights into the character of the prostitutes themselves. An important theoretical exploration from the viewpoint of the social scientist is W.I. Thomas' *The Unadjusted Girl* (1923). Using case studies of delinquent girls, Thomas describes prostitution as deviant behavior arising not only from economic circumstances but also from the process of "individualization." Sexual delinquency arises not from sexual desire or economic need, but from a desire for material goods. Sex is the young girl's capital, as Thomas realizes, though he does not relate this insight to Marxist thought.

BIBLIOGRAPHY

Addams, Jane. *A New Conscience and an Ancient Evil.*
    New York: Macmillan Co., 1912.

Chicago Vice Commission. *The Social Evil in Chicago: A Study
    of Existing Conditions with Recommendations by the Vice
    Commission of Chicago.* Chicago: Gunthorp-Warren Printing
    Co., 1911.

Ellington, George, [pseud.] *The Women of New York; or, the Underworld of the Great City.* Reprint. New York: Arno Press, 1972.

Feldman, Egal. "Prostitution, the Alien Woman and the Progressive Imagination." *American Quarterly* 19 (1967): 192-206.

Gardener, Helen Hamilton. *Is This Your Son, My Lord?* Boston: Arena Publishing Co., 1890.

Hadden, Maude Miner. *Slavery of Prostitution: A Plea for Emancipation.* New York: Macmillan Co., 1916.

Pivar, David J. *Purity Crusade: Sexual Morality and Social Control, 1868-1900.* Westport, Conn.: Greenwood Press, 1973.

Riegel, Robert. "Changing American Attitudes Toward Prostitution 1800-1920." *Journal of the History of Ideas* 29 (1968):437-452.

Rosebury, Theodore. *Microbes and Morals: The Strange Story of Venereal Disease.* New York: Viking Press, 1971.

Sanger, William W. *History of Prostitution: Its Extent, Causes, and Effects Throughout the World.* New York: Harper & Brothers, 1858.

Thomas, William I. *The Unadjusted Girl: With Cases and Standpoint for Behavior Analysis.* Boston: Little, Brown & Co., 1923.

Trumble, Alfred. *New York by Day and Night.* New York: R.K. Fox, 1881.

Washburn, Charles. *Come Into My Parlor: A Biography of the Aristocratic Everleigh Sisters of Chicago.* New York: Knickerbocker Publishing Co., 1934.

Winick, Charles, and Kinsie, Paul M. *The Lively Commerce: Prostitution in the United States.* Chicago: Quadrangle Books, 1971.

Woodruff, Charles S. *Legalized Prostitution; or Marriage as It is, and Marriage as It Should Be.* Boston: B. Marsh, 1862.

E. Industrialization After 1840

The so-called golden age of the working girl ended in
1840 with the influx of cheap immigrant labor. The Irish
migrations of the post-1840 period signaled the end of the
experimental period and heralded the intense period of industrialization in the United States. Women's waged work in the
post-Civil War period is dealt with by Joseph A. Hill in
Women in Gainful Occupations, 1870-1920 (1929). Based on
census data, this study analyzing occupational data provides
a discussion of the changing nature of women's work. Unfortunately the author does not provide the reader with information on wages, hours, or working conditions. However, this
work supplies a detailed commentary on the changing occupational structure.

Several firsthand accounts of the working conditions of
female workers appeared around the turn of the century. The
best of these was written by Dorothy Richardson, a middle-
class woman who lived as a working girl in New York. *The
Long Day* (1905) details the difficulties of women involved
in such seasonal work as flower making and hat making.

Middle-class women also involved themselves in the problems of sweated female labor by forming such organizations
as the Consumers' League. Maude Nathan's *The Story of an
Epoch-Making Movement* (1926) narrates the organization's
response to working conditions in retail stores. Consumer
pressure through the use of the "white list" served to expose
the abuses of store clerks forced to work long hours under
poor working conditions. The League extended its activities
to cover the products manufactured by female labor. At the
base of its critique, the consumer was responsible for the
worst of these evils. The history of the League represents
the first reformist response to the arrival of the consumer
economy. This, like other nineteenth-century reform efforts,
could be based upon an individual response to social injus-
tice.

Middle-class women reformers like Helen Campbell also
wrote articles on the working and living conditions of
working-class women. Campbell's study, *Prisoners of Poverty*
(1887), appeared in article form in the *New York Tribune* in
1886. She surveyed the needle trades and retail stores in
New York and concluded that philanthropy failed to remedy the
problems of working-class women. Her solutions included industrial education, immigration restriction, agitation for
better wages and shorter hours, and the need for cooperation,
perhaps even socialism. She later became an advocate of
Consumers' Unions influenced by consumers' reform movements.

Some of the best sources for information on the actual
conditions of employment for women are contained in the
various reports of governmental bureaus. Among these are
Carroll Wright's *Industrial Evolution of the United States*,
Chapter 16 (1895), the U.S. Bureau of Labor's *Work and Wages
of Men, Women and Children* (1897), Helen Sumner's *History of
Women in Industry in the United States* (1910), and the bulletins
of the Women's Bureau. Sumner's survey includes much important
information on average working hours, health, piece rates,
strikes, and family budgets. The study also includes an
examination of domestic service. The report draws together
from pamphlets, reports and newspapers much useful information on early nineteenth-century women's work. Wright's
survey from the colonial period to 1890 is based on government statistics and emphasizes the role of technological
improvements in opening up manufacturing to women and children.
The lower wages of women are explained by the newness of women
in the labor force, lack of training, expectation of marriage,
family support, competition, and lower standards of work
stemming from lower physical and mental capacities. However,
Wright maintains that woman's condition steadily improves as
women combine in associations which bring public attention to
their needs and as more protective legislation is passed.
This study was based on detailed research on urban working
women's lives carried out by settlement workers. It is less
reliable in its references to rural women. A more complete
listing of these pamphlets can be found in Mary Jane Soltow
et al., *Women in American Labor History, 1825-1935: An Annotated Bibliography* (1972). This bibliography draws together
many other books, articles, pamphlets, and government publications on the subject of women's industrial work.

Industrial work for women in the late nineteenth century
came under attack from doctors and reformers concerned with
the damaging consequences to female physiology and morals.
Dr. Edward Clarke's *Sex in Education* (1873) maintained that
women could engage in the same activities as men, but that a
woman must take care lest her physiology become damaged in
the crucial years of development between 14 and 20. Dr.
Clarke recommended a different educational system and curriculum for women which would take these factors into account.
His book influenced Azel Ames, the author of *Sex in Industry*
(1875), who applied Clarke's cautions to women workers. He
warned that the employment of young girls in shops and fac-
tories led to premature development of the sexual instincts
as well as possible damage to the reproductive organs.

The bulletins of the Women's Bureau are invaluable aids
to understanding the problems and working conditions of
working women in the twentieth century. The Bureau as an

always threatened agency within the Department of Labor saw
its role in publicizing information on women's working conditions and in educating the public in matters affecting
working women. Some of the most valuable publications deal
with local conditions in various industries or with special
status groups like married women or black women in the labor
force.

BIBLIOGRAPHY

Ames, Azel. *Sex in Industry: a Plea for the Working Girl.*
Boston: J.R. Osgood & Co., 1875.

Anderson, Mary. *Woman at Work: The Autobiography of Mary
Anderson as Told to Mary N. Winslow.* Minneapolis: University of Minnesota Press, 1951.

Butler, Elizabeth B. *Women and the Trades, Pittsburgh, 1907-
1908.* New York: Charities Publication Committee, 1909.

Campbell, Helen. *Prisoners of Poverty, Women Wage-Workers,
Their Trades and Their Lives.* Boston: Roberts Brothers,
1887.

Campbell, Helen. *Women Wage-Earners: Their Past, Their
Present and Their Future.* Boston: Roberts Brothers, 1893.

Clark, Sue Ainslie, and Wyatt, Edith. *Making Both Ends Meet:
The Income and Outlay of New York Working Girls.*
New York: Macmillan Co., 1911.

Clarke, Edward H. *Sex in Education; or, A Fair Chance for
Girls.* Boston: J.R. Osgood & Co., 1873.

Collins, Jennie. *Nature's Aristocracy; or, Battles and
Wounds in Time of Peace, A Plea for the Oppressed.*
Edited by Russell H. Conwell. Boston: Lee & Shepard,
1871.

Consumers' League of New York. *Behind the Scenes in a Hotel.*
New York: The Consumers' League of New York, 1922.

Dodge, Grace, ed. *Thoughts of Busy Girls. Written by a
Group of Girls Who Have Little Time for Study, and Yet
Who Find Much Time for Thinking.* New York: Cassell
Publishing Co., 1892.

Gilman, Charlotte Perkins. *Women and Economics; a Study of the Economic Relation Between Man and Women as a Factor in Social Evolution*. Boston: Small, Maynard & Co., 1898.

Hill, Joseph A. *Women in Gainful Occupations, 1870-1920*. Washington, D.C.: U.S. Government Printing Office, 1929.

Hughes, Gwendolyn. *Mothers in Industry: Wage Earning by Mothers in Philadelphia*. New York: New Republic, 1925.

Kelley, Florence. *Some Ethical Gains Through Legislation*. New York: Macmillan Co., 1905.

Lauck, William Jett, and Sydenstriker, Edgar. *Conditions of Labor in American Industries: A Summarization of the Results of Recent Investigations*. New York and London: Funk & Wagnalls Co., 1917.

MacLean, Annie M. *Wage-Earning Women*. New York: Macmillan Co., 1910.

MacLean, Annie M. *Women Workers and Society*. Chicago: A.C. McClurg & Co., 1916.

Nathan, Maude. *The Story of an Epoch-Making Movement*. Garden City, N.Y.: Doubleday, Page & Co., 1926.

New York State Legislature. *Report and Testimony Taken Before the Special Committee of the Assembly Appointed to Investigate the Condition of Female Labor in the City of New York*, transmitted to the Legislature, January 16, 1896. Albany, N.Y.: Wynkoop, Hallenbeck, Crawford Co., 1896.

Ormsbee, Hazel. *The Young Employed Girl*. New York: Womans Press, 1927.

Penny, Virginia. *Think and Act. A Series of Articles Pertaining to Men and Women, Work and Wages*. Philadelphia: Claxton, Remsen, & Haffelfinger, 1869.

Richardson, Dorothy. *The Long Day: The Story of a New York Working Girl, as Told by Herself*. New York: Century Co., 1905.

Riis, Jacob. *How the Other Half Lives; Studies Among the Tenements of New York*. New York: C. Scribner's Sons, 1890.

Tentler, Leslie. *Wage-earning Women: Industrial Work and Family Life in the United States, 1900-1930.* New York: Oxford University Press, 1979.

U.S., Congress, Senate. *Report on Conditions of Women and Child Wage Earners in the U.S.*: "History of Women in Industry in the United States," by Helen Sumner. Volume 9. 61st Congress, 2nd session, U.S. Senate Document 645, 1910.

U.S. Industrial Commission. *Reports of the Industrial Commission*: "Employment of Women in the U.S.,"pp. 923-932. Washington, D.C.: U.S. Government Printing Office, 1900-1902.

U.S. Women's Bureau. *Activities of the Women's Bureau of the United States,* by Agnes Lydia Peterson. Bulletin No. 86. Washington, D.C.: U.S. Government Printing Office, 1931.

U.S. Women's Bureau. *Bookkeepers, Stenographers, and Office Clerks in Ohio, 1914-1929.* Bulletin No. 95. Washington, D.C.: U.S. Government Printing Office, 1932.

U.S. Women's Bureau. *Chronological Development of Labor Legislation for Women in the United States.* Bulletin No. 66-II. Washington, D.C.: U.S. Government Printing Office, 1929.

U.S. Women's Bureau. *The Commercialization of the Home through Industrial Home Work.* Bulletin No. 135. Washington, D.C.: U.S. Government Printing Office, 1935.

U.S. Women's Bureau. *The Development of Minimum-Wage Laws in the United States, 1912-1927,* by Mildred Larcom (Jones) Gordon. Bulletin No. 61. Washington, D.C.: U.S. Government Printing Office, 1928.

U.S. Women's Bureau. *Domestic Workers and Their Employment Relations; a Study Based on the records of the Domestic Efficiency Association of Baltimore, Maryland,* by Mary V. Robinson. Bulletin No. 39. Washington, D.C.: U.S. Government Printing Office, 1924.

U.S. Women's Bureau. *The Employment of Women in Hazardous Industries in the United States.* Bulletin No. 6. Washington, D.C.: U.S. Government Printing Office, 1920.

U.S. Women's Bureau. *Facts About Working Women; A Graphic Presentation Based on Census Statistics and Studies of the Women's Bureau.* Bulletin No. 46. Washington, D.C.: Government Printing Office, 1925.

U.S. Women's Bureau. *The Family Status of Breadwinning Women: a Study of Material in the Census Schedules of a Selected Locality.* Bulletin No. 23. Washington, D.C.: U.S. Government Printing Office, 1922.

U.S. Women's Bureau. *Health Problems of Women in Industry.* Bulletin No. 18. Washington, D.C.: U.S. Government Printing Office, 1921.

U.S. Women's Bureau. *Hours and Conditions of Work for Women in Industry in Virginia.* Bulletin No. 10. Washington, D.C.: U.S. Government Printing Office, 1920.

U.S. Women's Bureau. *The Immigrant Woman and Her Job*, by Caroline Manning. Bulletin No. 74. Washington, D.C.: U.S. Government Printing Office, 1930.

U.S. Women's Bureau. *Industrial Accidents to Women in New Jersey, Ohio, and Wisconsin.* Bulletin No. 60. Washington, D.C.: U.S. Government Printing Office, 1927.

U.S. Women's Bureau. *Married Women in Industry*, by Mary Nelson Winslow. Bulletin No. 38. Washington, D.C.: U.S. Government Printing Office, 1924.

U.S. Women's Bureau. *Negro Women in Industry.* Bulletin No. 20. Washington, D.C.: U.S. Government Printing Office, 1922.

U.S. Women's Bureau. *The New Position of Women in American Industry.* Bulletin No. 12. Washington, D.C.: U.S. Government Printing Office, 1920.

U.S. Women's Bureau. *The Occupational Progress of Women, 1910-1930*, by Mary V. Dempsey. Bulletin No. 104. Washington, D.C.: U.S. Government Printing Office, 1933.

U.S. Women's Bureau. *A Physiological Basis for the Shorter Working Day for Women*, by George W. Webster. Bulletin No. 14. Washington, D.C.: U.S. Government Printing Office, 1921.

U.S. Women's Bureau. *Proceedings of Women's Industrial Con-
    ference, Called by the Women's Bureau of the U.S. Depart-
    ment of Labor.* Bulletin No. 33. Washington, D.C.: U.S.
    Government Printing Office, 1923.

U.S. Women's Bureau. *Proposed Employment of Women During the
    War in the Industries of Niagara Falls, N.Y.* Bulletin
    No. 1. Washington, D.C.: Government Printing Office,
    1919.

U.S. Women's Bureau. *The Share of Wage-Earning Women in
    Family Support.* Bulletin No. 30. U.S. Government
    Printing Office, 1923.

U.S. Women's Bureau. *Summaries of Studies on the Economic
    Status of Women* compiled by the American Association of
    University Women. Bulletin No. 134. Washington, D.C.:
    U.S. Government Printing Office, 1935.

U.S. Women's Bureau. *Wages of Candy Makers in Philadelphia
    in 1919.* Bulletin No. 4. Washington, D.C.: U.S. Govern-
    ment Printing Office, 1919.

U.S. Women's Bureau. *Women Who Work in Offices: I. Study
    of Employed Women: II. Study of Women Seeking Employ-
    ment.* Bulletin No. 132. Washington, D.C.: U.S. Govern-
    ment Printing Office, n.d.

U.S. Women's Bureau. *Women's Wages in Kansas.* Bulletin No.
    17. Washington, D.C.: U.S. Government Printing Office,
    1921.

VanVorst, Bessie. *The Woman Who Toils; Being the Experience
    of Two Ladies as Factory Girls.* New York: Doubleday,
    Page & Co., 1903.

Walkowitz, Daniel J. "Working-Class Women in the Gilded Age:
    Factory, Community and Family Life Among Cohoes, New York
    Cotton Workers." *Journal of Social History* 5 (1972):
    464-490.

Wright, Carroll D. *The Working Girls of Boston.* Boston:
    Wright & Potter Printing Co., 1889.

Wright, Carroll D. *Industrial Evolution of the United States.*
    New York: Flood & Vincent, 1895. Chapter 16.

For a more complete listing of the Women's Bureau publications, see
Mary Jane Soltow, Carolyn Forche, and Murray Massre,
Women in American Labor History, 1825-1935: An Annotated Bibliography, pp. 133-140 (East Lansing: School of Labor and Industrial Relations, Michigan State University, 1972).

F. White-Collar Work

By the turn of the century, white-collar work began to attract women into the offices of business and government. The invention of the typewriter in 1868 only partially explains the large influx of women into clerical work. A series of *Fortune* articles in 1935 is a valuable source on the feminization of the office. The prospect of eventual marriage was thought to encourage women to work for low wages and office work did not challenge but complemented male work roles. According to *Fortune* the office became a woman's world because men wanted to transport something of the home setting to the business world. The secretary replaced the wife as business partner. This series of articles provides portfolio biographies of office workers, discussion of the office girl's budget, and statistical information on women wage earners in 1930.

BIBLIOGRAPHY

Allen, Grant [Rayner, Olive Pratt]. *The Typewriter Girl*. London: C.A. Pearson, 1897.

Bliven, Bruce. *The Wonderful Writing Machine*. New York: Random House, 1954.

Davies, Margery. "Woman's Place is at the Typewriter: The Feminization of the Clerical Labor Force." *Radical America* 8 (1974):1-28.

Spillman, Harry C. "The Stenographer Plus." *Ladies Home Journal*, February 1916.

"Women in Business; I." *Fortune*, July 1935.

"Women in Business; II." *Fortune*, August 1935.

G. Technology and the Household

Sources in this field are of three kinds. Manuals directed toward housekeepers, propagandist works describing the social benefits of science and technology applied to domestic life, and technical works on architecture, sanitation, and domestic design. The secondary literature, weak in conceptualization because the field has rarely interested scholarly historians, is insensitive to the possible social losses of technological change and uncritically boasting of the marvels of progress.

The genre of the housekeeping manual is the most valuable source for the study of domestic work and its ethos from 1800 to the 1880s. Among the best instructors in this genre are Catharine E. Beecher (1800-1878) and Marion Terhune Harland (1830-1922). Beecher's *A Treatise on Domestic Economy* (1841) together with its revision as *The American Woman's Home* (1869) are perhaps the most influential of any works on American domestic life. Beecher saw domestic life as the underpinning of a stable democracy, and she is a key figure in the effort to delineate the nature of Republican society. Kathryn Kish Sklar's biographical study of Beecher, *Catharine Beecher: A Study in American Domesticity* (1973), is a sensitive analysis of the personal and social sources of Beecher's ideas. Marion Harland's guides to domestic work were the most influential works of the turn of the century. Her revised housekeeping manual for the household with gas or electricity is a key source for the impact of new sources of energy on housework.

Examples of the propagandist genre on science applied to domestic work abound. Ellen H. Richards (1842-1911) turned her scientific training at M.I.T. to the task of educating women to efficiency as consumers in the new urban domestic world. Her *Chemistry of Cooking and Cleaning* (1882) is a pioneer work in domestic science. Christine Frederick represents the attempt to transfer ideas of industrial efficiency to the home; *The New Housekeeping: Efficiency Studies in Home Management* (1913) shares with Richards' writing no sense that laboratory standards of cleanliness or factory-style efficiency might present new burdens for the housewife.

BIBLIOGRAPHY

Alcott, William A. *The Young Housekeeper; or, Thoughts on Food and Cookery.* 2nd ed. Boston: G.W. Light, 1838.

Austin, Rev. Principal, ed. *Woman, Her Character, Culture and Calling.* c. 1890.

Beecher, Catharine E. *A Treatise on Domestic Economy, for
    the Use of Young Ladies at Home, and at School.* Boston:
    Marsh, Capen, Lyon, & Webb, 1841.

Beecher, Catharine E. *Letters to the People on Health and
    Happiness.* New York: Harper & Brothers, 1855.

Beecher, Catharine E. *Woman's Profession as Mother and Edu-
    cator, with Views in Opposition to Woman Suffrage.*
    Boston: G. Maclean, 1872.

Beecher, Catharine E. *Miss Beecher's Housekeeper and Health-
    keeper: Containing Five Hundred Recipes for Economical
    and Healthful Cooking; Also Many Directions for Securing
    Health and Happiness.* New York: Harper & Brothers, 1873.

Beecher, Catharine E., and Stowe, Harriet Beecher. *The American
    Woman's Home: or Principles of Domestic Science; Being a
    Guide to the Formation and Maintenance of Economical,
    Healthful, Beautiful, and Christian Homes.* New York:
    J.B. Ford & Co., 1869.

Busbey, Katherine. *Home Life in America.* New York: Mac-
    millan Co., 1910.

Child, Lydia Maria. *The American Frugal Housewife.* 8th ed.
    Boston: Carter & Hendee, 1910.

Duff, Sister Loretto Basil. *A Course in Household Arts.*
    Boston: Whitcomb & Barrows, 1916.

Dwight, Theodore. *The Father's Book; or, Suggestions for the
    Government and Instruction of Young Children, on Princi-
    ples Appropriate to a Christian Country.* Springfield,
    Mass.: G. & C. Merriam, 1834.

Frederick, Christine. *The New Housekeeping: Efficiency
    Studies in Home Management.* Garden City, N.Y.: Double-
    day, Page & Co., 1913.

Goff, May Perrin, ed. *The Household (of the Detroit Free
    Press). A Cyclopedia of Practical Hints for Modern Homes.*
    Detroit: Detroit Free Press Co., 1881.

Hale, Sarah Josepha. *The Good Housekeeper, or the Way to Live
    Well and Be Well While We Live.* Boston: Weeks, Jordan
    & Co., 1839.

Hale, Sarah Josepha. *Manners; or, Happy Homes and Good Society All the Year Round*. Boston: J.E. Tilton and Co., 1868.

Humphrey, Herman. *Domestic Education*. c. 1840.

Lancaster, Maud. *Electric Cooking, Heating and Cleaning, etc.; Being a Manual of Electricity in the Service of the Home*. London: Constable & Co., 1914.

Parloa, Maria. *The Appledore Cook Book: Containing Practical Receipts for Plain and Rich Cooking*. Boston: Graves and Ellis, 1872.

Parloa, Maria. *Miss Parloa's New Cook Book - A Guide to Marketing and Cooking*. Boston: Estes & Lauriat, 1881.

Parloa, Maria. *Home Economics; A Guide to Household Management; including the Proper Treatment of the Materials Entering into the Construction and Furnishing of the House*. New York: The Century Co., 1898.

Richards, Ellen H. *The Chemistry of Cooking and Cleaning; a Manual for Housekeepers*. Boston: Estes & Lauriat, 1881.

Sklar, Kathryn Kish. *Catharine Beecher: A Study in American Domesticity*. New Haven: Yale University Press, 1973.

Terhune, Mary Virginia [Harland, Marion, pseud.] *Common Sense in the Household; A Manual of Practical Housewifery*. New York: C. Scribner's Sons, 1871.

Terhune, Mary Virginia [Harland, Marion, pseud.] *House and Home: A Complete Cook-book and Housewife's Guide*. Philadelphia: P.W. Ziegler & Co., 1889.

Terhune, Mary Virginia [Harland, Marion, pseud.] *The New Common Sense in the Household, Revised for Gas and Electricity by her Daughter C. Terhune Herrick*. New York: Frederick A. Stokes Co., 1926.

H.   Urbanization, Technological Change,
and Domestic Science

The works of Christine Frederick, Ellen Richards, and Marion Talbot should be consulted for a full understanding of the attempt to make cleaning and household management a form of science. See especially Frederick's *Household*

Engineering (1915), Richards' *Home Sanitation: A Manual for Housekeepers* (1887), and Talbot and Breckinridge's *The Modern Household* (1912).

Insight into domestic design and technological change can be gained from Lewis H. Gibson's *Convenient Houses with Fifty Plans for the Housekeeper* (1889). William P. Gerhard was the most dedicated publicist of the bathroom in domestic design, and his *Sanitary Engineering of Buildings* (1889) provides a wide range of information about bathrooms and their design.

Harry Blair Hull's *Household Refrigeration* (1924) gives vivid details about the impact of new appliances on domestic life, as does Maude Lancaster's study of household electrification, *Electric Cooking, Heating and Cleaning* (1914).

Students of the modern ethos of domestic efficiency in the United States will find the *Proceedings of the Lake Placid Conference on Home Economics* (1901-1908) an invaluable source. The only critic of the newly inflated female house-keeper/domestic scientist was Charlotte Perkins Gilman whose *The Home: Its Work and Influence* (1903) represents virtually the only voice raised against the new domesticity and its effects in secluding women in exclusively private life.

BIBLIOGRAPHY

Baker, Elizabeth F. *Technology and Women's Work*. New York: Columbia University Press, 1964.

Barger, Harold. *Distribution's Place in the American Economy Since 1869*. Princeton: Princeton University Press, 1955.

Barrett, John P. *Electricity at the Columbian Exposition*. Chicago: R.R. Donnelly & Sons Co., 1894.

Brown, Laura N. *Scientific Living for Prolonging the Term of Human Life. The New Domestic Science*. New York: The Health-culture Co., 1909.

Carpenter, Rolla C. *Heating and Ventilating Buildings*. New York: John Wiley & Sons, 1895.

Chapin, Charles V. *Municipal Sanitation in the United States*. Providence: Snow & Farnham, 1901.

Dyer, Annie Isabel (Robertson). *Guide to the Literature of Home and Family Life; A Classified Bibliography for Home Economics, with Use and Content Annotations*. Philadelphia: J.P. Lippincott Co., 1924.

Frederick, Christine. *Household Engineering: Scientific Management in the Home*. Chicago: American School of Home Economics, 1915.

Gerhard, William Paul. *Sanitary Engineering of Buildings*. New York: W.T. Comstock, 1889.

Gerhard, William Paul. *The Modern Rain-bath*. New York: reprinted from the *American Architect* of February 10, 1894, 1894.

Gerhard, William Paul. *On Bathing and Different Forms of Baths*. New York: N.T. Comstock, 1895.

Gibson, Louis H. *Convenient Houses with Fifty Plans for the Housekeeper*. New York: T.Y. Crowell & Co., 1889.

Gilbreth, Lillian M. *The Home-Maker and Her Job*. New York: D. Appleton & Co., 1927.

Gilman, Charlotte Perkins. *The Home, Its Work and Influence*. New York: McClure, Phillips, & Co., 1903.

Herrick, Christine. *In City Tents: How to Find, Furnish and Keep a Small House on Slender Means*. New York: G.P. Putnam & Sons, 1902.

Hull, Harry B. *Household Refrigeration: A Complete Treatise on the Principles, Types, Construction, and Operation of Both Ice and Mechanically Cooled Domestic Refrigerators, and the Use of Ice and Refrigeration in the Home*. Chicago: Nickerson & Collins Co., 1924.

Hunt, Caroline L. "Woman's Public Work for the Home: An Ethical Substitute for Co-operative Housekeeping." *Journal of Home Economics* 1 (1909):219-224.

Industrial Chicago. Chicago: Goodspeed Publishing Co., 1891.

Lake Placid Conference on Home Economics. *Proceedings of First, Second and Third Conferences*. Lake Placid, 1901.

Lake Placid Conference on Home Economics. *Proceedings of the Fourth Annual Conference*. Lake Placid, 1902.

Lake Placid Conference on Home Economics. *Proceedings of the Fifth Annual Conference*. Lake Placid, 1903.

Lake Placid Conference on Home Economics. *Proceedings of the Sixth Annual Conference.* Lake Placid, 1904.

Lake Placid Conference on Home Economics. *Proceedings of the Seventh Annual Conference.* Lake Placid, 1905.

Lake Placid Conference on Home Economics. *Proceedings of the Eighth Annual Conference.* Lake Placid, 1906.

Lake Placid Conference on Home Economics. *Proceedings of the Ninth Annual Conference.* Lake Placid, 1907.

Lake Placid Conference on Home Economics. *Proceedings of the Tenth Annual Conference.* Lake Placid, 1908.

Lancaster, Maude. *Electric Cooking, Heating and Cleaning, etc., Being a Manual of Electricity in the Service of the Home.* London: Constable & Co., Ltd., 1914.

Lawler, James J. *Lawler's American Sanitary Plumbing; A Practical Work on the Best Methods of Modern Plumbing.* New York: Excelsior Publishing House, 1896.

Lincoln, Edwin Stoddard. *The Electric Home: A Standard Ready Reference Book.* New York: Electric Home Publishing Co., 1933.

Pattison, Mary Stranahan. *Principles of Domestic Engineering; or, The What, Why and How of a Home.* New York: Trow Press, 1915.

President's Conference on Home Building and Home Ownership. *Household Management and Kitchens: Reports of the Committees on Household Management,* edited by John M. Gries and James Ford. Washington, D.C.: U.S. Government Printing Office, 1932.

Putnam, John Pickering. *Plumbing and Household Sanitation.* Garden City, New York: Doubleday, Page & Co., 1911.

Richards, Ellen H. *Home Sanitation: A Manual for Housekeepers.* Boston: Ticknor & Co., 1887.

Richards, Ellen H. *The Cost of Living as Modified by Sanitary Science.* New York: John Wiley & Sons, 1899.

Richards, Ellen H. *The Cost of Food: A Study in Dietaries.* New York: John Wiley & Sons, 1901.

Richards, Ellen H. *The Cost of Shelter*. New York: John
    Wiley & Sons, 1905.

Richards, Ellen H. "Ideal Housekeeping in the Twentieth Cen-
    tury." *Journal of Home Economics* 3 (1911):174-175.

Snyder, Edna B., and Bruing, M.P. *A Study of Washing Machines*.
    Lincoln, Neb.: Agricultural Research Station, Research
    Bulletin No. 56, 1931.

Swisher, Jacob A. "The Evolution of Wash Day." *Iowa Journal
    of History and Politics* 38 (1939):3-49.

Talbot, Marion. *More than Lore: Reminiscences of Marion
    Talbot, Dean of Women. University of Chicago, 1892-1925*.
    Chicago: University of Chicago Press, 1936.

Talbot, Marion, and Breckinridge, Sophonisba P. *The Modern
    Household*. Boston: Whitcomb & Barrows, 1912.

I. Histories of Technology, Biographical Writings,
    and Secondary Materials Dealing with
    Urbanization and Domestic Life

The secondary literature on this subject is not rich.
Siegfried Giedion's *Mechanization Takes Command* (1948)
amasses enormous amounts of information relating to technological change but relates the process as one of unending
progress. The work of Bemis and Burchard on *The Evolving
House* (1933-36) supplies a much needed survey of domestic
design. *American Building: The Forces that Shape It* (1948),
by James M. Fitch, attempts to relate design and construction
to social pressures. Sam B. Warner, Jr.'s pioneer study of
suburbanization, *Streetcar Suburbs: The Process of Growth in
Boston, 1870-1900* (1962), describes the process by which the
workplace was settled, a process which was contemporaneous
with the effort to give housework the aura of the laboratory
and the factory.

BIBLIOGRAPHY

Abbott, Edith. *The Tenements of Chicago, 1908-1935*. Chicago:
    University of Chicago Press, 1936.

Atkins, Gordon. "Health, Housing and Poverty in New York
    City, 1865-1898." Ph.D. dissertation, Columbia University,
    1947.

Barger, Harold. *Distribution's Place in the American Economy Since 1869*. Princeton, N.J.: Princeton University Press, 1955.

Bemis, Albert F., and Burchard, John. *The Evolving House*. 3 volumes. Cambridge, Mass.: Technology Press, 1933-36.

Burchard, John E., and Bush-Brown, Albert. *The Architecture of America: A Social and Cultural History*. Boston: Little, Brown, 1961.

Byington, Margaret F. *Homestead: The Households of a Mill Town*. New York: Charities Publication Committee, 1910.

Coolidge, John. *Mill and Mansion: A Study of Architecture and Society in Lowell, Massachusetts, 1820-1865*. New York: Columbia University Press, 1942.

Douglass, Harlan P. *The Suburban Trend*. New York: Century Co., 1925.

Ferry, John W. *A History of the Department Store*. New York: Macmillan Co., 1960.

Fitch, James M. *American Building: The Forces That Shape It*. Boston: Houghton Mifflin Co., 1948.

Giedion, Siegfried. *Mechanization Takes Command: A Contribution to Anonymous History*. New York: Oxford University Press, 1948.

Gifford, Don Creighton, ed. *The Literature of Architecture: The Evolution of Architectural Theory and Practice in Nineteenth Century America*. New York: E.P. Dutton & Co., 1966.

Gowans, Alan. *Images of American Living; Four Centuries of Architecture and Furniture as Cultural Expression*. Philadelphia: Lippincott, 1964.

Hayden, Dolores. *Seven American Utopias: The Architecture of Communitarian Socialism, 1790-1975*. Cambridge, Mass.: M.I.T. Press, 1976.

Holst, Hermann V. *Modern American Homes*. Chicago: American Technical Society, 1912.

Hunt, Caroline L. *The Life of Ellen H. Richards*. Boston: Whitcomb & Barrows, 1912.

Kellogg, Paul U. *The Pittsburgh Survey: Findings in Six Volumes*. New York: Charities Publication Committee, 1909-1914.

Lubove, Roy. *The Progressives and the Slums: Tenement House Reforms in New York City, 1890-1917*. Pittsburgh: University of Pittsburgh Press, 1962.

Lynes, Russell. *The Domesticated Americans*. New York: Harper & Row, 1963.

Perry, Clarence A. *Housing for the Machine Age*. New York: Russell Sage Foundation, 1939.

Presbrey, Frank. *The History and Development of Advertising*. Garden City, N.Y.: Doubleday, Doran & Co., 1929.

Rapoport, Amos. *House Form and Culture*. Englewood Cliffs, N.J.: Prentice-Hall, 1969.

Scully, Vincent J. *American Architecture and Urbanism*. New York: Praeger, 1969.

Sklar, Kathryn Kish. *Catherine Beecher: A Study in American Domesticity*. New Haven: Yale University Press, 1973.

Talbot, Marion. *The Education of Women*. Chicago: University of Chicago Press, 1910.

Warner, Sam B., Jr. *Streetcar Suburbs: The Process of Growth in Boston, 1870-1900*. Cambridge, Mass.: Harvard University Press, 1962.

Wendt, Lloyd and Kogan, Herman. *Give the Lady What She Wants!* . . . *The Story of Marshall Field and Co.* Chicago: Rand McNally, 1952.

Williamson, Jefferson. *The American Hotel: An Anecdotal History*. New York: Alfred A. Knopf, 1930.

Wood, Edith E. *The Housing of the Unskilled Wage Earner: America's Next Problem*. New York: Macmillan Co., 1919.

J. Women as Consumers

The literature on the nervous housewife and her role as anxious consumer is a product of the 1920s. Myerson's *The Nervous Housewife* (1920) is the classic account of the woman alone in suburbia and deprived of the stimulus of alternative roles. Lorinne Pruette's *Women and Leisure* (1924) is a polemical response to women's return to the workplace in the 1920s and a call for education for "leisure" and motherhood. Only Thorstein Veblen's essay "The Economic Theory of Women's Dress" in *Popular Science Monthly* (November 1894) 'drew attention to the ritual nature of much female consumption.

BIBLIOGRAPHY

Andrews, Benjamin. "The Home Woman as Buyer and Controller of Consumption." *Ladies Home Journal*, August 1924.

Lucas, Bertha. *The Woman Who Spends; A Study of Her Economic Function*. Boston: Whitcomb & Barrows, 1904.

Myerson, Abraham. *The Nervous Housewife*. Boston: Little, Brown & Co., 1920.

Parsons, Alice Beal. *Woman's Dilemma*. New York: Thomas Y. Crowell Co., 1926.

Pruette, Lorinne. *Woman and Leisure, A Study of Social Waste*. Reprint. New York: Arno Press, 1972.

Veblen, Thorstein. "The Economic Theory of Women's Dress." *Popular Science Monthly*, November 1894.

SECTION III

CULTURAL ROLES OF MIDDLE-CLASS WOMEN IN INDUSTRIALIZING AMERICA: SCHOOLS, LITERACY, AND WOMEN'S INTELLECTUAL WORK

In the preceding section we see the pattern of relationships which emerged between the industrial base of American society and the home. This was a relationship which utilized women's work in unskilled occupations and in service activities supporting the bureaucratic aspects of modern business organizations, and a relationship which came to rest on stimulating domestic consumption to provide the ever-expanding market for the products of the consumer economy. This section is devoted to examining the roles played by women in the cultural activities supported by the economic base of society during the period in which the industrial economy was built up and the modern business organizations that managed it took shape. During this process many formerly domestic activities concerned with the rearing of the young and the care of the sick were transferred from the home to special institutions, the school and the hospital, and these activities became the province of specially trained professionals. Women played a large part in defining the ethos of such professions and in redefining domestic life as aspects of domesticity were handed over to neutral professionals. The professionalized activities of the domestic sphere were not seen as part of the productive base of the economy, and their economic rewards were correspondingly marginal. Alongside those marginally rewarded professional activities, women took on a variety of voluntary activities, unrewarded by the market for labor and skills, activities that laid the basis for what we now see as the "not-for-profit" sector of American economic and cultural life. In so doing they played a significant part in defining the cultural institutions and activities of industrial and postindustrial America, and the woman writer emerged as an authoritative voice commenting on manners, morals, and taste.

It is helpful to see this emerging pattern of feminine activity as contributing to the moral economy of society alongside the clergy and clerical institutions. Unless we give serious attention to women's roles and products in this moral economy, we fail to grasp the significance of voluntarism in American history and the extent to which volunteer activity has brought women into positions of power and influence to which they had no access whatsoever in the sphere of profit-making institutions and politics. Since the voluntary sector of society is fueled by ideas of altruism, service, and social uplift on the one hand and aspirations toward beauty, the enhancement of life, and high culture on the other, this sector of society has functioned in very close relationship with intellectuals, artists, and those who live for and are supported by ideas. Thus the woman writer and intellectual, excluded from the formal institutions creating and validating ideas such as the university and the professional association, nonetheless had her niche and her audience.

We can see this characteristic moral economy taking shape in the early national period as women gain education and assume responsibility for teaching the young. It is expanded after the Civil War as secular philanthropy, modeled closely on the work of the Catholic religious orders and given its twentieth-century form in the service professions and the professions related to the arts. Along with this focus of activity went new forms of sociability for women in social and service clubs and a popular press and style of journalism directed toward this clearly defined audience. If we see women's sphere of competence being defined in the nineteenth century as moral and cultural, we can begin to understand why there was strong antifeminist opposition to the merging of male and female spheres of authority and to see just what the nature of the forces were that were to be pitted in the battle over the suffrage, a battle initially waged in the name of equality in competence between males and females.

A. Education and the Teaching Profession

Historical writing treating women's access to education and their entry into the predominant role of teacher of the young has generally been of two kinds: women are treated as part of the general account of the broadening of educational opportunity in the United States, or the subject is dealt with through biographical writing on the lives of important women educators. Thus writing on this subject has been responsive to whatever have been the dominant trends in interpreting American educational history. Thomas Woody's *A History of Women's Education in the United States* (1929) forms part of a larger oeuvre dedicated to chronicling the triumphs of an ever-expanding educational system striving to achieve the American ideal of equality of opportunity and universal popular education. Woody sees only progress in the opening of educational doors for women in the nineteenth century. He applauds the founding of coeducational and single-sex schools in equal terms, and, although the quotations he cites from legislative debates over opening high-school education to women suggest otherwise, he concludes that the broadening of access for women to primary and secondary education was brought about in response to a growing commitment to equality between the sexes. Eleanor Flexner's *Century of Struggle* (1959) reflects the interest of American historians in the fifties in the subject of political movements and political organizations and underlines the extent and range of opposition to the expansion of women's rights encountered by the feminist movement in the nineteenth and early twentieth century. Nonetheless Flexner subscribes to the general interpretation of American educational history in which access to educational institutions is the critical factor and in which the history of expanding access can be taken as one of progress. By the early 1960s we see a more complex view of educational institutions and their functions shaping the interpretation of educational history. Bernard Bailyn's *Education in the Forming of American Society* (1960) sees the breakdown in colonial society of traditional modes of education through family and craft as the key to a new set of attitudes about the individual and his potential that was to govern American ideas about education. In this context the school is seen as an emerging modern agency potentially at odds with the family and a radical force for the acceleration of individualism and social change. Although not specifically treated by Bailyn, the woman teacher in the dame school and the female child learning outside the home are subsumed within the interpretive sweep of the work. The same may be said of Rush Welter's *Popular Education and Democratic Thought in America* (1962), which traces the relationship between the movement for popular schooling and the institutions it spawned, and the development of democratic attitudes and beliefs. Michael Katz's *The Irony of Early School Reform* (1968) moves on from the concept of the creation of nonfamily agencies of socialization to examine the content of what was taught in the early common school, the recruitment of common school teachers, and the motives of school founders. In tune with the radical critique of the American past so characteristic of the 1960s, Katz finds that the chief function of the early tax-supported school was to tax the working class for a form of education which was of little value to workers and to expose the children of the working class to habits of

routine which prepared them to tolerate the boredom of the
industrial factory which was their eventual destiny. For
Katz the early woman school teacher, underpaid and low in
status, represented one more social group that was the victim
of the ambiguous motives of the early school reformers, more
interested in imposing mass discipline by the least costly
means than in the value of literacy for those formerly unedu-
cated. Katz's work introduces the reader to a new set of
questions about the meaning and value of literacy that are of
great importance for the interpretation of educational history.
Carlo Cipolla's *Literacy and Development in the West* (1969)
provides a summary of the basic connections assumed to link
the rise of literacy and modernization in the history of the
west. The literature laying out the standard view of the
relationship between literacy and the development of modern
society is subjected to rigorous questioning in Richard
Hoggart's *The Uses of Literacy: Changing Patterns in English
Mass Culture* (1957)* and in Harvey J. Graff's *The Literacy
Myth: Literacy and Social Structure in the Nineteenth Century
City* (1979).** These writers point out that our valuation on
literacy, and our sense that it is central to improved economic productivity and rising standards of life, comes from
the culture of the eighteenth-century Enlightenment and from
seventeenth-century Puritanism. Historians, by definition
persons who are products of cultural settings in which word
and text are highly valued, have tended to underestimate the
importance of oral culture for those for whom the manipulation of print had little meaning or value. Certainly we have
misunderstood the relationship between literacy and economic
mobility in the nineteenth century, a point which brings us
back to low status and the poorly paid school teacher, whose
command of print gave her no economic advantages comparable
with her less literate male working-class contemporaries.
Those who study the history of women's education have yet to in-
corporate this important perspective in their work and to raise
questions about the meaning of literacy to nineteenth-century
women. This question is of particular importance as we
analyze women's growing educational role in the nineteenth
century and the rise of the popular press written by and published for women. It may well be that literacy permitted
women of a wide variety of backgrounds to assume new positions

*Richard Hoggart. *The Uses of Literacy: Changing Patterns in
     English Mass Culture*. Fair Lawn, N.J.: Essential Books,
     1957.

**Harvey J. Graff. *The Literacy Myth: Literacy and Social
     Structure in the Nineteenth Century City*. New York:
     Academic Press, 1979.

of authority as writers directing their attention to the
moral economy of society. So far none of the studies of
literacy and mobility in the nineteenth century have paid
specific attention to women, and none have considered the
significance of literacy in terms other than the profit-making
economy.

Biographical studies of women educators, like the general
histories of education already discussed, reflect the dominant
historical questions of the authors and do not add up to a
cumulative understanding of the history of women's education
in the nineteenth and twentieth century. Beth B. Gilchrist's
The Life of Mary Lyon (1910) puts the reader in touch with a
substantial archive of material documenting the life of the
founder of Mount Holyoke. In tone, however, it resembles
the pious biographies of founders of nineteenth-century
Catholic religious orders. We are still awaiting the biography of Mary Lyon which would link her personal genius as a
builder of institutions to the intellectual and social forces
of her day. The student of women's education in the 1830s
and '40s will find that Alma Lutz's biography of the founder
of Troy Female Seminary, *Emma Willard* (1929), moves in the
direction of linking Emma Willard's life to the social forces
of her time. Willard's extraordinary career as a textbook
writer, celebrator of American republicanism, and her skill
as a teacher are chronicled in terms of the rise of the
common school, the nationalism of the new republic, and the
ease of building institutions in the early nineteenth cen-
try. However, there is no attempt to examine Willard and her
complicated human relationships with any attention to the
psychological dimensions of her remarkable career. The
reader sees Willard as an educational innovator in teaching
women mathematics and Greek, but the author shows no
apparent sense of contradiction in describing Willard's
weekly sermons on women's duty and on the need to reassure
society that the educated woman did not question her place
as man's subordinate. Such a life and such a set of values
immediately calls into question the "progressive" view of
women's education, which assumes that access to training in
reading, writing, and arithmetic was automatically access to
learning that would promote change in women's position.
However, the biographical approach obscures such questions,
as it does in Mae E. Harveson's biography of the founder of
the Hartford Seminary for Women and the proponent of women's
special role as educator of the young in the new republic,
Catharine Beecher. Harveson's *Catharine Esther Beecher,
Pioneer Educator* (1931) provides a detailed account of
Beecher's early family life, her first efforts to found a
school for women in Hartford, and the generalizing of her

drive to see women provide the training of the young, a
broadening of ambition which resulted from the move of the
Beecher family from New England to Lane Seminary in Cincinnati.
Beecher's interest in women's health is noted, but the link
between the wish to provide for independent roles for single
women teachers and the critique of the dominant view of women
contained in the health-reform movement is not made. The
reader is once again presented with a female figure who is
undoubtedly an innovator in education but a staunch supporter
of women's subordination, though the author fails to make any
connection between this contradiction and the general view of
the movement to educate women as one with progressive and
egalitarian motives. Louise H. Tharp's *Until Victory: Horace
Mann and Mary Peabody* (1953) is another example of the biographical genre unlinked to larger social movements. Peabody's role as the founder of the kindergarten movement in
the United States was one particularly sympathetic to the
social concerns of America in the fifties and the return to
the celebration of the large family. Mann's interest in
childhood is described without the analysis of motive or
class interest shortly to be developed by Katz in his *Irony
of Early American School Reform* (1968). Kathryn Kish
Sklar's *Catharine Beecher: A Study in American Domesticity*
(1973) is written with full recognition of the critique of
the motives of early educational reformers developed by Katz
and with appropriate questions on the meaning of literacy for
the objects of Beecher's fierce and effective campaign to
recruit and deploy a national body of young women teachers.
Sklar analyzes the ambiguities of Beecher's own motivations,
her failures as an organizer, and the forces in the contemporary family which set a career like Beecher's in motion.
She notes the cult of domesticity developed by a woman who
never established her own household and was typical of her
generation in fearing that the frontier might undermine the
integrity of middle-class family life. Sklar draws attention
to Beecher as the prototype of the woman reformer who enlarges
women's sphere in social territory by serving as a propagandist for the values of the home and domestic life that confine
her to a separate sphere. We have yet to see a biography of
Beecher which pays attention to her achievements as a detached student of the routines of domestic work and to the
significance of her early inventions of domestic labor-saving
devices. Beecher's maps of kitchens and laundries and of the
minimum number of steps necessary to carry out cooking and
cleaning functions may well represent the first American time-
and-motion studies, but as yet we have no treatment of domestic technology which links preindustrial inventions with the
labor-saving devices introduced after the arrival of

electricity and gas. Beecher represents an early stage of
domestic science when women could control their own domestic
technology and in this respect must be differentiated from
the later "domestic science" movement.

The reader will find a variety of periodical articles
discussing the founding years, trends in curriculum or the
evolution of various state systems as they affect the education of women. However, these are so episodic as to offer
little in the way of general interpretation. A valuable
source which provides the flavor of the movement to extend
education to all classes and in all regions is Emily N. Vanderpoel's *Chronicles of a Pioneer School* (1903) and *More
Chronicles of a Pioneer School* (1927). The letters and
diaries of some of the most outstanding early teachers will
also introduce the reader to the complicated set of social
forces which encouraged women to value education and see more
than personal service in teaching. Of these Nancy Hoffman,
ed., *Woman's True Profession: Voices from the History of
Teaching* (1981) and Alvira H. Phelps, *Hours With My Pupils*
(1859) are the most helpful, since they indicate the expectations women brought to the emerging role of teacher.

We know the main outlines of women's access to higher
education in the nineteenth century. Mabel Newcomer's
A Century of Higher Education of Women (1959) charts the history of access from the admission of women to the newly
founded Oberlin College in the 1830s through the establishment of the separate colleges for women in New England, the
middle states, and the South in the decades of the 1850s,
'60s, and '70s. Newcomer's account is accurate, though
marked by its time of writing, since Newcomer assumes that
access to public and private institutions represents the
only obstacle to equality in education for women, and that
the only viable form of education for Americans in the second
half of the twentieth century would be coeducation. Louise
S. Boas's *Women's Education Begins: The Rise of Women's
Colleges* (1935) is a detailed account of the founding of
colleges for women in the nineteenth century written by an
author sympathetic to the goal of separate education for
women. Arthur C. Cole's *A Hundred Years of Mount Holyoke
College* (1940) is a similarly detailed and sympathetic
account with an invaluable listing of sources on the founding
years of the college. James M. Taylor's *Before Vassar
Opened: A Contribution to the History of Higher Education in
America* (1914) describes the social and economic forces which
resulted in the foundation of one of the pioneers in women's
education. Laurenius Clarke Seelye's *The Early History of
Smith College* (1923) describes the founding years of Smith
College from the point of view of the first president of the

college. There are 25th, 50th, 75th, and centennial volumes
chronicling the history of the most prosperous and long-lived
colleges for women, which are notable for the excellence of
research and care in leading the reader to documentary sources.
Some of the flavor of contemporary comment on the access of
women to higher education can be found in May Wright Sewall,
Domestic and Social Effects of the Higher Education of Women
(1887) and Mabel L. Robinson's *The Curriculum of the Woman's
College* (1918). Robert S. Fletcher's *A History of Oberlin
College from Its Foundation through the Civil War* (1943)
deals meticulously with the first institution to attempt the
higher education of both sexes together, while Ronald W.
Hogeland treats the social ideas that encouraged coeducation
in "Coeducation of the Sexes at Oberlin College: A Study of
Social Ideas in Mid-Nineteenth Century America" (1972-73).
In general, these accounts have focused on questions of access
or curriculum, while those produced as institutional histories
have concentrated attention with much justification on the
achievements of alumnae.

Lee Tidball's article "The Search for Talented Women"
(1974) was the first step in redirecting attention to the
outcomes of higher education for women and in attempting a
more systematic examination of the woman achiever in the
nineteenth and twentieth century than any set of institutional
histories could manage. Her work prompted a reexamination of
the value of coeducation so favorably assessed by Newcomer in
1959. A first step in this reexamination is Jill K. Conway's
"Perspectives on the History of Women's Education in the
United States" (1974). A more extended examination of the
motives for coeducation and the comparative benefits of
single-sex education has been carried out by Patricia Albjerg
Graham in *Community and Class in American Education, 1865-1918*
(1974). Lynn D. Gordon has examined the early environment of
coeducation at Berkeley and Cornell in her "Co-Education on
Two Campuses: Berkeley and Chicago, 1890-1912," in *Woman's
Being, Woman's Place: Female Identity and Vocation in American
History* (1979, 171-192), and Patricia Palmieri has written a
history of Wellesley College which examines its culture on its
own terms and attempts to sketch out the kind of scholarly
life aspired to by women scholars before the scholarly life
became professionalized and ruled over by the male-dominated
professional scholarly associations. The current focus of
research is on the woman scholar and achiever and on the
various expedients adopted by colleges specifically for women
to bridge the gap between their mission to maximize women's
potential and a social order which would restrict that potential within a limited social territory upon graduation. Such
expedients as Vassar College's program in the study of

Euthenics or Smith College's Institute for the Coordination
of Women's Interests indicate early efforts to create new
institutions which would link women's nonprofit activities
with the life of the mind and the creation of new knowledge.
    However we look at the evidence, it is clear that the
movement to expand educational opportunity for women may be
understood in terms of two distinct stages in the nineteenth
and the early twentieth century. The first, from 1790 through
the Civil War, may be understood as the stage in which access
to education was argued for and achieved to enable women to
carry out their assigned function of educating the young and
shaping the domestic environment in which the citizen was
created. In the post-Civil War years we see a second stage
in this educational movement posed by the development of
institutions of higher education for women. Here two contradictory forces were at work. On the one hand, the social
forces which produced the search for order were also at work
with respect to women's sphere of competence, so that many
aspects of housekeeping and child-rearing were given new
professional shape and required new forms of preparation.
These forces were on the whole uncritical of women's special
sphere in American society and were a logical development of
the attitudes and goals of the early women educational pioneers. On the other hand, the evangelical culture which fostered the founding of colleges and linked future social perfection to better education and moral understanding combined
with the secular forces of the movement for women's rights,
and each in its way held utopian expectations for the kind
of society that would come into being if the moral and intellectual abilities related to women's nurturing and service
roles could be deployed as a check on the acquisitiveness and
competitiveness of American business culture. The beliefs
and goals of the women's rights movement drew on the radical
secular culture of the Enlightenment, while the evangelical
Christian drive to elevate women's qualities drew on the
popular religious rejection of the Enlightenment. Both impulses found uneasy partnership in the founding of new institutions for women's learning, and these were in place by the
closing decades of the nineteenth century. They served as
staging grounds for a wide variety of ideas about the possible
improvement of American society which could be brought about
by giving new forms of intellectual discipline to women. They
were not unified intellectual communities but pluralistic
ones in which the wish to strengthen women within their sphere
and the desire to free women for every kind of endeavor and
occupation appropriate to men could both be harnessed to
educational goals. By the opening decades of the twentieth
century, we see these two objectives coalescing in the

development of women's service professions where a secularized evangelical charity took professional form. In order to
understand this process, we must trace the development of
women's philanthropy and its intersection with formal institutions of higher education.

BIBLIOGRAPHY

Bailyn, Bernard. *Education in the Forming of American Soci-
    ety: Needs and Opportunities for Study.* Chapel Hill:
    University of North Carolina Press, 1960.

Baylor, Ruth M. *Elizabeth Palmer Peabody: Kindergarten
    Pioneer.* Philadelphia: University of Philadelphia Press,
    1965.

Boas, Louise S. *Woman's Education Begins: The Rise of
    Women's Colleges.* Norton, Massachusetts: Wheaton College
    Press, 1935.

Calhoun, Daniel. *The Intelligence of a People.* Princeton,
    N.J.: Princeton University Press, 1973.

Capen, Eliza P. "Zilpah Grant and the Art of Teaching: 1829."
    New England Quarterly 20:347-364.

Cipolla, Carlo. *Literacy and Development in the West.*
    Baltimore: Penguin Books, 1969.

Cole, Arthur C. *A Hundred Years of Mount Holyoke College:
    The Evolution of an Educational Ideal.* New Haven: Yale
    University Press, 1940.

Conrad, Susan. *Perish the Thought: Intellectual Women in
    Romantic America, 1830-1860.* New York: Oxford University
    Press, 1976.

Conway, Jill K. "Perspectives on the History of Women's
    Education in the U.S." *History of Education Quarterly*
    14 (1974):1-12.

Cross, Barbara. *The Educated Woman in America: Selected
    Writings of Catharine Beecher, Margaret Fuller, and M.
    Carey Thomas.* New York: Teachers College Press, 1965.

Eaton, John. *Illiteracy and Its Social, Political and Indus-
    trial Effects.* New York: Union League Club, 1883.

Eggleston, Edward. *The Hoosier School-Master: A Novel.* New York: Sagamore Press, 1957.

Elsbree, Willard S. *The American Teacher: Evolution of a Profession in a Democracy.* New York: American Book Co., 1939.

Elson, Ruth M. *Guardians of Tradition, American Schoolbooks of the Nineteenth Century.* Lincoln: University of Nebraska Press, 1964.

Fletcher, Robert S. *A History of Oberlin College from Its Foundation through the Civil War.* Oberlin, Ohio: Oberlin College, 1943.

Flexner, Eleanor. *Century of Struggle: The Woman's Rights Movement in the United States.* Cambridge, Mass.: Harvard University Press, Belknap Press, 1959.

Gilchrist, Beth B. *The Life of Mary Lyon.* Boston: Houghton Mifflin Co., 1910.

Gordon, Lynn D. "Co-education on Two Campuses: Berkeley and Chicago, 1890-1912," in *Woman's Being, Woman's Place: Female Identity and Vocation in American History*, pp. 171-192. Boston: Hall, 1979.

Graham, Patricia Albjerg. *Community and Class in American Education, 1865-1918.* New York: John Wiley & Sons, 1974.

Harveson, Mae E. "Catharine Esther Beecher, Pioneer Educator." Ph.D. dissertation, University of Philadelphia, 1931.

Hoffman, Nancy, ed. *Woman's True Profession: Voices from the History of Teaching.* Old Westbury, N.Y.: Feminist Press, 1981.

Hogeland, Ronald W. "Coeducation of the Sexes at Oberlin College: A Study of Social Ideas in Mid-Nineteenth Century America." *Journal of Social History* 6 (1972-1973): 160-176.

Hughes, Robert M., and Turner, Joseph A. "Notes on the Higher Education of Women in Virginia." *William and Mary College College Quarterly Historical Magazine* 9 (1929):325-334.

Kaestle, Carl F. *The Evolution of an Urban School System: New York City, 1750-1850.* Cambridge, Mass.: Harvard University Press, 1973.

Katz, Michael B. *The Irony of Early School Reform: Educational Innovation in Mid-Nineteenth Century Massachusetts.* Cambridge, Mass.: Harvard University Press, 1968.

Landes, W.M., and Solomon, Lewis C. "Compulsory Schooling Legislation." *Journal of Economic History* 32 (1972):36-91.

Lockridge, Kenneth. *Literacy in Colonial New England: An Enquiry into the Social Context of Literacy in the Early Modern West.* New York: W.W. Norton & Co., 1974.

Lutz, Alma. *Emma Willard, Daughter of Democracy.* New York: Houghton Mifflin Co., 1929.

MacLear, Martha. *The History of the Education of Girls in New York and New England, 1800-1870.* Washington, D.C.: Howard University Press, 1926.

McClellan, Bernard E. "Education for an Industrial Society: Changing Conceptions of the Role of Public Schooling, 1865-1900." Ph.D. dissertation, Northwestern University, 1972.

McClelland, Clarence P. "The Education of Females in Early Illinois." *Journal of the Illinois State Historical Society* 36 (1943):378-407.

Newcomer, Mabel. *A Century of Higher Education for American Women.* New York: Harper, 1959.

Phelps, Almira H. *Hours with My Pupils.* New York: C. Scribner, 1859.

Richardson, Eudora R. "The Case of the Women's Colleges in the South." *Southern Atlantic Quarterly* 29 (1930):126-139.

Roberts, Josephine. "Elizabeth Peabody and the Temple School." *New England Quarterly* 15 (1942):497-508.

Robinson, Mabel L. *The Curriculum of the Woman's College.* Washington, D.C.: U.S. Government Printing Office, 1918.

Sack, Saul. "The Higher Education of Women in Pennsylvania." *Pennsylvania Magazine of History and Biography* 83 (1959): 29-73.

Savin, Marion B., and Abrahams, Harold J. "The Young Ladies' Academy of Philadelphia." *History of Education Journal* 8 (1956):58-67.

Schultz, Stanley K. *The Culture Factory: Boston Public Schools, 1789-1860.* New York: Oxford University Press, 1973.

Seelye, Laurenius Clarke. *The Early History of Smith College, 1871-1910.* Boston: Houghton Mifflin Co., 1923.

Sewall, May Wright. *Domestic and Social Effects of the Higher Education of Women.* c. 1887.

Shephard, William. "Buckingham Female Collegiate Institute." *William and Mary College Quarterly Historical Magazine* 20 (1940):167-193.

Sherzer, Jane. "The Higher Education of Women in the Ohio Valley." *Ohio Historical Quarterly* 25 (1916):1-26.

Sklar, Kathryn Kish. *Catharine Beecher: A Study in American Domesticity.* New Haven: Yale University Press, 1973.

Strong, Floyd Bryan. "Ideas of the Early Sex Education Movement in America, 1890-1920." *History of Education Quarterly* 12 (1972):129-161.

Taylor, James Monroe. *Before Vassar Opened: A Contribution to the History of Higher Education in America.* Boston: Houghton Mifflin Co., 1914.

Tharp, Louise Hall. *Until Victory: Horace Mann and Mary Peabody.* Boston: Little, Brown, 1953.

Thompson, Eleanor W. *Education for Ladies, 1830-1860: Ideas on Education in Magazines for Women.* New York: King's Crown Press, 1947.

Tidball, M. Elizabeth. "The Search for Talented Women." *Change* 6 (1974):51-52.

Troen, Selwyn. "Popular Education in Nineteenth Century St. Louis." *History of Education Quarterly* 13 (1973):23-40.

Tully, Alan. "Literacy Levels and Educational Development in Rural Pennsylvania, 1729-1755. *Pennsylvania History* 39 (1973):301-302.

Vanderpoel, Emily N. *Chronicles of a Pioneer School from 1792 to 1833, Being the History of Miss Sarah Pierce and Her Litchfield School.* Cambridge, Mass.: University Press, 1903.

Vanderpoel, Emily N. *More Chronicles of a Pioneer School,
    from 1792 to 1833, Being Added History on the Litchfield
    Female Academy Kept by Miss Sarah Pierce and her Nephew,
    John Pierce Brace*. New York: Cadmus Book Shop, 1927.

Vinovskis, Maris A. "Trends in Massachusetts Education 1826-
    1860." *History of Education Quarterly* 12 (1972):501-530.

Warren, Charles. *Illiteracy in the U.S. in 1870 and 1880 with
    Diagrams and Observations*. Washington, D.C.: U.S. Govern-
    ment Printing Office, 1884.

Welter, Barbara. "Anti-Intellectualism and the American Woman,
    1800-1860." *American Quarterly* 28 (1966):151-174.

Welter, Barbara. *Dimity Convictions: The American Woman in
    the Nineteenth Century*. Athens: Ohio University Press, 1976.

Welter, Rush, ed. *Popular Education and Democratic Thought in
    America*. New York: Columbia University Press, 1962.

Wofford, Kate V. *An History of the Status and Training of
    Elementary Rural Teachers of the United States, 1860-1930*.
    Pittsburgh: Press of T. Siviter & Co., 1935.

Woody, Thomas. *A History of Women's Education in the United
    States*. 2 volumes. New York: Science Press, 1929.

B. Women's Philanthropy and the Emergence
of the Service Professions, 1830-1910

1. General Works

General histories of the charitable impulse and its organized expression in the service professions date from the era
of the New Deal. These works of the thirties such as Edith
Abbott's *Some American Pioneers in Social Welfare* (1937) and
Albert Deutsch's *The Mentally Ill in America* (1937) locate
the charitable impulse in the humanitarian concerns of the
1840s and trace it through the stages of individual effort,
the organization of volunteers, and the assumption of responsibility by the state for the elderly, the dependent, and the
handicapped, a responsibility they proudly saw as finally
located where it belonged with the federal government of the
New Deal period. Some interest in the role played by women
in the development of organized charity as a general social
phenomenon may be seen in the writing of the early forties

such as Henry Lee Swint's *The Northern Teacher in the South, 1862-1870* (1941), a work which traces the extraordinary exodus of single northern women to staff the schools of the Freedman's Aid Society, and Mary B. Truedley's valuable article "The Benevolent Fair: A Study of Charitable Organizations Among Women in the First Third of the Nineteenth Century" (1940). Treudley is concerned with the development of women's voluntary associations for charitable purposes such as the care of orphans or the reformation of prostitutes, and the development of the charity bazaar as a means of fund raising for women who controlled no private disposable income. The Second World War intervened and the history of philanthropy was not a subject of general study again until Robert Bremner's *From the Depths: The Discovery of Poverty in the United States* (1956) and *American Philanthropy* (1960). Bremner's work was part of the general discovery of the history of the immigrant in America which was of such universal interest in the fifties, and both works are part of the rewriting of American history in terms which made the city and its varied immigrant populations the main theme in the development of American institutions as opposed to the frontier and the patterns of farming life. Bremner duly notes the high level of participation by American women in the discovery of poverty and the voluntary associations created to relieve its effects, but he is more interested in the objects of philanthropy than the agents of philanthropic organization and their general place in the total context of American culture. Merle Curti's "American Philanthropy and the National Character" (1958) again demonstrates a concern with the place of voluntarism in shaping American culture, but he has only a passing interest with the relationship of voluntarism to gender and gender roles. Keith E. Melder's "Ladies Bountiful: Organized Women's Benevolence in Early Nineteenth Century America" (1967) focuses directly on voluntarism and gender and draws attention to the place assigned women's voluntarism in the culture of the early republic. Melder's work is followed by that of Carroll Smith-Rosenberg, whose *Religion and the Rise of the American City: The New York City Mission Movement, 1812-1870* (1971) links the assignment of benevolent activity to women in the early republic with the development of a consciousness of women's social position which was a prerequisite for the later feminist movement of the 1840s. Smith-Rosenberg's theme has been developed at length by Nancy Cott in *The Bonds of Womanhood: "Woman's Sphere" in New England, 1780-1835* (1977). A different view of the philanthropic impulse shaped by the new social consciousness of the 1970s is presented in David Rothman's *The Discovery of the Asylum* (1971) which, like Katz's work on the founders of the common school system, analyzes the motives of

the founders of the supposedly benevolent institution and
focuses on the discipline imposed and the manipulation of the
inhabitants of school or asylum in the interests of a dominant
educated middle class. Rothman's analysis requires us to move
cautiously in interpreting the motives of some of the outstanding early leaders of philanthropy directed toward the
care of the insane.

Certainly by far the most outstanding female figure in
American public life from the 1830s to her death in 1887 was
Dorothea Lynde Dix, whose single-minded campaign to create
state and federal institutions for the care of the insane
brought her to national prominence by 1843. Dix's life was
written shortly after her death by Francis Tiffany, a friend
and associate who drew copiously on Dix's diaries and letters
for his eulogistic account of her career. Tiffany's work is
in the standard style of Victorian biography in which the hero
or heroine of great talents is called by providence to fulfill
a God-given task. Nonetheless, by his generous quotations,
Tiffany gives the reader ample evidence that Dix's rapid rise
to prominence as the spokeswoman for the insane grew out of
some unstated needs in the emerging state and national polity.
Helen E. Marshall's *Dorothea Dix, Forgotten Samaritan* (1937),
though more apparently objective, is in many ways less useful
since its purpose is to describe in Dix the precursor of the
concern with social welfare which characterized the New Deal.
Neither writer is concerned with Dix as social type or with
the constellation of social and political needs which made
her achievement possible. Born in the early years of the
republic, educated by the generosity of prosperous relatives
and introduced by them to Boston intellectual life, Dix combined a highly developed religious sensibility with a drive
to earn her own place in society. This drive was mixed with
a semireligious patriotism and awe for the political institutions of the new republic and a profound wish to be of
service in her own right. Her role as spokeswoman for the
insane, persons who by definition could have no voice of
their own, illustrates the function women working out of
benevolence were to play in the national political system, as
it developed its characteristic forms of patronage and spoils.
Where political office was sought for purposes of patronage,
no individual within the political system could claim to be
"disinterested" or, like the reform-minded aristocracy,
interested in curbing capitalist exploitation in England
"above politics." Women could, however, play this role to
perfection, provided that they remained within their sphere
and did not have a vote which presumably could be bought.
When we see Dix as social type and examine the social and
political dynamics that played around her apolitical political

career, we see her use of the right of petition and her presumed political neutrality to represent interests that were
outside the economic system and found no representation in
state or federal legislatures. The voteless woman of benevolence thus played a weighty role in the moral economy of a
society struggling to come to terms with a political system
that had developed a strong party and spoils system. Dix as
reformer, using the strengths of women's sphere for the maxi-
mum of "influence," is an important social type, for she illustrates the way in which the strong-minded woman could build
an independent life by perceiving and fulfilling the needs of
society not met by the market and the capitalist economy.
There were many local, regional and national variants of Dix
as type, but they await their collective and individual biographers.* The social type of the benevolent woman sprang to
national consciousness during the Civil War when the organized
fund-raising abilities hitherto directed to isolated and local
charitable endeavors were focused on the support of the U.S.
Sanitary Commission or the support of the Confederate armies
in the field. L.P. Brockett's history of the Sanitary Commission contained in his *Philanthropic Results of the War*
(1863) describes the upsurge of female voluntarism evoked by
the war and the favorable reception given for the first time
to the woman who worked outside the home. The Civil War thus
became a turning point for the history of women's activity in
nonprofit functions outside the home, for it expanded the
sphere of women's competence and made service activities
acceptable out of patriotism as well as from religious motivations. We may thus date the new style secular benevolence
from the late 1860s carried out in the name of national service and social uplift.

BIBLIOGRAPHY

Abbott, Edith. *Some American Pioneers in Social Welfare:
    Selected Documents with Editorial Notes.* Chicago: Uni-
    versity of Chicago Press, 1937.

Bremner, Robert H. *From the Depths: The Discovery of Poverty
    in the United States.* New York: New York University
    Press, 1956.

Bremner, Robert H. *American Philanthropy.* Chicago: Univer-
    sity of Chicago Press, 1960.

*
See Edward T. James, ed. *Notable American Women, 1607-1950:
    A Biographical Dictonary.* Cambridge, Mass.: Belknap Press
    of Harvard University Press, 1971.

Brockett, Linus Pierrepont. *The Philanthropic Results of the War in America, Collected from Official and Other Authentic Sources.* New York: Press of Wynkoop, Hallenbeck Thomas, 1863.

Cott, Nancy. *The Bonds of Womanhood: "Woman's Sphere" in New England, 1780-1835.* New Haven: Yale University Press, 1977.

Curti, Merle. "American Philanthropy and the National Character." *American Quarterly* 10 (1958):420-437.

Deutsch, Albert. *The Mentally Ill in America: A History of Their Case and Treatment from Colonial Times.* Garden City, N.Y.: Doubleday, Doran & Co., 1937.

Marshall, Helen E. *Dorothea Dix, Forgotten Samaritan.* Chapel Hill: University of North Carolina Press, 1937.

Melder, Keith E. "Ladies Bountiful: Organized Women's Benevolence in Early Nineteenth Century America." *New York History* 48 (1967):231-254.

Rothman, David. *The Discovery of the Asylum: Social Order and Disorder in the New Republic.* Boston: Little, Brown, 1971.

Smith-Rosenberg, Carroll. *Religion and the Rise of the American City: The New York City Mission Movement, 1812-1870.* Ithaca, N.Y.: Cornell University Press, 1971.

Stearns, Bertha-Monica. "Reform Periodicals and Female Reformers, 1830-1860." *American Historical Review* 37 (1932):678-699.

Swint, Henry Lee. *The Northern Teacher in the South, 1862-1870.* Nashville, Tenn.: Vanderbilt University Press, 1941.

Tiffany, Francis. *Life of Dorothea Lynde Dix.* New York: Houghton Mifflin Co., 1890

Treudley, Mary B. "The Benevolent Fair: A Study of Charitable Organizations Among Women in the First Third of the Nineteenth Century." *Social Service Review* 14 (1940):509-522.

2. *Social Work*

The history of the establishment of the profession of social work is well documented by the copious memoirs of the founding generation and by the literature of advice and instruction the founders wrote for new practitioners. In many ways the founding documents for the new profession are to be found in the letters and papers of Josephine Shaw Lowell. Lowell, a privileged daughter of a Boston Brahmin family, looked to social service after the Civil War to commemorate the sacrifice of her husband killed in action as an officer in the Union army. Her search for service took her into the founding years of the American Charity Organization movement, an organization aimed at coordinating the charitable efforts of a city or region so as to ensure that charitable giving reached targets in an efficient manner and to expend the funds in ways calculated to eradicate, rather than foster, poverty. As head of the New York Charity Organization Society, Lowell carried on a lengthy correspondence describing the goals of the Society and her own views on the causes and cures of unemployment and pauperism. Her letters are generously quoted in William Rhinelander Stewart, *The Philanthropic Work of Josephine Shaw Lowell* (1911). Stewart's work describes her increasing role of leadership within the Charity Organization Society but is less satisfactory in tracing her progressive disenchantment with capitalism, her support for the nascent Women's Trade Union League, and her attempt, through the establishment of the National Consumers' League, to organize consumers to control the worst excesses of capitalism. Lowell resembles Dix in entering the world of benevolence in search of an important cause, but unlike Dix her encounters with the objects of her efforts, the working men and women who were the casualties of the business cycles of the early industrial state, led her to progressive, not to say radical, social and economic views. Thus we see that women's function in the moral economy could lead to both conservative and radical outcomes as in the case of Dix. The exercise of charity could either salve the practitioner's conscience or foster new perceptions of social reality as in the case of Josephine Shaw Lowell.

Jane Addams' *Philanthropy and Social Progress* (1893) was the first clearly articulated and self-aware statement of the motives that prompted women's philanthropic work. It is a transitional document that attempts to blend Christian ideas of charity with an evolutionary view of social progress through the mobilization of human resources for social uplift. Undoubtedly the most influential statement of its generation, it was followed by a series of works, *Democracy*

and Social Ethics (1902) and *Newer Ideals of Peace* (1907),
which attempted to explore the ethical dimensions of social
conflict and to locate the social forces which could mediate
the class struggles of the industrial state. Addams was quite
explicit about her view that the moral and intellectual concerns of educated women were the important balance weight of
the social system of the emerging industrial society. In her
Twenty Years at Hull House (1910) and *The Second Twenty Years
at Hull House* (1930), Addams returned to the analysis of personal motivations which took women into voluntarism in the
nonprofit sector. She described in secular terms a subjective
need for the fulfillment of meaningful work outside the
domestic setting, an emotional drive which could not be satisfied within the confines of the home.

Mary Richmond's essays on the practice of philanthropy
and her autobiographical writing parallels that of Jane Addams.
Her *Friendly Visiting Among the Poor* (1899) is a guide to conduct for the middle-class visitor to the pauper household.
The Good Neighbor in the Modern City (1907) expands on the
concept of what may be regarded as a helpful intervention
from a detached outsider in the lives of the urban poor. By
1917, when Richmond published *Social Diagnosis*, her notion of
intervention had taken on medical overtones, and the visitor
had evolved from a neighbor into a professional trained to
treat "social pathology." Richmond's autobiographical writing
contained in *The Long View* (1930) is valuable because it
offers the reader some insight into the interests and motives
of the benevolent woman turned professional whose origins
were not of the prosperous middle class.

Lillian D. Wald's *House on Henry Street* (1915) and
Windows on Henry Street (1934) are of the same genre as the
autobiographical writing of Addams and Richmond, but they are
important sources for understanding the stream of Jewish
philanthropy which converged with that generated by evangelical Protestantism to establish the profession of social work.
The emotional forces that motivated Wald to search for fulfilling work outside the home were identical with those of
her Protestant Christian sisters, but her intellectual stance
toward the task was different because many of the indigent
urban poor she aided were Jewish immigrants.

Students will find the Quaker tradition represented in
Florence Kelley's brief autobiographical sketches published
in *Survey* (1926 and 1927). These are notable for the impact
of Kelley's training as an economist and her access to social
theory critical of industrial capitalism through her study at
the University of Zurich. The parallel Catholic experience
can be found in Sister Maria Concepta, *The Making of a Sister-
Teacher* (1965), Sister M. Eulalia Herron, *The Sisters of Mercy*

in the United States (1929), Sister Mary Xavier Holworthy,
Diamonds for the King (1945), and Sister M. Rita Hefferman,
A Story of Fifty Years. The most striking difference between
the Catholic experience and that of Protestant or Jewish urban
reformers and public health workers was the sense of fulfilling
a traditional role which Catholic sisters carried into a wide
variety of new situations as teachers and hospital workers.
Mary E. Mannix's *Memoirs of Sister Louise, Superior of the
Sisters of Notre Dame, with Reminiscences of the Early Days
of the Order in the United States* (1907) and Mary Ewens' *The
Role of the Nun in Nineteenth Century America: Variations on
the International Theme* (1978) make clear the continuity of
the Catholic vocation to charity with the European roots of
Catholic religious communities, and the degree to which the
education and training of women religious prepared them to
assume new roles in nineteenth-century urban society.

Historians have written about the pioneers of social work
mainly as participants in wider movements of American reform.
Frank D. Watson's *The Charity Organization Movement in the
United States* (1922) is a study of transatlantic reform currents based on humanitarian reactions to the problems of
poverty in the modern industrial city. He notes the high
level of participation by women in charitable work in both the
British and the American city but does not trace the role of
American women in the industrial city to its earlier nineteenth-century origins. Lillian Wald's biographer, Robert L.
Duffus in *Lillian Wald, Neighbor and Crusader* (1938), sees
Wald's career as typical of the generation who were to be
leaders in the New Deal approach to a national welfare system.
Muriel W. and Ralph E. Pumphrey link Richmond's work to the
rise of the medical profession in the United States and the
influence of psychiatry on American society. Roy Lubove, in
his *The Professional Altruist: The Emergence of Social Work
as a Career, 1880-1930* (1965), studies the development of
social work toward systematic practice as an instance in the
general movement toward professionalization and the creation
of a society of technicians and experts. Allen F. Davis
analyzes the links between the pioneers of social work and
the Progressive movement in *Spearheads for Reform: The Social
Settlements and the Progressive Movement, 1890-1914* (1967),
treating the charitable impulse as one component of the status
changes, new social perceptions, and drive for organization
and control that made up Progressivism. Davis' biography of
Jane Addams, *American Heroine* (1973), takes Addams and her
career on its own terms and examines the larger social forces
that played into Addams' unusual career of public service,
rather than fitting the subject into the standard chronology
of American reform movements. Davis has most difficulty with

explaining why Addams' career should have gone into such a
startling decline in the 1920s and why she left no succeeding
generation of women reformers. This problem is treated in
William L. O'Neill's *Everyone Was Brave: The Rise and Fall of
Feminism in America* (1969). O'Neill has been much criticized
by feminist reviewers for announcing the demise of feminism
shortly before its lively renewal in the mid 1960s. Nonetheless his general analysis of feminist leaders and the organizations they led is one of the first historical narratives to
treat feminism as a movement on its own terms rather than as
an aspect of Progressivism. Jill K. Conway's "Women Reformers
and American Culture, 1870-1930" (1971-72) explores some of
the contradictions within the central beliefs of feminists of
the period 1870-1930 that resulted in their failure to recruit
disciples. Conway raises the question of role and consciousness and asks whether the woman reformer of this era who drew
her authority from the role of the benevolent woman could
analyze her life accurately or communicate her experience to
another generation, since she was the prisoner of the stereo-
typed role and moral assumptions of the early national period.
The profession of social work which in Weberian terms was the
routinized version of the lives of the late nineteenth-century
women reformers contained the altruistic and nurturing aspects
of their lives without the component of rebellion against
middle-class values, which took them on their particular path
out of acceptance of conventional family life.

BIBLIOGRAPHY

Addams, Jane. *Democracy and Social Ethics*. New York: Mac-
　　millan Co., 1902.

Addams, Jane. *Newer Ideals of Peace*. New York: Macmillan
　　Co., 1907.

Addams, Jane. *Twenty Years at Hull House, with Autobiographi-
　　cal Notes*. Macmillan Co., 1910.

Addams, Jane. *The Second Twenty Years at Hull House: Sep-
　　tember 1909 to September 1929, with a Record of Growing
　　World Consciousness*. New York: Macmillan Co., 1930.

Addams, Jane, et al. *Philanthropy and Social Progress; Seven
　　Essays . . . Delivered Before the School of Applied Ethics
　　at Plymouth, Mass., during the Session of 1892*. New York:
　　T.Y. Crowell & Co., 1893.

Conway, Jill K. "Women Reformers and American Culture: 1870-1930." *Journal of Social History* 5 (1971-1972):164-177.

Davis, Allen F. *Spearheads for Reform: The Social Settlements and the Progressive Movement, 1890-1914.* New York: Oxford University Press, 1967.

Davis, Allen F. *American Heroine: The Life and Legend of Jane Addams.* New York: Oxford University Press, 1973.

Duffus, Robert L. *Lillian Wald, Neighbor and Crusader.* New York: Macmillan Co., 1938.

Ewens, Mary. *The Role of the Nun in Nineteenth Century America: Variations on the International Theme.* New York: Arno Press, 1978.

Goldmark, Josephine. *Impatient Crusader: Florence Kelley's Life Story.* Urbana: University of Illinois Press, 1953.

Goodale, Frances A., ed. *The Literature of Philanthropy.* New York: Harper & Brothers, 1893.

Hefferman, Sister Mary Rita. *A Story of Fifty Years.* c. 1905.

Herron, Sister Mary Eulalia. *The Sisters of Mercy in the United States, 1843-1928.* New York: Macmillan Co., 1929.

Hollis, Ernest V., and Taylor, Alice L. *Social Work Education in the United States, the Report of a Study Made for the National Council on Social Work Education.* New York: Columbia University Press, 1951.

Holworthy, Sister Mary Xavier. *Diamonds for the King.* Corpus Christi, Tex.: n.p., 1945.

Kelley, Florence. "My Philadelphia." *Survey*, 1 October 1926.

Kelley, Florence. "My Novitiate." *Survey*, 1 April 1927.

Lubove, Roy. *The Professional Altruist: The Emergence of Social Work as a Career, 1880-1930.* Cambridge: Harvard University Press, 1965.

Mannix, Mary E. *Memoirs of Sister Louise, Superior of the Sisters of Notre Dame, with Reminiscences of the Early Days of the Order in the United States.* Boston: Angel Guardian Press, 1907.

Maria Concepta, Sister. *The Making of a Sister-Teacher.*

Notre Dame, Ind.: University of Notre Dame Press, 1965.

O'Neill, William L. *Everyone Was Brave: The Rise and Fall of Feminism in America.* Chicago: Quadrangle Books, 1969.

Pumphrey, Muriel W. *Mary Richmond and the Rise of Professional Social Work in Baltimore: The Foundations of a Creative Career.* Ann Arbor: University Microfilms, 1956.

Pumphrey, Ralph E., and Pumphrey, Muriel W., eds. *The Heritage of American Social Work: Readings in Its Philosophical and Institutional Development.* New York: Columbia University Press, 1961.

Richmond, Mary E. *Friendly Visiting Among the Poor: A Handbook for Charity Workers.* New York: Macmillan Co., 1899.

Richmond, Mary E. *The Good Neighbor in the Modern City.* Philadelphia: J.B. Lippincott Co., 1907.

Richmond, Mary E. *Social Diagnosis.* New York: Russell Sage Foundation, 1917.

Richmond, Mary E. *The Long View: Papers and Addresses by Mary E. Richmond.* New York: Russell Sage Foundation, 1930.

Ross, Ishbel. *Angel of the Battlefield: The Life of Clara Barton.* New York: Harper, 1956.

Stewart, William Rhinelander. *The Philanthropic Work of Josephine Shaw Lowell: Continuing a Biographical Sketch of Her Life, Together with a Selection of Her Public Papers and Private Letters.* New York: Macmillan Co., 1911.

Wald, Lillian D. *The House on Henry Street.* New York: H. Holt & Co., 1915.

Wald, Lillian D. *Windows on Henry Street.* Boston: Little, Brown & Co., 1934.

Watson, Frank D. *The Charity Organization Movement in the United States, a Study in American Philanthropy.* New York: Macmillan Co., 1922.

3. Nursing

The history of the establishment of the profession of nursing has attracted less attention from historians than that of social work. The nursing profession is usually viewed as developing alongside the modern concept of public health, and the public-health nurse is seen as a fieldworker for the modern institution of the hospital. Nursing as a profession is rarely treated as a twentieth-century variant of women's historic role as healer of the sick and midwife, and few historical accounts treat nursing as the lower-status occupation for women which emerged after the tradition of folk medicine had been suppressed and the male medical profession had taken over the study of illness and health. Yet the history of women's role in health care offers an important case study of the changes in status that affected women with the rise of the professions. The mystique of the late nineteenth-century nursing profession was a curious amalgam of the ideal of service delivered through an organization modeled on the disciplines of the army and the religious order. It took form during the Civil War when the Sisters of Charity performed notable service in caring for both the Union and Confederate wounded and when Dorothea Dix began to recruit and train a corps of women volunteers to deliver health care for the United States Sanitary Commission. In the immediate post-Civil War years, the development of concern for public health in the modern city offered the nurse the chance to serve in a disciplined war against disease and to participate in the idealism and belief in progress which recruited men into the career of scientist. Initially the public-health nurse was seen as an alternative to the male medical practitioner and as a deliverer of health care to the patient in the home rather than in the ambiguous and feared institution of the hospital. The developments in the control of infection and in medical research which changed this perception and downgraded the role of the nurse are traced in Ida M. Cannon's *On the Social Frontiers of Medicine* (1952). Cannon, the founder of medical social work and the sister of the famous medical researcher Walter B. Cannon, describes her own response to the development of the hospital as research laboratory and her own vivid conviction that healing is a social process involving patient, family, and those involved in giving health care in much more than the professional medical interactions. The idealism and fulfillment associated with entering the scientific struggle against disease is well described in Elizabeth Christophers Hobson's *Recollections of a Happy Life* (1916) and in Lavinia L. Dock and Mary A. Nutting's *A History of Nursing* (1907-12), one of the few works to link the modern nurse with the folk tradition of medicine. J. Warrington's *The Nurse's Guide* (1839) provides an early account of the role of the nurse in health care before the emergence of the modern hospital. Similar information may be found in all housekeeping manuals written

before the 1870s. Catharine E. Beecher's *The American Woman's
Home* (1869), for example, provides clear evidence of development in knowledge of health care through its various editions
from 1841 to 1874. The requirements of the curriculum in
nursing schools and the developing specialty of medical history have provided a regular crop of general histories of
nursing from the 1930s to the 1960s, when the profession began
to experience its crisis of identity associated with the
feminist critique of medicine and its treatment of women.
Francis R. Packard's *History of Medicine in the United States*
(1931) is the first in this genre, and Richard H. Shryock's
The History of Nursing (1959) is the most comprehensive.
There is, however, no systematic account of the process by
which the nurse became the adjunct of the doctor in the
delivery of health care in the hospital rather than retaining
her public-health and community role. Segments of the question are dealt with in the professional publications of organizations devoted to specialties such as public-health
nursing or psychiatric social work, e.g., *Visiting Nurse
Quarterly*, *Public Health Quarterly*, *The Public Health Nurse*,
Public Health Nursing, but no general study examines the entire system of health-care delivery from this point of view.

BIBLIOGRAPHY

Austin, Anne L. *History of Nursing Source Book.* New York:
    G.P. Putnam's Sons, 1957.

Beecher, Catharine E. *The American Woman's Home: or, Prin-
    ciples of Domestic Science; Being a Guide to the Formation
    and Maintenance of Economical, Healthful, Beautiful, and
    Christian Homes.* New York: J.B. Ford & Co., 1869.

Cannon, Ida M. *On the Social Frontier of Medicine: Pioneering
    in Medical Social Service.* Cambridge, Mass.: Harvard
    University Press, 1952.

Dock, Lavinia L., and Nutting, Mary A. *A History of Nursing:
    The Evolution of Nursing Systems from the Earliest Times
    to the Foundation of the First English and American
    Training Schools for Nurses.* 4 volumes. New York: G.P.
    Putnam's Sons, 1907-1912.

Hobson, Elizabeth Christophers. *Recollections of a Happy Life.*
    New York: G.P. Putnam's Sons, 1916.

Jolly, Ellen R. *Nuns of the Battlefield.* Providence:
    Providence Visitor Press, 1927.

Packard, Francis R. *History of Medicine in the United States.*
    2 volumes. New York: P.B. Hoeber, 1931.

Roberts, Mary K. *American Nursing: History and Interpretation.*
    New York: Macmillan Co., 1954.

Rodabaugh, James H., and Rodabaugh, Mary J. *Nursing in Ohio,*
    A History. Columbus: Ohio State Nurses Association, 1951.

Rosen, George. *A History of Public Health.* New York: M.D.
    Publications, 1958.

Shryock, Richard H. *The History of Nursing: An Interpretation*
    of the Social and Medical Factors Involved. Philadelphia:
    W.B. Saunders, 1959.

Visiting Nurse Quarterly (1909-1912); *Public Health Quarterly*
    (1913-1918); *The Public Health Nurse* (1918-1931);
    Public Health Nursing (1931-   ). Utica, N.Y.: National
    Organization for Public Health Nursing.

Waite, Frederick C. *History of the New England Female*
    Medical College, 1848-1874. Boston: Boston University
    School of Medicine, 1950.

Warrington, J. *The Nurse's Guide; Containing a Series of*
    Instructions to Females Who Wish to Engage in the Important
    Business of Nursing Mother and Child in the Lying-In
    Chamber. Philadelphia: Thomas Cowperthwait, 1839.

4. Librarianship

The development of the profession of librarian illustrates
with great clarity the manner in which women's role as guardian of culture and inculcator of noneconomic values tended
to be downgraded by the forces of professionalization. The
history of nursing shows us the potential for social change
embodied in the woman health professional who could spear-
head community health-care delivery and call into question a
male monopoly on the practice of medicine. We see this role
undermined by the emergence of the modern hospital with its
male hierarchies and its research orientation. In social
work we see professionalization emptying the role of social
worker of the resonance which the woman good-works volunteer
possessed and linking the caseworker to bureaucratic modes of

proceeding, so that the role was purged of its potential for
social criticism and rebelliousness. In the founding of the
modern public library and the training of the women who would
be its poorly paid staff, we see with even greater clarity
the process by which women's supposed altruism and interest in
cultural matters could be used to mask a simple economic
desire to found and operate cultural institutions for the
masses at the smallest possible cost to the public purse.

Historians have differed about the social impulses represented in the establishment of the public library in America.
Sidney H. Ditzion's *Arsenals of a Democratic Culture, A Social
History of the American Public Library Movement in New England
and the Middle States from 1850 to 1900* (1947) follows a
theme sketched by Samuel S. Green in *The Public Library Movement in the United States, 1853-1893* (1913). Both writers
treating the subject from the perspective of a wartime era in
which democratic institutions were on trial described the
foundation and elaboration of the public-library system as a
triumph of American democratic idealism, voluntarism, and
cultural progress. Although aware that women were the vast
majority of the professional staff of the public library,
neither Green nor Ditzion saw this occupational segregation
as anything but a benign social adjustment to the need for
educated women to find useful social occupations.

Ann Douglas in *The Feminization of American Culture*
(1977) and Dee Garrison in *Apostles of Culture: The Public
Librarian and American Society, 1876-1920* (1979) have seen
the public-library movement as an expression of the attempts
of the elite genteel culture of the affluent middle class to
impose cultural restraints on the working classes. Douglas
sees women as active participants in this activity working as
cultural missionaries to inculcate proper genteel values
through the reading materials made available through the public library. Garrison sees some women librarians as potential rebels who held working-class culture in high regard,
but is in general agreement that the public-library movement
was one more aspect of the Progressive impulse to discipline
and regulate the masses. Garrison concurs that the majority
of women attracted by the profession were cultural and social
conservatives who thoroughly supported the existing division
of social territory between males and females and who saw the
library not as new social territory but merely as an extension of the home. This view has been criticized in Phyllis
Dain's "Ambivalence and Paradox: The Social Bonds of the
Public Library" (1975). *Library Trends* 25 (July 1976) contains a selection of essays on library history in the United
States including John Colsen's "The Writing of American
Library History," which concludes that the weight of the

evidence supports the view of the library as an elite mechanism
of cultural control.

Laurel Ann Grotzinger's *The Power and the Dignity: Librarianship and Katherine Sharp* (1966) treats one of the pioneers
of the profession as feminist and inspired by the notion of
the dignity of independent occupations for women. Mary Jane
Regan, *Echoes from the Past* (1927), recalls the founding years
of the profession. Garrison's work contains a full bibliography listing useful sources in the extensive publications of
the library profession, but it is notable that the library
movement inspired far less autobiographical writing or social
commentary from women participants than did the professions of
social work and nursing.

BIBLIOGRAPHY

Colsen, John. "The Writing of American Library History."
    Library Trends 25 (1976):7-21.

Dain, Phyllis. "Ambivalence and Paradox: The Social Bonds of
    the Public Library." *Library Journal* 100 (1975):261-266.

Ditzion, Sidney H. *Arsenals of a Democratic Culture, A
    Social History of the American Public Library Movement
    in New England and the Middle States from 1850-1900.*
    Chicago: American Library Association, 1947.

Douglas, Ann. *The Feminization of American Culture.* New
    York: Alfred A. Knopf, 1977.

Duffus, Robert L. *Our Starving Libraries: Studies in Ten
    American Communities during the Depression Years.*
    New York: Houghton Mifflin Co., 1933.

Garrison, Dee. "The Tender Technicians: The Feminization of
    Public Librarianship, 1876-1905." *Journal of Social
    History* 6 (1972-1973):131-159.

Garrison, Dee. *Apostles of Culture: The Public Librarian
    and American Society, 1876-1920.* New York: Free Press,
    1979.

Green, Samuel S. *The Public Library Movement in the United
    States 1853-1893.* Boston: Boston Book Co., 1913.

Grotzinger, Laurel Ann. *The Power and the Dignity: Librarian-
    ship and Katherine Sharp.* New York: Scarecrow Press, 1966.

Regan, Mary Jane. *Echoes from the Past: Reminiscences of the
     Boston Athenaeum.* Boston: The Boston Athenaeum, 1927.

Williamson, Charles C. *Training for Library Service: A Report
     Prepared for the Carnegie Corporation of New York.*
     Boston: D.P. Updike, Merrymount Press, 1923.

C. Women's Clubs

An important aspect of women's position in the moral
economy of society was the sociability that accompanied the
role of volunteer or professional concerned with either social
uplift or cultural affairs. Julia Ward Howe in her memoirs
described the women's club as the equivalent of college for
women of her generation who had not had the opportunity for
formal education. Whether in an old East Coast city such as
Boston or the new and rapidly growing Chicago, the women's
club provided the network of women of money and influence who
could mobilize resources for good causes and enjoy the company of like-minded women in the process. Much has been made
of the male sociability of the men's club seen as a center of
influence where business contacts were made and outsiders
excluded. The history of women's clubs is an important chapter in the narrative of women's roles as volunteers or founders of the service professions. The city women's club was
the setting for the study of social issues and for education
in the fine and decorative arts, the appreciation of music
and literary culture. Its counterpart in the small town
played the same role on a smaller scale and proved the launch-
ing pad for many national careers in the nonprofit sector.
The club was an almost exclusively middle-class phenomenon,
though the city women's club might interest itself in questions relating to working women and child labor. The white
women's club had its counterpart for affluent black women,
and the black women's clubs played a significant role in
publicizing the horrors of lynch law and violence against the
Negro in the north.
     Mary I. Wood's *History of the General Federation of Women's
Clubs* (1912) is a straightforward institutional history exhibiting justifiable pride in the role the social organizations of
justifiable pride at the role the social organizations of
women had played in the peak years of Progressive urban
reform. Mildred White Wells' *Unity in Diversity* (1953) analyzes the women's-club movement from the point of view of its
relationship to contemporary reform movements, and Martha
Strayer's *The D.A.R.: An Informal History* (1958) relates the
links of the Daughters of the American Revolution to

conservative political issues. None of these histories has
been written with any of the central questions about the history of women's organizations in mind. The secular club and
the religious women's association are not seen as variants of
the same drive to female sociability. The informal politics
of "influence" associated with women's sphere is not examined,
nor is the question raised as to whether or not separate organizations represented a sounder strategy towards achieving
women's political and social goals than the counter expedient
to be followed in the 1960s of attempting to outlaw exclusively
male associations.

A number of biographies illustrate the importance of the
women's club for the lives of women who were of national or
regional importance in politics and the arts. Julia Ward
Howe's *Reminiscences, 1819-1899* (1899) is particularly valuable
for identifying the educational benefits of the club and the
excitement of discovering one's own identity through sharing
experience with other women of one's generation. Ida Wells
Barnett's autobiography, *Crusade for Justice* edited by
Alfreda M. Duster (1970), describes the parallel experience
for black women and Louise de Koven Bowen's *Growing Up With
a City* (1926) suggests the particular importance of the Chicago
Women's Club in the founding and support of Chicago's major
cultural and social welfare institutions.

Students of the suffrage and antisuffrage movements would
do well to consult the anniversary histories of the principal
women's clubs such as the Chilton Club of Boston, the Chicago
Woman's Club, the Colony Club of New York City, the Cosmopolitan Club of New York City, the Sulgrave Club of Washington, D.C., and Sorosis of New York City, for these were the
central networks of influence in the sphere of women and key
centers for the exchange of ideas and the mobilizing of energies. A typical listing of women's clubs derived from Massa-
chusetts sources follows: the Afternoon Club of Gardner, the
Cabot Club of Middleboro, Friends in Council of Turners Falls,
Home Study Club of Ashland, Kosmos Club of Wakefield, Medford
Women's Club, Middlesex Women's Club of Lowell, Milford
Women's Club, New England Women's Club of Boston, Old and New
Club of Malden, Springfield Women's Club, Sunderland Women's
Club, Thursday Club of Westborough, Waltham Women's Club,
Wellesley Hills Women's Club, West Concord Women's Club,
Woburn Women's Club, and Worcester Women's Club. The student
may consult a similar list for any state or region and will
find that archival materials documenting the history of the
nineteenth-century women's club are not difficult to locate.

BIBLIOGRAPHY

Abrahall, Frances H., ed. *Club-Women of New York, 1919-1920.* New York: New York City Federation of Women's Clubs, 1919.

Bailey, Nettie F. "The Significance of the Woman's Club Movement." *Harper's Bazaar* 39: 204-209.

Barnett, Ida Wells. *Crusade for Justice.* Edited by Alfreda M. Duster. Chicago: University of Chicago Press, 1970.

Bartlett, Mary K. "The Philanthropic Work of the Chicago Women's Club." *The Outlook* 49: 827-828.

Beadle, Muriel, and the Centennial History Committee. *The Fortnightly of Chicago: The City and Its Women, 1873-1973.* Chicago: Henry Regnery, 1973.

Benton, Caroline French. *Complete Club Book for Women.* Boston: L.C. Page, 1915.

Blair, Emily Newell. "Why Clubs for Women?" *The Forum* 77: 354-363.

Blair, Karen J. "Origins of the General Federation of Women's Clubs." Paper read at Berkshire Conference on the History of Women, June 9-11, 1976, at Bryn Mawr College. Mimeographed.

Blair, Karen J. *The Clubwoman as Feminist: True Womanhood Defined, 1868-1914.* New York: Holmes & Meier, 1980.

Bowen, Louise de Koven. *Growing Up with a City.* New York: Macmillan Co., 1926.

Bryce, Mary E. "The Club as an Ally to Higher Education." *Arena* 6: 378-380.

Cass, Alice Hazen. *Practical Programs for Women's Clubs.* Chicago: A.C. McClurg, 1915.

Clapp, Roger T. *The Hope Club: A Centennial History, 1875-1975.* E.A. Johnson, 1975.

Cleveland, Grover. "Woman's Mission and Woman's Clubs." *Ladies' Home Journal* 22: 3-4.

"The Club Movement among Colored Women of America." Chapter 17 in Booker T. Washington, *A New Negro for a New Century.* Chicago: American Publishing House, 1900.

Croly, Mrs. Jane Cunningham. *Sorosis, Its Origin and History*. New York: Press of J.J. Little, 1886.

Croly, Mrs. Jane Cunningham. *The History of the Woman's Club Movement in America*. New York: Henry G. Allen, 1898.

Davis, Elizabeth L. *Lifting as They Climb*. Washington, D.C.: National Association of Colored Women, n.d.

Denison, Dimies F.S. "The President of the General Federation of Women's Clubs." *Outlook* 78: 267-269.

Diaz, A.M. "Women's Clubs: Their True Character." *National Magazine* 3: 59-63.

Dunbar, Olivia Howard. "The Woman's University Club." *Harper's Bazaar* 42: 1111-1114.

Francis, M.C. "The Federation of Women's Clubs." *The Review of Reviews* 12: 720-721.

Frank, Henriette Greenebaum, and Jerome, Amalie Hofer, comp. *Annals of the Chicago Women's Club for the First Forty Years of Its Organization, 1876-1916*. Chicago: Chicago Women's Club, 1916.

Granger, Mrs. A.O. "The Effect of Club Work in the South." *American Academy of Political and Social Science Annals* 28: 248-256.

Hartt, Mary Bronson. "Work for Women's Clubs to Do." *Good Housekeeping* 49: 245-247.

Hawthorne, Hildegarde. "The General Federation of Women's Clubs: A Great Altruistic Movement." *The Century Magazine* 80: 832-837.

Henrotin, Ellen M. "The Attitudes of Women's Clubs and Associations toward Social Economics." *Bulletin of the Department of Labor* 23: 501-545.

Henrotin, Ellen M. "General Federation of Women's Clubs." *Outlook* 55: 442-446.

Howe, Julia Ward. *Reminiscences, 1818-1899*. New York: Houghton Mifflin and Co., 1899.

Howe, Julia Ward. "A Chronicle of Boston Clubs." *New England Magazine* 34: 610-615.

Johnson, Helen Louise. "The Work of the Home Economics Department, General Federation of Women's Clubs." *Journal of Home Economics* 5: 153-155.

Lerner, Gerda. "Early Community Work of Black Club Women." *Journal of Negro History* 59: 158-167.

Lockwood, Florence. "Working Girl's Clubs." *Century Magazine* 41: 793-794.

MacLean, Annie Marion. "A Progressive Club of Working Women." *Survey* 15: 299-302.

Mason, Amelia Gere. "Woman's Clubs." (From *Woman in the Golden Age* , The Century Company, 1901.) In *Living Age* 231: 656-658.

Matthews, S. "The Woman's Club and the Church." *Independent* 103: 12-13.

May, E. Anne S. "The Woman's Club Movement." *The Vermonter* 3: 167-172.

Merrill, Margaret Manton. "Sorosis." *Cosmopolitan* 15: 153-158.

Miller, Oliver Thorne. *The Woman's Club: A Practical Guide and Handbook*. New York: United States Book Co., 1891.

Mumford, Mary E. "The Civic Club of Philadelphia." *Outlook* 52: 588-589.

Nobles, Katherine. "Club Life in the South." *Arena* 6: 374-378.

Richmond, Mary E. "Working Women's Clubs." *Charities Review* 6: 351-352.

Roberts, Kate Louise. *The Club Woman's Handbook of Programs and Club Management*. New York: Funk and Wagnalls, 1914.

Sargent, Mrs. John T., ed. *Sketches and Reminiscences of the Radical Club of Chestnut Street, Boston*. Boston: James R. Osgood, 1880.

Severance, Mrs. Caroline M. "The Genesis of the Club Idea." *Woman's Journal* 33: 174.

Sewall, May Wright. "Women's Clubs--A Symposium." *Arena* 6: 362-368.

Strayer, Martha. *The D.A.R.: An Informal History*. Washington, D.C.: Public Affairs Press, 1958.

Talbot, Marion, and Rosenberry, Lois I. *The History of the A.A.U.W., 1881-1931*. Boston: Houghton Mifflin, 1931.

Ward, Mary Alden. "The Influence of Women's Clubs in New England and in the Mid-Eastern States." *American Academy of Political and Social Science Annals* 28: 205-226.

Wells, Mildred White. *Unity in Diversity: The History of the General Federation of Women's Clubs*. Washington, D.C.: General Federation of Women's Clubs, 1953.

Williams, Fannie Barrier. "Club Movement among Negro Women." In *Progress of a Race*. Edited by John W. Gibson and William H. Crogman. Miami: Mnemosyne, 1969; reprint of 1902 ed.

Winant, Marguerite Dawson. *Century of Sorosis, 1868-1968*. Uniondale, N.Y.: Salisbury Printers, 1968.

Winter, Alice Ames. *The Business of Being a Club Woman*. New York: Century, 1925.

Wood, Mary I. *The History of the General Federation of Women's Clubs*. New York: Norwood, 1912.

Wood, Mary I. "Civic Activities of Women's Clubs." *American Academy of Political and Social Science Annals* 28: 78-87.

Woolley, Mary E. "The Woman's Club Woman." *Good Housekeeping* 50: 559-565.

Students may also consult the anniversary histories of the principal women's clubs such as the Chilton Club of Boston, the Colony Club of New York, the Cosmopolitan Club of New York, and the Sulgrave Club of Washington, D.C.

D. Women Writers and Journalists

1. General Works

The dominating position assigned women within the moral economy solved the problem of women's literary voice, since women were expected to preach, to practice moral uplift, and to instruct in the noneconomic sphere of life, provided they avoided comment on economic and political questions. While the sentimental novel may be regarded as derivative from the writing of eighteenth-century England and the moral essay from the evangelical culture typified by Hannah More, the American variants of these forms developed a logic of their own related to the emotional climate and constellation of social forces within which the American woman writer worked.

The women writers of the pre-Civil War period have been studied as a general phenomenon in American culture though relatively infrequently from the prespective of the feminist movement, since their unrelenting sentimentality and glorification of women's domesticity has not seemed fertile ground for feminist scholarship, which has to its detriment neglected to understand the social forces that supported antifeminist views. Caroline H. Dall saw the link between the movement for women's education and the earlier discontents of romantic heroines in her *The Romance of the Association; or, One Last Glimpse of Charlotte Temple and Eliza Wharton* (1875). At the University of Maine in the twenties and thirties, a series of monographs were published on the women writers who shaped the early American novel. Of these the most useful are V.B. Field, *Constantia: A Study of the Life and Works of Judith Sargent Murray, 1751-1820* (1931) and E. Pendleton and M. Ellis, *Philenia: The Life and Works of Sarah Wentworth Morton* (1931).

Meade Minnigerode drew attention to the breadth of circulation of the works of the women writers of the forties and the crushing sentimentality of their work in *The Fabulous Forties, 1840-1850* (1924). Herbert Brown's *The Sentimental Novel in America, 1789-1860* (1940) places the work of the woman novelist in the general context of the development of American fiction and focuses attention on its glorification of the woman within the domestic sphere. Mrs. Stowe's words in *The Minister's Wooing* (1859) about the Christian home, "the appointed shrine for women, more holy than cloister, more saintly and pure than church or altar.... Priestess, wife and mother, there she ministers daily in works of household peace...." (pp. 567-68), are quoted without reference to the degree to which Stowe found her own role within her domestic setting intolerable, to be escaped by trips to water cures, rests after nervous prostration and fits of depression. Yet Stowe represents the paradox that many of the creators of the myth of the perfect domestic woman were themselves escaping through illness or other expedients from the very role they gave almost sacramental significance.

Helen Papashvily writing in 1956 pointed out in *All the Happy Endings* that the fiction of women writers tended to

treat in searing detail the problems of the nineteenth-century
woman. Heroines were robbed by designing husbands, deprived
of children by heartless spouses who claimed offspring as
theirs no matter what philandering or fecklessness on their
part broke up a family. Men were unfaithful, cruel, and
physically intimidating, and yet the woman writer of the
sentimental novel brought the plot to a conclusion not with
rebellion against women's subordination but with a mechanically
happy ending. In Papashvily's view the novel was a prefeminist examination of women's situation with the happy
ending cranked into place to forestall reaching revolutionary
conclusions.

Shortly after Papashvily wrote, William R. Taylor began
to examine the function of the image of home and family life
in the emerging sense of regional and cultural differences
which began to separate north and south in the early nineteenth century. Taylor also drew attention to the degree to
which women were the forgers of the differing images of the
two regions in the popular imagination and to the ideological
significance of the concept of domesticity, a concept around
which a variety of economic and political values coalesced.

While Taylor was interested in the ideological significance of the sentimentalized northern and southern family,
Ann Douglas in *The Feminization of American Culture* (1977)
was concerned with the degree to which women's exclusion from
economic and political realities in the pre-Civil War era
produced false consciousness and prevented them from any
clear analysis of the contradictions in American society.
Douglas is particularly interested in the saccharine sentimentality with which mother-child and husband-wife relationships are treated and the papering over of harsh reality
which eventually transformed a Puritan sense of death into
the plush lined coffin and the romantically planted cemeteries
that were the predecessors of twentieth-century slumberlands.
Douglas's criticisms of the shallowness of the emotional level
at which women's literature operated is the first Marxist
critique to be developed of the sentimental woman writer, and
it may be added the first to operate on the assumption that
women might have had a better hold on reality than pre-Civil
War culture appeared to offer them.

Students of the period have thus tended either to segregate the woman writer and the sentimental world view she
represented or to examine it as an aspect of a larger cultural transformation such as the emergence of sectional
conflict or the cheapening and decline of religious sensibility before the forces of capitalism and secularism. Little
attention has been devoted to the social forces which produced
the woman writer and to the cultural contradictions contained

within her fiction. We need to know why writers of the order
of Harriet Beecher Stowe and second-rate imaginations like
that of Lydia Sigourney both passed over the disillusionment
of unhappy marriage to focus obsessively on the redemptive
family. They did so at a time when the demographic balance
of American society was so disrupted by the westward movement
that marriage and the formation of a family was not a possibility for many eastern women and when utopian experiments
with sexuality and child-rearing seemed a serious threat to
older mores. Their response to these social forces appears
to have been to find an accommodation for the single woman as
school teacher or domestic scientist and to give overwhelming
emphasis to women's role as moral guardian within the family.
By so doing they mobilized the predominant social opinion
behind some modified expansion of social territory for the
single woman provided that this expansion went along with
renewed emphasis on the temporary nature of the adjustment
and the ultimate importance of the traditional family.

Thus we should link the sentimental fiction of the
period with the most common response to industrialization and
the disturbances of population that went along with it. These
population movements and the new opportunities for women's
work that accompanied them have long been thought to result
in the rise of modern feminism. Women's place in the moral
economy, however, required that a different response be the
dominant one in the United States. Since the threats to
established values embodied in capitalism and urban industrial
society were grave, indeed, many linked their perception of
these threats to an increased need to counterbalance them with
the moral weight of women's sphere. Far from wishing to dis-
mantle it, they wished to strengthen it and by so doing increase the redemptive power of the female in society's moral
economy. Those who saw the threats most clearly by reason of
failing to form or maintain a family could thus become the
most articulate and emotionally committed promoters of the
myth of sacramental domesticity. In one sense, we may agree
with Papashvily and Douglas that sentimental views of the
family limited women's ability to understand urban capitalist
society. Yet we may also see in the sentimental novelist an
individual wrestling with the perception of just how acquisitive and competitive the economic and political world of
mid-nineteenth-century America was and engaged in a desperate
search for countervailing social forces. Once we examine the
sentimental writer from this point of view, she does not represent Douglas's false consciousness or Brown's failure of
analysis, but a phenomenon in her own terms, a critic of
American capitalism able to call on neither the aristocracy
nor the organized working class as opposing social forces.

We may then examine this response with greater curiosity and more openness to the points women writers were attempting, however gushing the prose conventions of the day, to make. There were, of course, incandescent imaginations and literary powers which transcended the contemporary situation such as we find in the work of Emily Dickinson. Yet, for the historian the second-rate artist who is bound by time and culture is often the most fruitful source.

BIBLIOGRAPHY

Brown, Herbert Ross. *The Sentimental Novel in America 1789-1860.* Durham, N.C.: Duke University Press, 1940.

Dall, Caroline H. *The Romance of the Association; or, One Last Glimpse of Charlotte Temple and Eliza Wharton.* Cambridge, Mass.: Press of J. Wilson & Son, 1875.

Douglas, Ann. *The Feminization of American Culture.* New York: Alfred A. Knopf, 1977.

Field, Vera Bernadette. *Constantia: A Study of the Life and Works of Judith Sargent Murray, 1751-1820.* Orono, Maine: Printed at the University Press, 1931.

Minnigerode, Meade. *The Fabulous Forties, 1840-1850, a Presentation of Private Life.* New York: G.P. Putnam's Sons, 1924.

Papashvily, Helen W. *All the Happy Endings: A Study of the Domestic Novel in America, the Women Who Wrote It, the Women Who Read It, in the Nineteenth Century.* New York: Harper, 1956.

Pattee, Fred L. *The Feminine Fifties.* New York: Appleton-Century Co., 1940.

Pendleton, Emily and Ellis, Milton. *Philenia: The Life and Works of Sarah Wentworth Morton, 1759-1846.* Orono, Maine: Printed at the University Press, 1931.

Stowe, Harriet Beecher. *The Minister's Wooing.* New York: Derby & Jackson, 1859.

Taylor, William Robert. *Cavalier and Yankee: The Old South and American National Character.* Garden City: Anchor Books, 1961.

2. *Selected Authors and Works of Importance for the Study of Women's Fiction, Poetry and Journalism*

Lydia Maria Child

The Adventures of Jamie and Jeannie, and Other Stories. Boston: D. Lothrop & Co., 1876.

The American Frugal Housewife. 8th ed. Boston: Carter, Hendee & Co., 1832.

Anti-Slavery Catechism. Newburyport: C. Whipple, 1836.

An Appeal in Favor of that Class of Americans Called Africans. Boston: Allen & Ticknor, 1833.

Aspirations of the World. A Chain of Opals. Boston: Roberts Brothers, 1878.

Authentic Anecdotes of American Slavery. No. 1-2. Newburyport: C. Whipple, 1835.

Autumnal Leaves: Tales and Sketches in Prose and Poetry. New York: C.S. Francis & Co., 1857.

Biographical Sketches of Great and Good Men. Boston: Putnam & Hunt, 1828.

Biographies of Good Wives. New York: C.S. Francis & Co., 184-.

The Biographies of Lady Russell, and Madame Guyon. Boston: Carter, Hendee & Co., 1832.

The Biographies of Madame de Staël, and Madame Roland. Boston: Carter, Hendee & Co., 1832.

Brief History of the Condition of Women, in Various Ages and Nations. 5th ed. New York: C.S. Francis & Co., 1835.

The Brother and Sister: and Other Stories. Philadelphia: New Book Store, 1852.

The Children of Mount Ida, and Other Stories. New York: C.S. Francis & Co., 1871.

The Christ-Child, and Other Stories. Boston: D. Lothrop, 1869.

The Coronal. A Collection of Miscellaneous Pieces. Boston: Carter, 1831.

Domestic Economy. Boston: n.p., 1830.

*Elizabeth Haddon; A True Narrative of the Early Settlement of
New Jersey*. Philadelphia, 1898.

Emily Parker, or Impulse, Not Principle. Boston: Bowles and
Dearborn, 1827.

The Evils of Slavery and the Cure of Slavery. Newburyport:
C. Whipple, 1836.

Fact and Fiction: A Collection of Stories. New York: C.S.
Francis & Co., 1846.

The Family Nurse, or Companion of the Frugal Housewife.
Boston: C.J. Hendee, 1837.

*The First Settlers of New England; or, Conquest of the Pequods,
Narragansetts and Pokanokets*. New York: C.S. Francis &
Co., 1828.

Flowers for Children. New York: C.S. Francis & Co., 1844-45.

The Freedmen's Book. Boston: Ticknor & Fields, 1865.

The Frugal Housewife. Boston: Marsh & Capen, 1829.

The Girl's Own Book. New York: Clark Austin & Co., 1833.

Good Wives. Boston: Carter, Hendee & Co., 1833.

*The History of the Condition of Women in Various Ages and
Nations*. Boston: J. Allen & Co., 1835.

Hobomok, A Tale of Early Times. Boston: Cummings, Hilliard
& Co., 1824.

Isaac T. Hopper. A True Life. Boston: J.P. Jewett & Co., 1853.

Letters from New York. London: R. Bentley, 1843.

The Little Girl's Own Book. Boston, 1831.

Looking Toward Sunset. Boston: Ticknor & Fields, 1865.

The Magician's Show Box, and Other Stories. Boston: Ticknor
& Fields, 1856.

Married Women: Biographies of Good Wives. New York: C.S.
Francis & Co., 1871.

Memoirs of Madame de Staël and Madame Roland. New York: C.S.
Francis & Co., 1847.

The Mother's Book. Boston: Carter, Hendee & Babcock, 1831.

A New Flower for Children. New York: C.S. Francis & Co., 1856.

The Oasis. Boston: Allen and Ticknor, 1834.

*The Patriarchal Institution as Described by Members of Its
Own Family*. New York: American Anti-Slavery Society,
1860.

Philothea, a Romance. Boston: Otis, Broaders, 1836.

The Power of Kindness; and Other Stories. Philadelphia: W.P.
Hazard, 1857.

The Progress of Religious Ideas through the Successive Ages.
New York: C.S. Francis & Co., 1855.

Rainbows for Children. New York: James Miller, 184-.

The Rebels; or, Boston, before the Revolution. Boston:
Cummings, Hilliard, and Co., 1825.

*The Right Way, the Safe Way, Proved by the Emancipation in
the British West Indies, and Elsewhere*. New York:
n.p., 1860.

A Romance of the Republic. Boston: Ticknor & Fields, 1867.

Rose Marian, and the Flower Fairies. Boston: Crosby &
Ainsworth, 1865.

Sketches from Real Life. Philadelphia: Hazard & Mitchell,
1850.

A Tribute to Colonel Robert G. Shaw. Cambridge, Mass.:
Harvard University Press, 1864.

Emily Dickinson

Bolts of Melody; New Poems of Emily Dickinson. Edited by Mabel
Loomis Todd and Millicent Todd Bingham. London: J. Cape, 1945.

The Complete Poems of Emily Dickinson, with an Introduction

by her Niece, Martha Dickinson Bianchi. Boston: Little,
Brown, & Co., 1924.

A Cycle of Sonnets. Edited by Mabel Loomis Todd. Boston:
Roberts Brothers, 1896.

Emily Dickinson. New York: Simon & Schuster, 1927.

*Emily Dickinson, Face to Face: Unpublished Letters with Notes
and Reminiscences,* by her niece Martha Dickinson Bianchi.
Boston: Houghton Mifflin Co., 1932.

An Emily Dickinson Year Book. Edited by Helen H. Arnold.
Northampton, Mass.: Hampshire Bookshop, 1948.

*Eternity; Chorus for Women's Voices, Flute, Two Horns, and
Brass.* Poem by Emily Dickinson, music by Wallingford
Rieger. New York: H. Flammer, 1945.

Five Poems by Emily Dickinson. Set to music by Ernst Bacon.
New York: G. Schirmer, 1944.

*Further Poems by Emily Dickinson Withheld from Publication by
her Sister Lavinia.* Edited by her niece Martha Dickinson
Bianchi and Alfred Leite Hampson. Boston: Little, Brown
& Co., 1929.

Letters of Emily Dickinson. Edited by Mabel Loomis Todd.
Boston: Roberts Brothers, 1894.

Letters to Dr. and Mrs. Josiah Gilbert Holland. Edited by
their granddaughter Theodora Van Wagenen Ward. Cambridge,
Mass.: Harvard University Press, 1951.

*The Life and Letters of Emily Dickinson, by her niece Martha
Dickinson Bianchi.* Boston: Houghton Mifflin Co., 1924.

Love Poems. Mount Vernon, New York: Peter Pauper Press, 1952.

Poems, by Emily Dickinson. Edited by two of her friends,
Mabel Loomis Todd and T.W. Higginson. Series 1-3.
Boston: Roberts Brothers, 1891-96.

*Poems and Letters; Together with Miscellaneous Correspondence
of the Editors of Her Own Work.* Given to the Public
Library of the City of Boston. Galatea Collection,
Manuscripts. 1911.

Poems for Youth. Edited by Alfred Leite Hampson. Boston:
Little, Brown, & Co., 1934.

Poems, Hitherto Published Only in Part. Edited by Millicent Todd Bingham, 1947.

Poems: Including Variant Readings Critically Compared with All Known Manuscripts. Edited by Thomas H. Johnson. Cambridge: Harvard University Press, Belknap Press, 1955.

The Poems of Emily Dickinson. Edited by Martha Dickinson Bianchi and Alfred Leite Hampson. Centenary ed. Boston: Little, Brown, & Co., 1930.

Poems: Selected and Edited with a Commentary by Louis Untermeyer. New York: Heritage Press, 1952.

Selected Poems of Emily Dickinson. Edited by Conrad Aiken. London: J. Cape, 1924.

The Single Hound; Poems of a Lifetime. Introduction by her niece, Martha Dickinson Bianchi. Boston: Little, Brown, & Co., 1914.

The Unbound Anthology. New York: The Poet's Guild, 19--.

Unpublished Poems of Emily Dickinson. Edited by her niece Martha Dickinson Bianchi and Alfred Leite Hampson. Boston: Little, Brown, & Co., 1935.

Copland, Aaron. *Twelve Poems of Emily Dickinson, Set to Music*. New York: Boosey & Hawkes, 1956.

Margaret Fuller (Ossoli)

Art, Literature, and the Drama. Edited by her brother, Arthur B. Fuller. Boston: Brown, Taggard & Chase, 1860.

At Home and Abroad; or, Things and Thoughts in America and Europe. Edited by her brother, Arthur B. Fuller. Boston: Crosby, Nichols, 1856.

The Dial: A Magazine for Literature, Philosophy, and Religion. Boston: Weeks, Jordan & Co., 1841-44.

Life Without and Life Within: Or, Reviews, Narratives, Essays, and Poems. Edited by her brother, Arthur B. Fuller. Boston: Brown, Taggard & Chase, 1859.

Literature and Art. With an Introduction by Horace Greeley. New York: Fowler & Wells, 1852.

Love-Letters of Margaret Fuller, 1845-46, With an introduction by Julia Ward Howe. New York: D. Appleton & Co., 1903.

Memoirs of Margaret Fuller Ossoli. Boston: Phillips, 1851.

Memoirs of Margaret Fuller Ossoli. London: R. Bentley, 1852.

Papers on Literature and Art. New York: Wiley & Putnam, 1846.

Summer in the Lakes, in 1843. Boston: C.C. Little & J. Brown, 1844.

Woman in the Nineteenth Century. London: H.G. Clarke & Co., 1845.

Woman in the Nineteenth Century, and Kindred Papers Relating to the Sphere, Condition and Duties of Woman. Edited by her brother, Arthur B. Fuller. New York: Sheldon, Lamport & Co., 1855.

The Writings of Margaret Fuller. Edited by Mason Wade. New York: Viking Press, 1941.

Sarah Orne Jewett

The Best Stories of Sarah Orne Jewett. Selected by Willa Cather. Boston: Houghton Mifflin Co., 1925.

Betty Leicester: A Story for Girls. Boston: Houghton Mifflin Co., 1889.

Betty Leicester's Christmas. Boston: Houghton Mifflin Co., 1889.

County By-ways. Boston: Houghton Mifflin Co., 1881.

A Country Doctor. Boston: Houghton Mifflin Co., 1884.

The Country of the Pointed Firs. Boston: Houghton Mifflin Co., 1896.

Deephaven. Boston: J.R. Osgood Co., 1877.

Katy's Birthday. Boston: D. Lothrop & Co., 1883.

The King of Folly Island, and Other People. Boston: Houghton Mifflin Co., 1888.

Letters of Sarah Orne Jewett. Edited by Annie Fields. Boston: Houghton Mifflin Co., 1911.

The Life of Nancy. Boston: Houghton Mifflin Co., 1895.

A Marsh Island. Boston: Houghton Mifflin Co., 1885.

The Mate of Daylight and Friends Ashore. 9th ed. Boston: Houghton Mifflin Co., 1883.

A Native of Winby, and Other Stories. Boston: Houghton Mifflin Co., 1893.

The Night Before Thanksgiving. Boston: Houghton Mifflin Co., 1910.

The Normans; Told Chiefly in Relation to Their Conquest of England. New York: G.P. Putnam's Sons, 1886.

Old Friends and New. Boston: Houghton, Osgood & Co., 1879.

Play Days. A Book of Stories for Children. Boston: Houghton, Osgood and Co., 1878.

The Queen's Twin, and Other Stories. Boston: Houghton Mifflin Co., 1899.

Strangers and Wayfarers. Boston: Houghton Mifflin Co., 1890.

Tales of New England. Boston: Houghton Mifflin Co., 1890.

The Tory Lover. Boston: Houghton Mifflin Co., 1901.

A White Heron, and Other Stories. Boston: Houghton Mifflin Co., 1886.

Lucy Larcom

As It Is in Heaven. Boston: Houghton Mifflin Co., 1891.

At the Beautiful Gate, and Other Songs of Faith. Boston: Houghton Mifflin Co., 1892.

Beckonings for Everyday, a Calendar of Thought. Boston: Houghton Mifflin Co., 1886.

Easter Gleams. Boston: Houghton Mifflin Co., 1890.

Easter Messengers; A New Poem of the Flowers. New York: White, Stokes & Allen, 1886.

Hillside and Seaside in Poetry. Boston: J.R. Osgood & Co., 1877.

An Idyl of Work. Boston: J.R. Osgood & Co., 1875.

Landscape in American Poetry. New York: D. Appleton & Co., 1879.

A New England Girlhood; Outlined from Memory. Boston: Houghton, Mifflin Co., 1889.

Our Young Folks. An Illustrated Magazine for Boys and Girls. Boston: Ticknor & Fields, 1865-73.

Poems. Boston: Fields, Osgood & Co., 1868.

Roadside Poems for Summer Travelers. Boston: J.R. Osgood & Co., 1876.

Similitudes. Boston: J.P. Jewett & Co., 1854.

The Unseen Friend. Boston: Houghton Mifflin Co., 1892.

Wheaton Seminary, a Semi-Centennial Sketch. Cambridge, Mass.: Printed at Riverside Press, 1885.

Wild Roses of Cape Ann, and Other Poems. Boston: Houghton Mifflin Co., 1881.

Kate Chopin

At Fault. A Novel. St. Louis: Nixon-Jones Printing Co., 1890.

The Awakening. Chicago: H.S. Stone & Co., 1899.

Bayou Folk. Boston: Houghton Mifflin Co., 1894.

In and Out of Natchitoches. Boston, 1893.

A Night in Acadie. Chicago: Way & Williams, 1897.

Sarah Josepha Hale

Alfred Greeley's Northwood; A Tale of New England. Boston: Bowles & Dearborn, Ingraham & Hewes, Printers, 1827.

Alice Ray: A Romance in Rhyme. Philadelphia, 1845.

The American Ladies' Magazine. Boston: J.B. Dow, 1828–36.

Aunt Mary's New Stories for Young People. Boston: J. Munroe
    & Co., 1849.

*Biography of Distinguished Women, or, Women's Record, from the
    Creation to AD 1869.* New York: Harper, 1876.

"Boarding Out." A Tale of Domestic Life. New York: Harper,
    1846.

The Book of Flowers. London: Saunders & Otley, 1836.

*A Complete Dictionary of Poetical Quotations: Comprising the
    Most Excellent and Appropriate Passages in the Old British
    Poets; with Choice and Copious Selections from the Best
    Modern British and American Poets.* Philadelphia: Claxton,
    Remsen & Haffelfinger, 1849.

*Conversations on the Burman Mission. By a Lady of New Hamp-
    shire.* Boston: Massachusetts Sabbath School Union, 1830.

Countries of Europe. New York: McLoughlin Brothers, n.d.

The Crocus; A Fresh Flower for the Holidays. New York:
    E. Dunigan & Brother, 1849.

Flora's Interpreter, and Fortuna Flora. Boston: Sanborn,
    Carter & Bazin, 1848.

*Flora's Interpreter: Or, The American Book of Flowers and
    Sentiments.* Boston: Marsh, Capen & Lyon, 1832.

The Genius of Oblivion; and Other Original Poems. Concord:
    J.B. Moore, 1823.

*The Gift for Good Boys, Containing the Good Little Boy's
    Book, and the Wise Boys.* New York: E. Dunigan & Brothers,
    n.d.

The Gift for Good Little Girls. New York: E. Dunigan &
    Brothers, 18––.

*The Gift for Juveniles, Containing Gift to Young Friends and
    Three Baskets.* New York: E. Dunigan & Brothers, 1849.

Gift to Young Friends; or, the Guide to Good. New York:
    E. Dunigan, 1842.

Godey's Magazine. New York: The Godey Co., 1830-1898.

The Good Housekeeper; or, the Way to Live Well and to be Well While We Live Containing Directions for Choosing and Preparing Food in Regard to Health, Economy, and Taste. Boston: Weeks, Jordan & Co., 1839.

Happy Changes, or Pride and Its Consequences, etc. New York: E. Dunigan & Brothers, n.d.

Harry Guy, the Widow's Son. A Story of the Sea. Boston: B.B. Mussey & Co., 1848.

Infant School Management; with Notes of Lessons and on the Phenomena of Nature and Common Life. London: E. Stanford, 1886.

The Juvenile Budget Opened: Being Selections from the Writing of Dr. John Aiken, with a Sketch of his Life. Boston: Marsh, Capen, Lyon, & Webb, 1840.

Keeping House and House Keeping; a Story of Domestic Life. New York: Harper, 1845.

The Ladies' Magazine, and Literary Gazette. Boston: Putnam & Hunt, 1828-34.

The Ladies' New Book of Cookery: A Practical System for Private Families in Town and Country: with Directions for Carving, and Arranging the Table for Parties, etc. New York: H. Long & brother, 1852.

The Ladies' Wreath: A Selection from the Female Poetic Writers of England and America. Boston: Marsh, Capen & Lyon, 1837.

Lessons from Women's Lives. Edinburgh: W.P. Nimmo & Co., 1880.

The Letters of Lady Mary (Pierrepont) Wortley. Boston: Roberts Brothers, 1876.

The Letters of Madame de Sevigne to her Daughter and Friends. Rev. ed. Boston: Little, Brown & Co., 1900.

Liberia; or, Mr. Peyton's Experiments. New York: Harper & Brothers, 1853.

Mrs. Hale's Little Boys and Girls Library. New York, 1843.

Love; or, Woman's Destiny. Philadelphia: D. Ashmead, 1870.

Manners; or, Happy Homes and Good Society all the Year Round.
    Boston: J.E. Tilton & Co., 1868.

Mary Had a Little Lamb. London: M. Ward, 1891.

Modern Household Cookery: A New Work for Private Families.
    New York: T. Nelson & Sons, 1863.

My Cousin Mary: Or, The Inebriate. Boston: Whipple &
    Darrell, 1839.

My Little Song Book: Adapted to Children and Youth. Boston:
    J.B. Dow, 1841.

Mrs. Hale's New Cook Book. Rev. ed. Philadephia: T.B.
    Peterson & Brothers, 1873.

*The New Household Receipt-Book: Containing Maxims, Directions,
    and Specifics for Promoting Health, Comfort, and Improve-
    ment in the Homes of People.* New York: H. Long, 1853.

Northwood; a Tale of New England. Boston: Bowles & Dearborn,
    1827.

*Northwood; or, Life, North and South; Showing the True
    Character of Both.* New York: H. Long, 1852.

The Opal: A Pure Gift for the Holy Days. New York: J.C.
    Riker, 1844-49.

*Poems for our Children: Designed for Families, Sabbath
    Schools, and Infant Schools.* Boston: Marsh, Capen
    & Lyons, 1830.

The Poet's Offering: for 1850. Philadelphia: Grigg, Elliot
    & Co., 1850.

Mrs. Hale's Receipts for the Million. Philadelphia: T.B.
    Peterson, 1857.

*The School Song Book. Adapted to the Scenes of the School
    Room.* Boston: Allen & Ticknor, 1834.

Short Tales in Short Words. New York: E. Dunigan, 18--.

Sketches of American Character. Boston: Putnam & Hunt, and
    Carter & Hendee, 1829.

Sketches of Distinguished Women from the Beginning to 1850.
New York: Harpers, 1853.

Spring Flowers, or the Poetical Bouquet: Easy, Pleasing and Moral Rhymes and Pieces of Poetry for Children.
New York: E. Dunigan, 18--.

Things by Their Right Names, and Other Stories, Fables and Moral Pieces, in Prose and Verse, Selected and Arranged from the Writings of Mrs. Barbauld. Boston: Marsh, Capen, Lyon & Webb, 1840.

The Three Baskets; or How Henry Richard, and Charles were Occupied while Papa Was Away. New York: E. Dunigan, 18--.

Three Hours; or, The Vigil of Life: and Other Poems.
Philadelphia: Carey & Hart, 1848.

Traits of American Life. Philadelphia: Carey & Hart, 1835.

Uncle Bunde's True and Instructive Stories, about Animals, Insects and Plants. New York: E. Dunigan, n.d.

The White Veil: A Bridal Gift. Philadelphia: E.H. Butler & Co., 1854.

The Wise Boys, or the Entertaining Histories of Fred Forethought, Matt Manythought, Luke Lovebook, and Ben Bee.
New York: E. Dunigan, n.d.

Woman's Record; or Sketches of All Distinguished Women, from "the Beginning" till AD 1850. New York: Harper & Brothers, 1853.

Susan Warner

American Female Patriotism. New York: Edward H. Fletcher, 1852.

Bread and Oranges. Boston: Bradley & Woodruff, 1875.

The Broken Walls of Jerusalem and the Rebuilding of Them.
New York: R. Carter & Co., 1879.

Carl Krinken: His Christmas Stocking. Boston: DeWolfe, Fiske, 1853.

Daisy. Continued from "Melbourne House." Philadelphia: Lippincott & Co., 1868-69.

Daisy in the Field. London: J. Nisbet & Co., 1874.

Daisy Plains. New York: R. Carter & Brothers, 1885.

Diana (A Novel). New York: G.P. Putnam's Sons, 1877.

Ellen Montgomery's Bookshelf. London: F. Warne, 1879.

The End of a Coil. London: F. Warne, 1880.

The Flag of Truce. New York: R. Carter & Brothers, 1875.

Gertrude and Her Bible. London: Routledge, Warne, & Routledge, 1865.

Giving Trust; Tales Illustrating the Lord's Prayer. London: Nisbet, 1875.

The Gold of Chickaree. London: J. Nisbet, 187-.

The Golden Ladder; Stories Illustrative of the Eight Beatitudes. London: F. Warne, 1887.

The Hills of Shatemuc. New York: D. Appleton & Co., 1856.

The House in Town. New York: R. Carter & Brothers, 1872.

The House of Israel. New York: R. Carter & Brothers, 1867.

Hymns for Mothers and Children. Boston: Walker, Wise, 1861.

The Kingdom of Judah. New York: R. Carter & Brothers, 1878.

The Law and the Testimony. New York: R. Carter & Brothers, 1853.

Lessons on the Standard Bearers of the Old Testament. New York, 1872.

The Letter of Credit. Boston: DeWolfe, Fiske & Co., 1881.

The Little American; A Series of Stories and Sketches for Young Folk. West Point, N.Y.: 18--.

The Little Black Hen. London: George Routledge & Sons, 1870.

The Little Camp on Eagle Hill. New York: R. Carter & Brothers, 1874.

The Little Nurse of Cape Cod. Philadelphia: American Sunday-School Union, 1863.

Maggie's Christmas; or the Rose in the Desert. London, 18--.

Melbourne House. London, 1864.

Mr. Rutherford's Children. Boston: Shepard, Clark & Brown, 1853.

My Desire. Boston: DeWolfe, Fiske, & Co., 1879.

Nobody. London: J. Nisbet & Co., 1882.

The Old Helmet. London: G. Routledge, n.d.

Opportunities. New York: R. Carter & Brothers, 1871

Pine Needles. New York: R. Carter & Brothers, 1877.

Queechy. New York: G.P. Putnam, 1852.

The Rapids of Niagara. Boston: Bradley & Woodruff, 1875.

A Red Wallflower. Boston: DeWolfe, Fiske & Co., 1884.

Robinson Crusoe's Farmyard, or, Stories and Anecdotes, Illustrating Their Habits. Philadelphia: Davis, Porter & Coates, 1866.

Say and Seal. Philadelphia: J.B. Lippincott & Co., 1860.

Sceptres and Crowns. New York: R. Carter & Brothers, 1875.

Stephen, M.D. Boston: DeWolfe, Fiske & Co., 1883.

Trading: Finishing the Story of "The House in Town." New York: R. Carter & Brothers, 1873.

The Two School Girls, and Other Tales. London: G. Routledge, 1867.

Walks from Eden. New York: R. Carter & Brothers, 1866.

"What She Could." New York: R. Carter & Brothers, 1871.

The Wide, Wide, World. New York, 1851.

Willow Brook, a Sequel to The Little Camp. London: Hutchinson, n.d.

Wych Hazel. London: F. Warne, 1876.

Ann Stephens

Alice Copley. Philadelphia, 184-.

Amos's Plot; or, The Governor's Indian Child. New York: Beadle, 1860.

Bellehood and Bondage. Philadelphia: T.B. Peterson & Brothers, 1873.

Bertha's Engagement. Philadelphia: T.B. Peterson & Brothers, 1875.

The Cable Odes. New York: Wynkoop, Hallenbeck, & Thomas, 1858.

The Curse of Gold. Philadelphia: T.B. Peterson & Brothers, 1869.

David Hunt. A Novel. New York: The F.M. Lupton Publishing Co., 1892.

The Diamond Necklace: and Other Tales. Boston: Gleason's Publishing Hall, 1846.

Doubly False. Philadelphia: T.B. Peterson & Brothers, 1868.

Esther: A Story of the Oregon Trail. London: Beadle, 1862.

Fashion and Famine. New York: Bunce & Brother, 1854.

Frank Leslie's Portfolio of Fancy Needlework. New York: Stringer & Townsend, 1855.

The Gold Brick. New York: Lupton, 1866.

Graham's American Monthly Magazine of Literature, Art, and Fashion. Philadelphia: G.R. Graham, 1841- .

The Heiress of Greenhurst. An Autobiography. New York: Edward Stephens, 1857.

Henry Longford, or, The Forged Will. A Tale of New York City. Boston: Gleason, 1847.

High Life in New York. New York: E. Stephens, 1843.

The Indian Princess. New York: Beadle & Adams, 1863.

The Indian Queen. New York: Beadle & Adams, 1864.

The Ladies' Complete Guide to Crochet, Fancy Knitting and Needlework. New York: Garrett & Co., 1854.

The Lady Mary. A Novel. New York: F.M. Lupton Publishing Co., 1892.

The Lady's World. Philadelphia, 18--.

Lily. In Memoriam. New York: J.J. Little & Co., 1884.

Lord Hope's Choice. Philadelphia: T.B. Peterson & Brothers, 1873.

Mabel's Mistake. Philadelphia: T.B. Peterson & Brothers, 1868.

Mahaska, the Indian Princess: A Tale of the Six Nations. London: Beadle, 1863.

Maleaska; or the Indian Wife of the White Hunter. New York: Beadle, 1873.

Married in Haste. Philadelphia: T.B. Peterson & Brothers, 1870.

Mary Derwent. Philadelphia: T.B. Peterson & Brothers, 1858.

Mrs. Stephens' Illustrated New Monthly. New York, 1856- .

Myra, the Child of Adoption. A Romance of Real Life. New York: Beadle & Adams, 1856.

A Noble Woman. Philadelphia: T.B. Peterson & Brothers, 1876.

Norston's Rest. Philadelphia: T.B. Peterson & Brothers, 1877.

The Old Countess; or, The Two Proposals. Philadelphia: T.B. Peterson & Brothers, 1873.

The Old Homestead. New York: Bunce, 1855.

The Outlaw's Wife; or The Valley Ranch. New York: Beadle & Adams, 1874.

Palaces and Prisons. Philadelphia: T.B. Peterson & Brothers, 1871.

The Peterson Magazine. Philadelphia: C.J. Peterson, 1894-98.

Phemie Frost's Experiences. New York: G.W. Carleton & Co., 1874.

Pictorial History of the War for the Union. New York: J.G. Wells, 1862.

The Portland Magazine; Devoted to Literature. Portland, Maine: E. Stephens, 1834-36.

The Portland Sketch Book. Portland: Colman & Chisholm, 1836.

The Queen of a Week. New York: W.W. Snowden, 1839.

The Red Coats; or, The Sack of Ungowa. A Tale of the Revolution. New York: Williams, 1848.

The Reigning Belle. Philadelphia: T.B. Peterson & Brothers, 1872.

The Rejected Wife. Philadelphia: T.B. Peterson & Brothers, 1863.

Rock Run; or, The Daughter of the Island. New York: F.M. Lupton, 1893.

Ruby Gray's Strategy. New York: F.M. Lupton, 1869.

Silent Struggles. Philadelphia: T.B. Peterson & Brothers, 1865.

The Soldier's Orphans. Philadelphia: T.B. Peterson & Brothers, 1866.

Sybil Chase; or, The Valley Ranch. A Tale of California Life. New York: Beadle & Co., 1861.

The Tradesman's Boast. Boston: Gleason's Publishing Hall, 1846.

The Wife's Secret. Philadelphia: T.B. Peterson & Brothers, 1864.

Wives and Windows; or, The Broken Life. Philadelphia: T.B. Peterson & Brothers, 1869.

The Works of Mrs. Ann S. Stephens. Philadelphia: T.B. Peterson & Brothers, 1859-86.

Zana; or, The Heiress of Clair Hall. London: Wood & Lock, 1854.

Anna Cora Mowatt

Armand; or, The Peer and the Peasant. London: W. Newbery, 1849.

Autobiography of an Actress; or, Eight Years on the Stage. Boston: Ticknor, Reed, & Fields, 1853.

The Clergyman's Wife, and Other Sketches. New York: G.W. Carleton & Co., 1867.

Evelyn; or, A Heart Unmasked. A Tale of Domestic Life. Philadelphia: G.B. Zieber & Co., 1845.

Fairy Fingers. A Novel. New York: Carleton, 1865.

Fashion; or, Life in New York. New York: S. French, 1849.

The Fortune Hunter; or, The Adventures of a Man About Town. A Novel of New York Society. New York: J. Winchester, New World Press, 1844.

Italian Life and Legends. New York: Carleton, 1870.

Life of Goethe. From His Autobiographical Papers and the Contributions of His Contemporaries. New York: J. Mowatt, 1844.

Memoirs of Madame d'Arblay ... Compiled from Her Voluminous Diaries and Letters, and from Other Sources. New York: J. Mowatt, 1844.

Mimic Life; or, Before and Behind the Curtain. Boston: Ticknor & Fields, 1856.

The Mute Singer. A Novel. New York: Carleton, 1866.

Pelayo: or, The Cavern of Covadonga. A Romance. New York: Harper & Brothers, 1836.

Plays. Boston: Ticknor & Fields, 1855.

Reviewers Reviewed: A Satire: by the Author of Pelayo. New York, 1837.

Twin Roses. A Narrative. Boston: Ticknor & Fields, 1857.

Harriet Beecher Stowe

Agnes of Sorrento. Boston: Houghton Mifflin Co., 1862.

Anti-Slavery Recollections. London: T. Hatchard, 1854.

Anti-Slavery Tales and Papers. Boston, 1896.

Augusta Howard ... Glasgow, Scottish Temperance League.
    Edinburgh: J. Dickson, 1853.

Betty's Bright Idea and Other Ideas. New York: National
    Temperance Society and Publication House, 1875.

*Bible Heroines, Being Narrative Biographies of Prominent
    Hebrew Women in the Patriarchal, National, and Christian
    Eras, Giving Views of Women in Sacred History, as Re-
    vealed in the Light of the Present Day.* New York: Fords,
    Howard & Hulbert, 1878.

A Budget of Christmas Tales. New York: The Christian Herald,
    1895.

The Chimney Corner. Boston: Ticknor & Fields, 1868.

The Christian Slave. Boston: Phillips, Sampson & Co., 1855.

Christ's Christmas Gifts. Columbus, Ohio: 1876.

The Coral Ring. Glasgow: Scottish Temperance League, 1853.

The Daisy's First Winter, and Other Stories. London: William
    P. Nimmo, 1875.

Deacon Pitkin's Farm. London: J. Clarke, 1875.

A Dog's Mission; or, The Story of the Old Avery House.
    New York: Fords, Howard & Hulbert, 1880.

Dred. Boston: Phillips, Sampson & Co., 1856.

Earthly Care, a Heavenly Discipline. Boston: American Tract
    Society, 1845.

The Edmonson Family, and the Capture of the Schooner Pearl.
    Cincinnati: American Reform Tract and Book Society, 1854.

*A Fifth Example of Observing the Sabbath Day; A Narrative
Founded on Facts; Intended as a Sequel to Mrs. Stowe's
"Four Ways of Observing the Sabbath."* London, n.d.

First Geography for Children. New York: J.C. Derby, 1855.

Flowers and Fruit from the Writings of Harriet Beecher Stowe.
Boston: Houghton Mifflin Co., 1888.

Footsteps of the Master. New York: Fords, Howard & Hulburt,
1876.

Four Ways of Observing the Sabbath. Liverpool: E. Howell,
1853.

The Ghost in the Mill, and Other Stories. London: S. Low,
Marston, Searle & Rivington, 1876.

House and Home Papers. Boston: Ticknor & Fields, 1865.

Household Papers and Stories. Boston: Houghton Mifflin Co.,
1896.

How to Spend the Sabbath. Liverpool: Pearce & Brewer, 1853.

The Key to Uncle Tom's Cabin. Boston, 1853.

*Lady Byron Vindicated; A History of the Byron Controversy
from Its Beginning in 1816 to the Present Time.* Boston:
Osgood, Fields & Co., 1870.

Light after Darkness; Religious Poems. London: S. Low &
Marston, 1867.

*Little Foxes; or, The Insignificant Little Habits which Mar
Domestic Happiness.* Boston: Ticknor & Fields, 1866.

Little Pussy Willow. New York: Fords, Howard & Hulbert, 1870.

The Lives and Deeds of Our Self-Made Men. Hartford, Conn.:
Worthington, Dustin & Co., 1872.

The May Flower, and Miscellaneous Writings. Boston: Phillips,
Sampson, & Co., 1855.

*The Mayflower; or Scenes and Sketches among the Descendants
of the Pilgrim Fathers.* London: Knight & Son, 1852.

Men of Our Times; or, Leading Patriots of the Day. Hartford, Conn.: Hartford Publishing Co., 1868.

The Minister's Wooing. Chicago: W.B. Conkey, 185-.

Ministration of Departed Spirits. Boston, 18--.

Mrs. Harriet Beecher Stowe on Dr. Monod and the American Tract Society; Considered in Relation to American Slavery. Edinburgh, 1858.

My Wife and I: or, Harry Henderson's History. Boston: Houghton Mifflin Co., 1871.

Nelly's Heroics with Other Heroic Stories. Boston: D. Lothrop, 1883.

A New England Sketch. A. Gilman, 1834.

A New Geography for Children. London: Sampson, Low, 1855.

The New Housekeeper's Manual; Embracing a New Revised Edition of The American Woman's Home; or, Principles of Domestic Science. New York: J.B. Ford & Co., 1874.

Nina Gordon: A Tale of the Great Dismal Swamp. Boston: Ticknor & Fields, 1866.

Novels and Stories. Boston: Houghton Mifflin Co., 1910.

Oldtown Fireside Stories. Boston: J.R. Osgood, 1871.

Oldtown Folks. Boston: Fields, Osgood & Co., 1869.

Our Charley, and What to Do with Him. Boston: Phillips, Sampson, 1858.

Our Famous Women; Comprising the Lives and Deeds of American Women. Hartford, Conn.: A.D. Worthington, 1883.

Palmetto-Leaves. Boston: J.R. Osgood & Co., 1873.

The Pearl of Orr's Island: A Story of the Coast of Maine. London: Sampson & Low, 1861.

Pink and White Tyranny. A Society Novel. Boston: Roberts Brothers, 1871.

Poganuc People: Their Loves and Lives. Boston: D. Lothrop & Co., 1878.

The Popular Tales. Glasgow: T.D. Morison, n.d.

Principles of Domestic Science. New York: J.B. Ford & Co., 1870.

Prize tale. A New England Sketch. Lowell, Mass.: A. Gilman, 1834.

Queer Little People. Boston: Ticknor & Fields, 1867.

Religious Poems. Boston: Ticknor & Fields, 1867.

Religious Studies, Sketches, and Poems. Boston: Houghton Mifflin Co., 1896.

Sam Lawson's Oldtown Fireside Stories. Boston: Houghton, Osgood, & Co., 1872.

Six of One by Half a Dozen of the Other--an Every Day Novel. Boston: Roberts Brothers, 1872.

Stories about Our Dogs. Edinburgh: William P. Nimmo, 1865.

Stories and Sketches for the Young. Boston: Houghton Mifflin Co., 1855.

Stories, Sketches, and Studies. Boston: Houghton Mifflin Co., 1896.

The Story of Little Eva from Uncle Tom's Cabin. Boston: D. Estes & Co., 1902.

Sunny Memories of Foreign Lands. Boston: Phillips, Sampson & Co., 1854.

A Tale of New England. Portland: S.H. Colesworthy, 1847.

Tales and Sketches of New England Life. London: S. Low & Co., 1855.

Temperance Tales. London: J. Cassell, 1853.

The Two Altars; or, Two Pictures in One. Boston, 1852.

Uncle Tom's Cabin. Boston, 1852.

*We and Our Neighbors: or, The Records of an Unfashionable
Street.* Boston: Houghton Mifflin Co., 1875.

*Women in Sacred History: A Series of Sketches Drawn from
Scriptural, Historical and Legendary Sources.* New York:
Fords, Howard, and Hulbert, 1873.

*The Writings of Harriet Beecher Stowe: with Biographical
Introductions, Portraits and Other Illustrations.*
Boston: Houghton Mifflin Co., 1896.

E.D.E.N. Southworth

Allworth Abbey. Philadelphia: T.B. Peterson & Brothers, 1865.

The Arrested Bride; or, The Lady of the Isle. London:
Milner, n.d.

The Artist's Love. Philadelphia: T.B. Peterson & Brothers, 1872.

A Beautiful Fiend, a Novel. Chicago: M.A. Donohue, 19--.

Between Two Loves; or, The Slave to Woman's Beauty. London:
Milner, n.d.

Brandon Coyle's Wife; A Sequel to "A Skeleton in the Closet."
New York: R. Bonner's Sons, 1893.

The Bridal Eve. Philadelphia: T.B. Peterson & Brothers, 1864.

The Bride of Llewellyn; or, Left Alone. Chicago: M.A.
Donohue, 1866.

The Bride's Dowry, a Novel. Chicago: M.A. Donohue, n.d.

The Bride's Fate; Sequel to "The Changed Brides."
New York: Federal Book Co., n.d.

The Broken Engagement; or, Speaking the Truth for a Day.
Philadelphia: T.B. Peterson & Brothers, 1862.

Broken Pledges. Philadelphia: T.B. Peterson & Brothers, 1891

Capitola the Madcap. New York: Hurst, n.d.

Capitola's Peril. Chicago: M.A. Donohue, 18--.

The Changed Brides; or, Winning her Way. New York: F.M.
Lupton Publishing Co., 1869.

The Christmas Guest, a Novel. Philadelphia: T.B. Peterson & Brothers, 1870.

The Cord Lady; or, The Bronzed Beauty of Paris. Philadelphia: C.W. Alexander, 1867.

Cruel as the Grave. New York: Grossett & Dunlap, n.d.

The Curse of Clifton: A Tale of Expiation and Redemption. London: Clarke, Beeton & Co., 1852.

David Lindsay; A Sequel to "Gloria." New York: R. Bonner's Sons, 1891.

A Deed Without a Name. New York: A.L. Burt Co., 1886.

The Deserted Wife. New York: D. Appleton & Co., 1850.

The Discarded Daughters; or, The Children of the Isle. Philadelphia: A. Hart, 1852.

The Doom of Devillo. New York: Street & Smith Corp., n.d.

Dorothy Harcourt's Secret; Sequel to "A Deed Without a Name." New York: A.L. Burt Co., 1880.

"Em." New York: G.W. Dillingham Co., 1898.

Em's Husband. New York: R. Bonner's Sons, 1892.

Eudora; or, The False Princess. New York: F.M. Lupton, 1894.

Fair Play; A Novel. New York: F.M. Lupton, 1894.

Fallen Pride; or, The Mountain Girl's Love. Philadelphia: T.B. Peterson & Brothers, 1868.

The Family Doom; or, The Sin of a Countess. Philadelphia: T.B. Peterson & Brothers, 1869.

The Fatal Marriage. Philadelphia: T.B. Peterson & Brothers, 1863.

The Fatal Secret. Chicago: M.A. Donohue & Co., 1877.

For Whose Sake? A Sequel to "Why Did He Wed Her?" New York: A.L. Burt Co., 1884.

For Woman's Love. A Novel. New York: R. Bonner's Sons, 1890.

The Fortune Seeker. Philadelphia: T.B. Peterson & Brothers, 1866.

Gertrude Haddon. "Only a Girl's Heart." New York: R. Bonner's Sons, 1894.

The Gipsy's Prophecy. A Tale of Real Life. Philadelphia: T.B. Peterson & Brothers, 1861.

Gloria. A Novel. New York: R. Bonner's Sons, 1891

Hagar; or, The Deserted Wife. London: Milner, n.d.

The Haunted Homestead; and Other Nouvellettes. Philadelphia: T.B. Peterson & Brothers, 1860.

Her Love or Her Life; A Sequel to "The Bride's Ordeal." New York: A.L. Burt & Co., 1877.

Her Mother's Secret. New York: A.L. Burt & Co., 1910.

Hickory Hall; or, The Outcast. Philadelphia: T.B. Peterson & Brothers, 1861.

The Hidden Hand. New York: Grosset & Dunlap, 1880.

How He Won Her, a Novel. Chicago: M.A. Donohue, n.d.

"I Will Marry You"; or, David Lindsay. London: Milner, n.d.

India; the Pearl of Pearl River. Philadelphia: T.B. Peterson & Brothers, 1856.

The Initials: A Story of Modern Life. Philadelphia: T.B. Peterson & Brothers, 18--.

Ishmael. Philadelphia: T.B. Peterson & Brothers, 1876.

The Lady of the Isle. A Romance from Real Life. Philadelphia: T.B. Peterson & Brothers, 1859.

A Leap in the Dark. New York: R. Bonner's Sons, 1889.

Lilith; A Sequel to "The Unloved Wife." New York: A.L. Burt Co., 1891.

Little Nea's Engagement; A Sequel to "Nearest and Dearest."

New York: A.L. Burt Co., 1889.

The Lost Bride; A Tale of Luckenough Hall. London: H. Lea, n.d.

The Lost Heir of Linlithgow. Chicago: M.A. Donohue & Co., 1872.

The Lost Heiress. Philadelphia: T.B. Peterson & Brothers, 1854.

The Lost Lady of Lone. New York: R. Bonner's Sons, 1890.

Love's Bitterest Cup; A Sequel to "Her Mother's Secret."
New York: A.L. Burt Co., 1910.

Love's Labor Won. Philadelphia: T.B. Peterson & Brothers, 1862.

The Maiden Widow. Philadelphia: T.B. Peterson & Brothers, 1870.

Miriam, the Avenger; or, The Missing Bridge. Philadelphia:
T.B. Peterson & Brothers, 187-.

The Mistaken Bride, or Lost Lady of Lone. Chicago: M.A.
Donohue, 1855.

The Mother-in-Law; or, The Isle of Rays. New York: D. Appleton
& Co., 1851.

The Mysterious Marriage; A Sequel to "A Leap in the Dark."
New York: A.L. Burt Co., 1893.

The Mystery of Dark Hollow. New York: Hurst & Co., 1875.

The Mystery of Raven Rock; Sequel to Unknown. Chicago:
M.A. Donohue, 1880.

Nearest and Dearest; or, The Restored Bridegroom. New York:
R. Bonner's Sons, 1889.

A Noble Lord. New York: Hurst & Co., 1872.

*Old Neighborhoods and New Settlements, or Christmas Evening
Legends.* Philadelphia: A. Hart, 1853.

Only a Girl's Heart. New York: R. Bonner's Sons, 1893.

The Phantom Wedding; or, The Fall of the House of Flint.
Philadelphia: T.B. Peterson & Brothers, 1878.

The Prince of Darkness; A Romance of the Blue Ridge.
Chicago: M.A. Donohue, 1869.

The Red Hill Tragedy. New York: F.M. Lupton, 1893.

The Rejected Bride. New York: Street & Street, 1893.

Retribution: A Novel. New York: Harper & Brothers, 1849.

Rock Run; or, The Daughter of the Island. New York: F.M. Lupton, 1893.

Self-Raised; or, From the Depths. Philadelphia: T.B. Peterson & Brothers, 1876.

Shannondale. New York: D. Appleton & Co., 1850.

A Skeleton in the Closet. New York: R. Bonner's Sons, 1893.

The Spectre Lover. Philadelphia: T.B. Peterson & Brothers, 1875.

The Struggle of a Soul, a Sequel to the Lost Lady of Lone. New York: A.L. Burt Co., 1904.

Sweet Love's Atonement, a Novel. New York: A.L. Burt Co., 1904.

Sybil Brotherton. A Novel. Philadelphia: T.B. Peterson & Brothers, 1879.

The Test of Love. New York: A.L. Burt Co., 1907.

The Three Beauties. Philadelphia: T.B. Peterson & Brothers, 1858.

The Three Sisters; or, New Year in the Little Rough-cast House. New York: Street, 19--.

To His Fate; Sequel to "Dorothy Harcourt's Secret." New York: A.L. Burt Co., 1886.

A Tortured Heart. New York: Street & Smith, 1907.

The Trail of the Serpent; or, The Homicide at Hawke Hall. New York: A.L. Burt Co., 1880.

Tried for Her Life. New York: Grosset & Dunlap, 1871.

The Two Sisters. Philadelphia: T.B. Peterson & Brothers, 1858.

Unknown; or, The Nobleman's Bride. Chicago: M.A. Donohue, 1880.

The Unloved Wife. New York: A.L. Burt Co., 1890.

An Unrequited Love. New York: A.L. Burt Co., 1890.

Victor's Triumph; The Sequel to "A Beautiful Friend." New York: F.M. Lupton Publishing Co., 1874.

Virginia and Magdalene, or The Foster Sisters. Philadelphia: T.B. Peterson & Brothers, 1851.

Vivia, or the Secret of Power. Philadelphia: T.B. Peterson & Brothers, 1857.

When Love Commands. New York: A.L. Burt Co., 1880.

When Shadows Die. New York: A.L. Burt Co., 1889.

Why Did He Wed Her? New York: A.L. Burt Co., 1884.

The Widow's Son; or, Left Alone. Philadelphia: T.B. Peterson & Brothers, 1867.

The Wife's Victory. Chicago: M.A. Donohue, 1854.

Will You Marry Me? London: Milner, n.d.

Zenobia's Suitors. New York: A.L. Burt Co., 1904.

Catharine Sedgwick

Amy Cranstoun. New York, 1841.

Biography of Lucretia Maria Davidson. Philadelphia, 1841.

The Boy of Mount Rhigi. Boston: Crosby & Nichols, 1847.

Charlie Hathaway; or, The City Clerk and His Sister; and Other Stories. New York: Allen Brothers, 1869.

Clarence; or, A Tale of Our Times. Philadelphia: Carey & Lea, 1830.

Daniel Prime. New York, 1837.

The Deformed Boy. Brookfield: E.G. Merriam, 1826.

Facts and Fancies, and Other Stories. New York: J. Miller, 1864.

Home. Boston: J. Munroe, 1835.

Hope Leslie; or, Early Times in the Massachusetts. New York:
  White, Gallaher, & White, 1827.

The Irish Girl, and Other Tales. London: Kent & Richards,
  1850.

Letters from Abroad to Kindred at Home. New York: Harper &
  Brothers, 1841.

The Linwoods; or, "Sixty Years Since." New York: Harper &
  Brothers, 1835.

Live and Let Live; or, Domestic Service Illustrated.
  New York: Harper & Brothers, 1837.

A Love Token for Children. New York: Harper & Brothers, 1837.

Married or Single? New York: Harper & Brothers, 1857.

Mary Dyre. Boston, 1890.

Mary Hollis; an Original Tale. New York: New York Unitarian
  Book Society, 1822.

Means and Ends, or, Self-Training. Boston: Marsh, Capen,
  Lyon & Webb, 1839.

Memoir of Joseph Curtis, a Model Man. New York: Harper &
  Brothers, 1858.

A Memoir of Lucretia Maria Davidson. New York: Harper &
  Brothers, 1854.

Morals of Manners; or Hints for Our Young People. New York:
  G.P. Putnam, 1846.

*A New England Tale; or, Sketches of New England Character and
  Manner.* New York: E. Bliss & E. White, 1822.

Pleasant Sundays. Boston: L.C. Bowles, 1832.

Poetical Remains of the Late Lucretia Maria Davidson.
  Philadelphia: Lea & Blanchard, 1843.

The Poor Rich Man and the Rich Poor Man. New York: Harper
  & Brothers, 1836.

Redwood; A Tale. London: J. Miller, 1824.

A Short Essay to Do Good. Stockbridge, Mass.: Republished from the Christian Teacher's Manual, 1826.

Stories for Young Persons. New York: Harper & Brothers, 1840.

Tales and Sketches by Miss Sedgwick. Philadelphia: Carey, Lea, and Blanchard, 1835.

Tales of City Life. Philadelphia: Hazard and Mitchell, 1850.

The Travellers. A Tale. Designed for Young People. New York: E. Bliss & E. White, 1825.

An Unsolved Riddle. New York: 1837.

Lydia Sigourney

Biographies of the Great and Good. Glasgow: W. Collins, 1855.

Biographies of Pious Persons. Springfield: G. & C. Merriam, 1833.

A Book for Boys; Consisting of Original Articles in Prose and Poetry. New York: Turner & Hayden, 1835.

A Book for Girls; Consisting of Original Articles in Prose and Poetry. New York: Orville Taylor, 1837.

The Child's Book, Consisting of Original Articles in Prose and Poetry. New York: Turner & Hayden, 1844.

The Christian Keepsake. New York: Leavitt & Allen, 1856.

The Coronal; or, Tales and Pencillings in Poetry and Prose. London: T. Nelson, 1848.

The Daily Counselor. Hartford, Conn.: Brown & Gross, 1858.

Examples from the 18th and 19th Centuries. New York: Charles Scribner, 1857.

Examples of Life and Death. New York: Charles Scribner, 1851.

The Faded Hope. New York: R. Carter & Brothers, 1853.

The Farmer and the Soldier. Hartford, Conn.: William Watson, 1835.

Gleanings. Hartford, Conn.: Brown & Gross, 1860.

Great and Good Women; Biographies for Girls. Edinburgh:
    W.P. Nimmo, 1866.

History of Marcus Aurelius, Emperor of Rome. Hartford, Conn.:
    Belknap & Hamersley, 1836.

*How to Be Happy. Written for the Children of Some Dear
    Friends.* Hartford, Conn.: D.F. Robinson, 1833.

*The Illuminated American Primer; Being an Introduction to
    Mrs. Sigourney's Pictorial Reader.* New York: Turner &
    Hayden, 1844.

Illustrated Poems. Philadelphia: Carey & Hart, 1849.

*The Intemperate, and The Reformed. Shewing the Awful Conse-
    quences of Intemperance and the Blessed Effects of Tem-
    perance Reformation.* Boston: S. Bliss, 1833.

Invitation for May Morning   Roxbury, Mass.: Press of T.R.
    Marvin.

*The Ladies' Companion, and Literary Expositor; a Monthly
    Magazine Embracing Every Department of Literature.*
    New York: W.W. Snowden, 1834–44.

Lays from the West: Poems. London: Thomas Ward & Co., 1834.

Letters of Life. New York: D. Appleton & Co., 1866.

Letters to Mothers. Hartford, Conn.: Hudson & Skinner, 1838.

*Letters to My Pupils: With Narratives and Biographical
    Sketches.* New York: R. Carter & Brothers, 1851.

Letters to Young Ladies. Hartford, Conn.: P. Canfield, 1833.

The Lovely Sisters, Margaret and Henrietta. Hartford, Conn.:
    H.S. Parsons & Co., 1845.

Lucy Howard's Journal. New York: Harper & Brothers, 1858.

The Man of Uz, and Other Poems. Hartford, Conn.: Williams,
    Wiley & Waterman, 1862.

Mary Rice. London: T. Nelson, 1859.

Memoir of Mrs. Harriet Newell Cook. New York: R. Carter & Brothers, 1853.

Memoir of Phebe P. Hammond, a Pupil in the American Asylum at Hartford. New York: Sleight & Van Norden, 1833.

Myrtis, with Other Etchings and Sketchings. Hartford, Conn.: Sheldon & Goodwin, 1846.

Olive Buds. Hartford, Conn.: W. Watson, 1836.

Olive Leaves. New York: R. Carter & Brothers, 1831.

Past Meridian. New York: D. Appleton & Co., 1854.

The Pastor's Return. New York, 1839.

The Pictorial Reader, Consisting of Original for the Instruction of Young Children. New York: Turner & Hayden, 1844.

Pleasant Memories of Pleasant Lands. Boston: J. Munroe & Co., 1842.

Pocahontas, and Other Poems. London: R. Tyas, 1841.

Poems. Boston: S.G. Goodrich, 1827.

Poems for Children. Hartford, Conn.: Canfield & Robins, 1836.

Poems for the Sea. Hartford, Conn.: H.S. Parsons & Co., 1850.

Poems, Religious and Elegaic. London: R. Tyas, 1841.

Poetical Works. Philadelphia: J.E. Potter, n.d.

Poetry for Children. Hartford, Conn.: Robinson & Pratt, 1834.

Poetry for Seamen. Boston: J. Munroe & Co., 1845.

The Poet's Books. New York, 1840.

The Poor Rich Man and the Rich Poor Man. New York, 1837.

The Religious Souvenir for Christmas and New Year's Presents. Hartford, Conn.: S. Andrus, 1800.

Sayings of Little Ones. New York: Blakeman & Mason, 1864.

Scenes in My Native Land. Boston: J. Munroe & Co., 1845.

The Sea and the Sailor. Hartford, Conn.: F.A. Brown, 1857.

Select Poems. Philadelphia: F.W. Greenough, 1938.

Selections from Various Sources. Worcester, Mass.: J.H. Turner, 1863.

Sketch of Connecticut, Forty Years Since. Hartford, Conn.: O.D. Looke & Sons, 1824.

Sketches. Philadelphia: Key & Biddle, 1834.

Stories for Youth; Founded on Fate. Hartford, Conn.: W. Watson, 1836.

Tales and Essays for Children. Hartford, Conn.: F.J. Huntington, 1835.

Traits of the Aborigines of America. A Poem. Cambridge, Mass.: Hilliard & Metcalf, printers, 1822.

The Voice of Flowers. Hartford, Conn.: H.S. Parsons & Co., 1846.

Water-Drops. New York: R. Carter, 1848.

The Weeping Willow. Hartford, Conn.: H.S. Parsons & Co., 1847.

The Western Home, and Other Poems. Philadelphia: Parry & McMillan, 1854.

Whisper to a Bride. Hartford, Conn.: H.S. Parsons & Co., 1850.

The Young Lady's Offering; or Gems of Prose and Poetry. Boston: Phillips, Sampson & Co., 1854.

Zinzendorff, and Other Poems. New York: Leavitt, Lord, & Co., 1835.

Elizabeth Oakes Prince Smith

Bald Eagle; or, The Last of the Ramapaughs. A Romance of Revolutionary Times. New York: Beadle & Adams, 1867.

Bertha and Lily; or, The Parsonage of Beech Glen. A Romance. New York: J.C. Derby, 1854.

The Dandelion. Boston: Saxton & Kelt, 1846.

Dew-Drops of the 19th Century; Gathered and Preserved in Their Brightness and Purity. New York: J.K. Wellman, 1846.

Hints on Dress and Beauty. New York: Fowler & Wells, 1852.

Hugo: A Legend of Rockland Lake. New York: J.S. Taylor, 1851.

The Keepsake: A Wreath of Poems and Sonnets. New York: Leavitt & Co., 1849.

The Lover's Gift; or, Tributes to the Beautiful. Hartford, Conn.: H.S. Parsons & Co., 1850.

Mary and Hugo; or, The Lost Angel, a Christmas Legend. New York: Derby & Jackson, 1857.

The Moss Cup. Boston: Saxton & Kelt, 1846.

The Newsboy. New York: J.C. Derby, 1854.

Old New York: or, Democracy in 1689. New York: Stringer & Townsend, 1853.

The Poetical Writings of Elizabeth Oakes Smith. New York: J.S. Redfield, 1845.

Riches Without Wings, or The Cleveland Family. Boston: G.W. Light, 1838.

Rose Bud, or, The True Child. Buffalo: G.H. Derby & Co., 1849.

The Sagamore of Saco. New York: Beadle & Co., 1868.

The Salamander; A Legend of Christmas. New York: G.P. Putnam, 1848.

Sanctity of Marriage. Syracuse, N.Y.: Lathrop's Print, 18--.

Shadow Land; or, The Seer. New York: Fowler & Wells, 1852.

The Sinless Child, and Other Poems. New York: Wiley & Putnam, 1843.

Stories for Good Children. Buffalo: G.H. Derby & Co., 1851.

The True Child. Boston: Saxton & Kelt, 1845.

The Western Captive, or The Times of Tecumseh. A Tale.
New York: J. Winchester, 1842.

Woman and Her Needs. New York: Fowler & Wells, 1851.

3. *Secondary Works on Women's Fiction and Journalism*

Studies of the woman writer are generally biographical,
derived from the subject's letters, and are mostly episodic.
The one splendid exception to this generalization is the study
of Emily Dickinson's poetry and life, a subject which has
attracted the mind of the literary scholar since the rise of
the new criticism in the fifties. Richard Chase and Thomas
H. Johnson have written standard biographies. Both works of
the fifties, Chase's *Emily Dickinson* (1951) is the more
straightforward account, while Thomas H. Johnson's *Emily
Dickinson: An Interpretive Biography* (1955) moves more in the
direction of psychohistory. Albert J. Gelpi's *Emily Dickinson: The Mind of the Poet* (1965) treats Dickinson's artistic
and intellectual development on their own terms while bringing the reader into familiarity with Dickinson's formidable
world of learning. David J. Higgins' *Portrait of Emily
Dickinson* (1961) draws on and attempts a synthesis of earlier
biographical and critical works.
    Apart from Dickinson only Margaret Fuller has attracted
continuing attention from biographers and literary scholars.
Shortly after Fuller's death William H. Channing's carefully
edited memorial volume recorded her extraordinary life and
searching criticism of the genteel woman's role (William H.
Channing et al., *Memoirs of Margaret Fuller Ossoli* [1874]).
Julia Ward Howe edited Fuller's love letters to Count Ossoli with the title *Love Letters of Margaret Fuller 1845-
1846* (1903). Boston propriety prevented either Channing
or Howe from discussing the combination of radicalism and
nineteenth-century romantic passion which led Fuller to con-
ceive and bear an illegitimate child only legitimized after
her lover could escape the political consequences of participation in the short-lived Roman Republic. This remarkable
journey from the life of the genteel Boston intelligentsia
to romantic liberalism and political rebellion is fully and
sympathetically chronicled in Mason Wade's *Margaret Fuller,
Whetstone of Genius* (1940), and Fuller's complete works are
splendidly edited in Wade's *The Writings of Margaret Fuller*
(1941).
    Catharine Maria Sedgwick's letters were edited with
eulogistic sketches of her life by Mary E. Dewey in 1872
(*Life and Letters of Catharine Sedgwick*). These show Sedgwick's broad and catholic tastes in reading, her lively

intellectual life, and her sense of the erosion of values in
contemporary society which led her to evoke in her fiction
the integrity and dignity of the Puritan past. Sedgwick's
novel, *Married or Single?* (1857), stressing the dignity of
the single life, has been taken as a feminist statement as is
implied by Sister Mary Michael Welsh in her *Catharine Maria
Sedgwick, Her Position in the Literature and Thought of Her
Time up to 1860* (1937). However, Sedgwick's single women
are tireless supporters of the conventional family rather
than rebels against its constraints. Lydia Maria Child's
correspondence was likewise edited by a close friend, John
Greenleaf Whittier, in 1883 (*Letters of Lydia Maria Child*)
while Child's life is also the subject of a modern biography
by Milton Meltzer, *Tongue of Flame* (1965). Meltzer attempts
to place Child in the reform culture of her day, but, like
other historians of the sentimental women writers, he is
unable to resolve the contradictions involved in Child's
strenuous and unyielding commitment to abolition and humanitarian social reform with her highly moralistic and sentimental guides to housekeeping for the young mother and her exaltation of the Christian home in her children's stories. Future
studies must elucidate in more detail how the views of a
Sedgwick or a Child may be seen, not as aberrant and contradictory, but part of a coherent world view espoused by intel-
ligent and highly educated women.
   Harriet Tubman's life is similarly drawn from letters and
memoirs in Sarah H. Bradford's *Harriet, Moses of Her People*
(1886). Bradford's commentary takes no note of the extent to
which Tubman's consciousness differed from that of her white
contemporaries, yet the historian needs to know more about
the reasons Tubman was so admired for exhibiting masculine
virtues like fearlessness, endurance, and readiness to face
death for principle. Earl Conrad's *Harriet Tubman* (1943)
separates fact from antislavery mythology in Tubman's life
but does not address the question of why black women in
Tubman's era could so effectively fuse anger and family feeling into systematic plans of action.
   Lucy Larcom's autobiography, *A New England Girlhood* (1889),
may be supplemented by Daniel Dulany Addison's *Lucy Larcom:
Life, Letters and Diary* (1894). Both should be studied by
those who interpret women's access to education as the source
of feminist perceptions and emotions. Larcom reveals the
passion for learning that motivated the pioneers in women's
education, but this passion is linked with an intense evangelical piety which led her to regard training of the mind
and access to learning as increased opportunity to refine and
deepen the religious sensibilities and greater capacity to
assist in the regeneration of the world. Larcom's sensibility

may well be compared with Harriet Beecher Stowe's revealed in her son Charles E. Stowe's *Life of Harriet Beecher Stowe, Compiled from Her Letters and Journals by Her Son* (1889). Robert Forrest Wilson's *Crusader in Crinoline, the Life of Harriet Beecher Stowe* (1941) concentrates on Stowe's literary development and on the explanation of Stowe's remarkably wide readership. Charles H. Foster in *The Rungless Ladder: Harriet Beecher Stowe and New England Puritanism* (1954) traces the sources of the Beecher family's religious sensibility in Puritan beliefs and attitudes, but is less concerned with the progressive and future directed ideas generated by women's education and their sense of enlarged power within women's traditional sphere. Stowe's literary talents and readership may make her a unique figure, but we must also ask what were the larger social and intellectual forces that link her to her generation and found expression through her art.

In searching for these links, it is useful to compare Stowe's development at the center of New England Puritan culture with that of Lydia Sigourney, the self-taught poet and essayist of Hartford. Sigourney's sentimentality and compulsive hack writing set her far apart from Stowe as an artist, but her sentimental attitudes toward death, her romantic idealization of childhood, her glorification of home and maternity, and her sense of female faith as a powerful source of social regeneration make them clearly examples of the same literary impulses. Gordon Haight's *Mrs. Sigourney, The Sweet Singer of Hartford* (1930) treats Mrs. Sigourney as an isolated phenomenon and does not examine closely the social context which played on Sigourney's cloyingly sentimental imagination. Ann Douglas Wood's article, "Mrs. Sigourney and the Sensibility of Inner Space" (1972) attempts an Eriksonian analysis of Sigourney fascination with the enclosed sentimental home, but the larger context of Sigourney's generation is not developed.

Sarah Josepha Hale is another vivid example of the woman required by widowhood and economic circumstance to break up her family who devoted her life as a journalist to promoting the cult of the redemptive Christian home. Hale's life is the subject of Ruth Finley's *The Lady of Godey's. Sara Josepha Hale* (1931). Finley chooses to focus attention on Hale's interest in healthy dress for women, her support for women's education, and for health reform. This treatment tends to make Hale a precursor of feminism and to gloss over her opposition to the suffrage and most of the campaigns for women's rights. These contradictions may be resolved by analyzing Hale as a critic of the emerging capitalist society of her adult life. Hale saw the counterforce for the capitalist acquisitive drive to be the moral strength of the healthy educated woman in the Christian home.

The fiction of E.D.E.N. Southworth is analyzed in Regis Louise Boyle's *Mrs. E.D.E.N. Southworth, Novelist* (1939). Boyle, like Papashvily, sees Southworth's happy endings and melodramatic treatment of women's trials in marriage as evidence of a prefeminist consciousness. While this may appear to be the case, if Southworth is studied in isolation, she may more usefully be seen as a variant of her generation's imaginative concern with the redemptive female.

Sarah Orne Jewett is also the subject of a biographical treatment which sees her in isolation and focuses on her fiction as an effort to reassert the integrity of rural life against the powerful forces of urbanization. While Jewett is thus made a vital character in regional fiction by F.O. Mathiessen in his biography, *Sarah Orne Jewett* (1929), and Jewett's development as a writer is carefully described in Frederic C. Jewett's *Sarah Orne Jewett* (1960), only Richard Cary's *Sarah Orne Jewett* (1962) attempts to place Jewett's work in a wider literary context. Cary passes lightly over Jewett's stories for children which are straight from the moralizing tradition of Beecher and Sigourney and focuses critical attention on Jewett's self-reliant and strong-minded female characters. These may be seen as descendants of Stowe's and Southworth's characters with the sentimental tradition of the redemptive female now subjected to the first hints of literary realism.

The most important work to be undertaken to place the sentimental women writers within a context that makes them comprehensible on the same terms as their contemporary advocates of women's rights and the suffrage is a generational analysis and collective biography. Their fictional treatment of women's place within the moral economy of nineteenth-century American society has much to offer the historian and can make comprehensible the social forces which made women so long uninterested and unconcerned with the suffrage movement.

BIBLIOGRAPHY

Lydia Maria Child

Meltzer, Milton. *Tongue of Flame: the Life of Lydia Maria Child.* New York: Cromwell, 1965.

Whittier, John G. *Letters of Lydia Maria Child, with a Biographical Introduction.* Boston: Houghton Mifflin Co., 1883.

Kate Chopin

Wolff, Cynthia Griffin. "Thanatos and Eros: Kate Chopin's The Awakening." *American Quarterly* 25 (1973):449-471.

Emily Dickinson

Chase, Richard V. *Emily Dickinson*. New York: Sloane, 1951.

Gelpi, Albert J. *Emily Dickinson: The Mind of the Poet*.
Cambridge, Mass.: Harvard University Press, 1965.

Higgins, David J. *Portrait of Emily Dickinson; the Poet and Her
Prose*. New Brunswick, N.J.: Rutgers University Press, 1967.

Johnson, Thomas Herbert. *Emily Dickinson: An Interpretive
Biography*. Cambridge, Mass.: Belknap Press, 1955.

Margaret Fuller (Ossoli)

Channing, William H., et al. *Memoirs of Margaret Fuller Ossoli*.
Boston: Roberts Brothers, 1874.

Howe, Julia Ward, ed. *Love Letters of Margaret Fuller, 1845-1846*.
New York: D. Appleton, 1903.

Wade, Mason. *Margaret Fuller, Whetstone of Genius*. New York:
Viking Press, 1940.

Wade, Mason, ed. *The Writings of Margaret Fuller*. New York:
Viking Press, 1941.

Sarah Josepha Hale

Finley, Ruth. *The Lady of Godey's. Sara Josepha Hale*.
Philadelphia: J.B. Lippincott Co., 1931.

Godey's Magazine. Volumes 1-137. First known as *Godey's
Lady's Book*. New York: The Godey Co., 1830-1898.

Sarah Orne Jewett

Cary, Richard. *Sarah Orne Jewett*. New York: Twayne Publishers, 1962.

Cary, Richard, ed. *Letters of Sarah Orne Jewett, 1849-1909*.
Waterville, Maine: Colby College Press, 1956.

Jewett, Frederic C. *Sarah Orne Jewett*. 1960.

Mathiessen, Francis O. *Sarah Orne Jewett*. Boston: Houghton
Mifflin Co., 1929.

Lucy Larcom

Addison, Daniel Dulany. *Lucy Larcom: Life, Letters and Diary.* Boston: Houghton Mifflin Co., 1894.

Larcom, Lucy. *A New England Girlhood, Outlined from Memory.* Boston: Houghton Mifflin Co., 1889.

Catharine Sedgwick

Dewey, Mary E., ed. *Life and Letters of Catharine Sedgwick.* New York: Harper & Brothers, 1872.

Sedgwick, Catharine M. *Married or Single?* New York: Harper & Brothers, 1857.

Welsh, Sister Mary Michael. *Catharine Maria Sedgwick, Her Position in the Literature and Thought of Her Time up to 1860.* Washington, D.C.: Catholic University of America Press, 1937.

Lydia Sigourney

Haight, Gordon S. *Mrs. Sigourney, the Sweet Singer of Hartford.* New Haven: Yale University Press, 1930.

Wood, Ann Douglas. "Mrs. Sigourney and the Sensibility of the Inner Space." *New England Quarterly* 45 (1972):163-181.

E.D.E.N. Southworth

Boyle, Regis Louise. *Mrs. E.D.E.N. Southworth, Novelist.* Washington, D.C.: Catholic University of America Press, 1939.

Harriet Beecher Stowe

Foster, Charles H. *The Rungless Ladder: Harriet Beecher Stowe and New England Puritanism.* Durham, N.C.: Duke University Press, 1954.

Stowe, Charles E. *Life of Harriet Beecher Stowe, Compiled from Her Letters and Journals by Her Son.* Boston: Houghton Mifflin Co., 1889.

Wilson, Robert Forrest. *Crusader in Crinoline, the Life of Harriet Beecher Stowe.* Philadelphia: J.B. Lippincott Co., 1941.

Harriet Tubman

Bradford, Sarah H. *Harriet, The Moses of Her People.*
    New York: G.R. Lockwood & Son, 1886.

Conrad, Earl. *Harriet Tubman.* Washington, D.C. Associated
    Publishers, 1943.

Women's Magazines

Mott, Frank Luther. *A History of American Magazines.* 5
    volumes. Cambridge, Mass.: Harvard University Press, 1938–
    1968.

Stearns, Bertha M. "Early Western Magazines for Ladies."
    Mississippi Valley Historical Review 28 (1931):319–330.

Stearns, Bertha M. "Philadelphia Magazines for Ladies,
    1830–1860." *Pennsylvania Magazine of History and Biography*
    69 (1945):207–219.

Wood, Ann D. "The 'Scribbling Women' and Fanny Fern: Why
    Women Wrote." *American Quarterly* 23 (1971):3–24.

SECTION IV

WOMEN'S RELIGIOUS LIFE AND THE
REFORM TRADITION, 1790-1860

A. General Works

Although it is generally conceded by historians of American religion that the participation of women in both revival and traditional forms of worship and church membership was high numerically, and that women's organizations were important supports for the American Protestant missionary endeavor and for the antislavery movement, there is no general history treating the religious impulse within women's sphere of society and covering its spectrum of radical and conservative manifestations. Interest in the religious origins of the reform impulse has fluctuated with the contemporary issues whose roots the cultural historian has sought to trace in the past. In the 1920s and '30s historians of American religion saw their work as an extended footnote to Frederick Jackson Turner's* frontier thesis or as a commentary on the significance of New England transcendentalism. For both the commenter on Turner or the chronicler of New England's cultural hegemony, only the mainstream of Protestant religion has seemed significant, and until very recently there was no effort to see the entire spectrum of religious experience in the formative years of the republic as an anthropologist would, linking fringe sects and mainstream in one structural analysis. Thus there has been only episodic interest in the millennial sects of the 1830s and '40s or in the secular proponents of the perfected society such as Robert Dale Owen. Since Turner's frontier thesis neglected the domestic and nurturing sphere of human experience entirely, and since transcendentalism was mainly the product of male intellectuals, we find only passing references to women in general histories of religion, though they made up the majority of most congregations and their role in the moral economy was central to almost every variant of perfectionism, secular or sacred.

*Frederick Jackson Turner. "The Significance of the Frontier in American History." *American Historical Association Annual Report* (1894):197-227.

Students will find Edward Branch's *The Sentimental Years,
1836-1860* (1934) an early effort to describe the character,
dominating emotions, and forms of expression of the emerging
middle-class society of mid-nineteenth-century America.
Branch attempts to treat the technical and decorative arts
alongside the religious and social movements of the period,
but since his text lacks extensive citations or bibliography,
it is not possible for the reader to benefit from the formidable range of materials Branch consulted. Henry Steele Commager's *Theodore Parker* (1936) is one of the gems of American
biography and a splendidly condensed introduction to the intellectual forces which shaped transcendentalism. Since
Parker's ideas were the inspiration which moved many New
England women into philanthropy, the reader will find Commager's biography a useful introduction to an intellectual
figure whose influence shaped careers as different as those
of Dorothea Dix, Julia Ward Howe, and Margaret Fuller.

The historians of the 1940s had their interest sparked
in nineteenth-century reform through the heritage of the New
Deal and through the need to describe the ways in which American democracy was different from the European mass culture
which had given rise to fascism. Alice Felt Tyler's *Freedom's
Ferment: Phases of American Social History to 1860* (1944) was
an attempt to link the religious utopianism of the mid-century,
the secular drive for the rights of women and the dependent,
and the shaping of American democracy in the Jacksonian era.
Richard Leopold's *Robert Dale Owen* (1946) describes the career
of one of the major male reformers committed to women's rights,
pacifism, and the elevation of the working class. Owen was
one of the forgotten heroes of American democracy, and Leopold
thought him important as one of the inheritors of an Anglo-
American humanitarian social tradition. Neither Tyler nor
Leopold wrote with a strong awareness of the problems of bias
or discrimination still faced by women contemporaries, and
neither, therefore, examined the forces opposed to women's
rights or the contradictions between the secular rationalism
of a Robert Dale Owen and the views of the Christian per-
fectionists.

In the fifties the focus of attention for cultural historians shifted to the American national character, the importance of urban culture in shaping the national identity,
and the contribution of the urban immigrant to American life.
William W. Sweet, in *Religion in the Development of American
Culture, 1765-1840* (1952), attempts to identify the part
played by religion in the movement of the American nation
westward, leading him to define the American character as
an amalgam of frontier experience and religious motivations.
His account devotes less than a page to the experience of

women, an omission he regrets as a necessity because of "the absence of written records" documenting that experience. The bibliography that follows this section will introduce the reader to the varieties of sources Sweet overlooked. Harold Schwartz's *Samuel Gridley Howe, Social Reformer, 1801-1876* (1956) links Howe's concern for the education of the deaf and dumb with the emerging democratic culture of Jacksonian America and locates the reform impulse squarely in the urban culture of Boston. Timothy L. Smith, in his *Revivalism and Social Reform in Mid-Nineteenth-Century America* (1957), draws attention to the importance of eastern urban centers for the development and propagation of Christian perfectionist ideas and to the role of women as teachers and preachers of perfectionist beliefs.

The decade of the sixties saw the renewed battle for the civil rights of blacks and a growing awareness of the degree to which the movement for women's rights had failed to secure them equal rights under the law. Thus Oscar Sherwin's study of Wendell Phillips, *Prophet of Liberty: The Life and Times of Wendell Phillips* (1958), pays almost as much attention to Phillips' involvement in the women's rights movement as it does to his leadership of the extreme wing of the antislavery movement. The emerging sense of the failure of America's elites to carry out the intent of nineteenth-century reform movements shaped the approach to the reformer's motivation expressed in Clifford S. Griffin's *Their Brothers' Keepers* (1960) and *The Ferment of Reform, 1830-1860* (1967). Griffin saw the missionary and tract societies as networks to extend and exert control over the behavior of the western settlements along lines congenial to eastern elites. He saw women as participants in this effort as tools of male elites who shared the fear that frontier society would lapse into anarchy. J.F.C. Harrison's *Robert Owen and the Owenites in Britain and America* (1969) draws on a wide range of theoretical approaches to the study of popular culture and places the Owenites in the general context of communitarian movements designed to recreate a balanced agrarian society in North America in protest against the emerging character of industrial society in Great Britain and western Europe. Harrison thus sees the millennial impulse translated from popular protest against industrialization, a protest which in the Owenite form is now connected with the secular drive to perfectibility.

Sydney E. Ahlstrom's two-volume *A Religious History of the American People* (1972) is an admirable synthesis of the approach to religious history developed by social and intellectual historians informed by the disciplines of anthropology and demography. All forms of belief including those involving

faith in the state or the community as the source of meaning
or transcendence in life are taken as falling within the
bounds of religious history, while the demographic and social
events prompting different definitions of the quest for meaning are considered relevant to the history of religion. Ahlstrom departs from a long tradition in taking the religious
experience of women to be a serious subject of concern, and
he devotes attention to women religious leaders and the importance of women's religious associations in the history
of American Protestantism. Ahlstrom sees the period from the
founding of the colonies to the 1960s as a Protestant epoch
in American history, an epoch which concluded with the convergence of international events and internal contradictions
within American society to separate religious experience from
belief in the chosen nature of the American political experiment, a cultural crisis permitting the first popular (as opposed to minority) expression of women's protest against the
hostility of Protestantism to women. Writing in the 1960s
and early 1970s, Ahlstrom took no note of the development of
the Total Woman Movement in the south which signified the continuing dominance among many segments of American society of
the Protestant idea that women's place was in the family.

How may we approach the question of women's deep involvement in a religious culture, which in its dominant Protestant
form was fearful of women as witnesses to religious experience and which distrusted women in any social setting but the
properly subordinate one of wife and mother lodged within the
institution of the family? Both Karl Mannheim and Max Weber
have drawn attention to the tendency of subordinate groups
to adopt otherworldly explanations of experience and to be
attracted to salvation religions that promise triumph in
another world. Moreover, the development of a new political
significance for the home and the family in the American republic permitted women to rise in status within the domestic
sphere and to achieve through "influence" forms of power not
open to women through participation in the money economy or
attempts at formal political participation. The benevolent
woman unmotivated by acquisitive drives could enter politics
as an advocate, could express her managerial talents through
building volunteer organizations, and could act on many basic
tenets of Christian ethics in ways not open to males in the
competitive world of the emerging corporation and machine
politics. Even more important, the rich diversity of sectarian life in nineteenth-century America permitted women to
use religious affiliation in ways which challenged male authority and male patterns of behavior. The women who attended
Methodist camp meetings and Methodist classes were asserting
their right to move outside the family to seek a perfected

life, and in both revival meeting and classes they had a form
of sociability not provided in other denominations. Methodism,
by permitting women to testify, provided an organizational
setting more open to women's religious experience than other
mainstream denominations. There was thus forged a powerful
link between evangelical culture and the traditional family,
since women could claim the moral authority that went with
their role in the family and yet look for individual salvation through revival and class meetings. The Methodist class
meetings may be seen as a form of later consciousness-raising
sessions, since class members were encouraged to share moral
dilemmas, problems of the unperfected will, and difficulties
within the family. The more radical sects provided an even
broader scope for questioning male authority, while the
openness of society to the formation of new religious associations permitted new versions of worship to develop, including female-led ones such as Christian Science, which may
be seen in part as a protest against the developing profession of medicine which enshrined many values hostile to women
and which certainly neglected the spiritual aspects of healing so central to the Christian message. Finally, the student
of women's religious life in nineteenth-century America must
recognize that, though formally Trinitarian, Protestant evangelical preaching and worship was focused on the figure of
Jesus and on the exaltation of the Christlike characteristics
of redemptive suffering, obedience, and compassion, all of
which formed the ideal of feminine behavior and were sharply
distinguished from those supposedly characteristic of males
engaged literally or metaphorically in battling the wilder-
ness. Thus the exclusively male imagery of Protestant worship was much modified in this social context. In Unitarianism this emphasis on Jesus found its fullest expression, and
not surprisingly, it proved dynamising for many women leaders
of nineteenth-century philanthropy. It is important for the
student of the history of American women to be sensitive to
the many positive, identity-forming aspects of women's religious participation in order to interpret correctly the
implications of women's involvement in reform movements, for
in many respects that participation could come from a powerful identity formed within the characteristic patterns of
evangelical culture and not in opposition to it.

BIBLIOGRAPHY

Ahlstrom, Sydney. *A Religious History of the American People.*
    New Haven: Yale University Press, 1972.

Branch, Edward Douglas. *The Sentimental Years, 1836-1860.*
    New York: D. Appleton-Century Co., 1934.

Commager, Henry Steele. *Theodore Parker*. Boston: Little, Brown, & Co., 1936.

Griffin, Clifford S. *Their Brothers' Keepers: Moral Steward-ship in the United States, 1800-1865*. New Brunswick, N.J.: Rutgers University Press, 1960.

Griffin, Clifford S. *The Ferment of Reform, 1830-1860*. New York: Crowell, 1967.

Harrison, John Fletcher Clews. *Robert Owen and the Owenites in Britain and America: The Quest for the New Moral World*. London: Routledge & Kegan Paul, 1969.

Leopold, Richard W. *Robert Dale Owen, a Biography*. Cambridge, Mass.: Harvard University Press, 1940.

Power, Richard L. "A Crusade to Extend Yankee Culture, 1820-1865." *New England Quarterly* 13 (1940):638-653.

Schwartz, Harold. *Samuel Gridley Howe, Social Reformer, 1801-1876*. Cambridge, Mass.: Harvard University Press, 1956.

Sherwin, Oscar. *Prophet of Liberty: The Life and Times of Wendell Phillips*. New York: Brookman Associates, 1958.

Smith, Timothy L. *Revivalism and Social Reform in Mid-Nineteenth-Century America*. New York: Abingdon Press, 1957.

Sweet, William W. *Religion in the Development of American Culture, 1765-1840*. New York: Charles Scribner's Sons, 1952.

Tyler, Alice Felt. *Freedom's Ferment: Phases of American Social History to 1860*. Minneapolis: The University of Minnesota Press, 1944.

B. Women in the Antislavery Movement

1. Secondary Sources

Historians of the abolition movement have fluctuated between the two poles of interpretation, focussing either on the intransigence of the abolitionists that prevented com-promise solutions and the slow evolution of change or on the

economic and cultural strength of slavery as an institution
and the corresponding moral imperative that drove the abolitionists. While that historical debate has been impassioned,
it is noteworthy that there has been little variation in the
interpretation of women's motives for joining the movement or
of the critical nature of women's participation in the abolition movement. The varying schools of opinion respecting
men's participation in the movement and the nature of slavery
as a cultural and economic force may be sampled in Gilbert H.
Barnes, *The Anti-Slavery Impulse, 1830-1844* (1933); Dwight L.
Dumond, *Anti-Slavery Origins of the Civil War in the United
States* (1939); Kenneth Stampp, *The Peculiar Institution:
Slavery in the Ante-bellum South* (1956); Stanley L. Elkins,
*Slavery: A Problem in American Institutional and Intellec-
tual Life* (1959); Leon Litwack, *North of Slavery: The Negro
in the Free States, 1790-1860* (1961); Eugene Genovese, *The
Political Economy of Slavery: Studies in the Economy and
Society of the Slave South* (1965); Eugene Genovese, *The World
the Slaveholders Made: Essays in Interpretation* (1969);
Eugene Genovese, *Roll Jordan Roll: The World the Slaves Made*
(1974); Herbert Gutman, *The Black Family in Slavery and Freedom, 1750-1925* (1976); and Leon Litwack, *Been in the Storm
So Long* (1979). These works, with the exception of Gutman's
study of the black family, neglect to examine whether women's
participation in the abolition movement came from a single
cause linked to gender or from a multiplicity of ideological
forces. This oversight has tended to obscure the spectrum of
opinion of women abolitionists and to link women's participation to the women's rights views associated with the Grimké
sisters and William Lloyd Garrison, though historians are
always clear that Garrison himself stood at the far left of
the spectrum of antislavery opinion.

    The treatment of women abolitionists has been mainly epi-
sodic and biographical and focused around the pole of interpretation which sees the abolition movement as a necessary
expression of principle directed against a strong and growing
economic institution. Catherine Gilbertson's biography,
Harriet Beecher Stowe (1937), is of this school. Arthur H.
Fauset's *Sojourner Truth, God's Faithful Pilgrim* (1938),
one of the few biographies of black women abolitionists, is
of the same genre. Lillian O'Connor's sketch of women abolitionists in her *Pioneer Women Orators* (1954) does not speculate about motives other than those of principle that might
have led her orators to espouse the cause. Otelia Cromwell's
biographical study, *Lucretia Mott* (1958), does recognize
schools of opinion within the Quaker community with respect
to slavery, and she links Mott's questioning of slavery to
a general disposition to question authority and subordination.

Elinor Hays, tracing Lucy Stone's motivations in *Morning Star:
A Biography of Lucy Stone* (1961), sees Stone's abolitionism
as a principled conclusion drawn from her questioning of male
authority. Alma Lutz's *Women of the Anti-Slavery Movement*
(1968) links participation in the movement to incipient feminism, as does Gerda Lerner in her study of the Grimkés, *The
Grimké Sisters from South Carolina* (1967). Elizabeth Cady
Stanton's biographers have focused attention on her complicated family life, her sense of obligation to live out the
life of the sons of her family lost to death in childhood,
and her unhappiness in marriage, all three of which are seen
as predisposing her to question women's subordination and by
extension to question the morality of slavery. Alma Lutz's
Created Equal: A Biography of Elizabeth Cady Stanton (1940)
describes Stanton's "instinctive" questioning of authority.
Lois W. Banner's *Elizabeth Cady Stanton, A Radical for Women's
Rights* (1980) examines Stanton's role in her family with
greater thoroughness and concludes that intellect, energy,
and unfulfilled emotional needs carried Stanton into the
abolition movement because that movement's questions about
slavery as an institution were congruent with her questions
about religion and about marriage as an institution. Students
should be wary of Theodore Stanton and Harriet Stanton
Blatch's *Elizabeth Cady Stanton as Revealed in Her Letters,
Diary and Reminiscences* (1922) because this collection has
been carefully edited to reveal Stanton in the light her
grandchildren favored.

General treatments of women abolitionists have varied on
the matter of motivation somewhat in terms of the sex of the
author. Alice F. Tyler in *Freedom's Ferment* (1944) and
Margaret F. Thorp in *Female Persuasion: Six Strong-Minded
Women* (1949) have taken their characters' statements at face
value with respect to their moral crises about the evil of
slavery and the necessity of opposition. Robert Riegel, in
his *American Feminists* (1963), implies that failures of adjustment produced initial feminist questioning of society
and that abolition offered a cause through which much rebelliousness could be acceptably dissipated. Andrew Sinclair
in *The Better Half: The Emancipation of the American Woman*
(1965) draws attention to the variety of political opinions
brought together by abolitionism and the failures of strategy
which led feminists to identify with the slave and permit the
black cause to siphon off organizing power and energy that
might have been directed to feminism. Only Hazel Wolf has
taken the enquiry into motivation further in her *On Freedom's
Altar: The Martyr Complex in the Abolition Movement* (1952),
which treats the wish to suffer for the cause present in
many male and female adherents.

As we may see from the antislavery writing by women listed
below, there is a world of difference between the broader social views of women abolitionists on issues other than slavery.
The motives which drew them into the movement ranged from evangelical piety and the need to keep the will "perfected" through
Sarah Grimké's Christian argument against the subjection of
any of God's creatures to Frances Wright's secular rationalism.
The generally radicalizing aspect of women's participation in
the abolition movement came from the discovery that moral insights, conceded to women within their sphere, could not be
acted upon if they touched on economic institutions. While
it is correct that many women found in abolition a form of
attacking male domination and male exploitation of women, it
must be remembered that for every woman who traveled from that
perception to criticism of the family and institutional Christianity there were several who made the attack in the name of
the Christian will "perfected in Christ" and who accepted
the family and Christian marriage as divinely inspired institutions. Furthermore, women who worked for the underground
railroad of necessity kept their participation secret, and
thus did not encounter the prescriptions against speaking in
public which moved the Grimkés to a new analysis of their
situation. We thus make a mistake to assume that the abolition movement was automatically a source of feminist criticism of women's position, as the subsequent history of the
movement for women's rights makes abundantly clear. As to
the motivations of women abolitionists, we must improve on the
historical analysis to date. Some benevolent women never
took up the cause. Dorothea Dix could travel through the
Union and Confederate lines recognized merely as the friend of
the insane. Sarah Josepha Hale kept the discussion of slavery
out of *Godey's Ladies Book,* aiming to keep her magazine national. We need to know more than the simple fact that women
abolitionists were strong-minded. What changes of status,
what intellectual or religious experiences, what drive for
power, what psychological forces produced both the abolitionist who became a feminist and the abolitionist who did not?
How important was women's participation in Methodism to their
recruitment into the antislavery ranks? Once recruited, what
factors proved radicalizing for women? Unless we can formu-
late a theoretical understanding of the process of radicalization for women, our explanations of the actions and motives
remain primitive and undifferentiated as though gender alone
explained all female acts both radical and conservative.

BIBLIOGRAPHY

Banner, Lois W. *Elizabeth Cady Stanton, A Radical for Women's Rights*. Boston: Little, Brown, & Co., 1980.

Barnes, Gilbert H. *The Anti-slavery Impulse, 1830-1844*. New York: D. Appleton Co., 1933.

Beach, Seth Curtis. *Daughters of the Puritans: A Group of Brief Biographies*. Freeport, N.Y.: Books for Libraries Press, 1967.

Cromwell, Otelia. *Lucretia Mott*. Cambridge, Mass.: Harvard University Press, 1958.

Drake, Thomas E. *Quakers and Slavery in America*. New Haven: Yale University Press, 1950.

Dumond, Dwight L. *Anti-Slavery Origins of the Civil War in the United States*. Ann Arbor: University of Michigan Press, 1939.

Dumond, Dwight L. *Antislavery: The Crusade for Freedom in America*. Ann Arbor: University of Michigan Press, 1961.

Elkins, Stanley L. *Slavery: A Problem in American Institutional and Intellectual Life*. Chicago: University of Chicago Press, 1959.

Fauset, Arthur H. *Sojourner Truth, God's Faithful Pilgrim*. Chapel Hill: University of North Carolina Press, 1938.

Filler, Louis. *The Crusade Against Slavery, 1830-1860*. New York: Harper, 1960.

Genovese, Eugene. *The Political Economy of Slavery: Studies in the Economy and Society of the Slave South*. New York: Pantheon Books, 1965.

Genovese, Eugene. *The World the Slaveholders Made: Essays in Interpretation*. New York: Pantheon Books, 1969.

Genovese, Eugene. *Roll Jordan Roll: The World the Slaves Made*. New York: Pantheon Books, 1974.

Gilbertson, Catherine. *Harriet Beecher Stowe*. New York: D. Appleton Co., 1937.

Gutman, Herbert. *The Black Family in Slavery and Freedom, 1750-1925*. New York: Pantheon Books, 1976.

Hays, Elinor R. *Morning Star: A Biography of Lucy Stone, 1818-1893*. New York: Harcourt, Brace & World, 1961.

Lerner, Gerda. *The Grimké Sisters from South Carolina: Rebels Against Slavery*. Boston: Houghton Mifflin Co., 1967.

Litwack, Leon F. *North of Slavery: The Negro in the Free States, 1790-1860*. Chicago: University of Chicago Press, 1961.

Litwack, Leon F. *Been in the Storm So Long: The Aftermath of Slavery*. New York: Alfred A. Knopf, 1979.

Lutz, Alma. *Created Equal: A Biography of Elizabeth Cady Stanton*. New York: John Day Co., 1940.

Lutz, Alma. *Crusade for Freedom: Women of the Antislavery Movement*. Boston: Beacon Press, 1968.

Muelder, Hermann R. *Fighters for Freedom: The History of Antislavery Activities of Men and Women Associated with Knox College*. New York: Columbia University Press, 1959.

O'Connor, Lillian. *Pioneer Women Orators: Rhetoric in the Ante-bellum Reform Movement*. New York: Columbia University Press, 1954.

Pease, Jane H., and Pease, William H. "The Role of Women in the Antislavery Movement." *Canadian Historical Association, Historical Papers* (1967):167-183.

Riegel, Robert E. *American Feminists*. Lawrence: University of Kansas Press, 1963.

Sinclair, Andrew. *The Better Half: The Emancipation of the American Woman*. New York: Harper & Row, 1965.

Stampp, Kenneth. *The Peculiar Institution: Slavery in the Ante-Bellum South*. New York: Alfred A. Knopf, 1956.

Stanton, Theodore, and Blatch, Harriet Stanton. *Elizabeth Cady Stanton as Revealed in Her Letters, Diary and Reminiscences*. 2 volumes. New York: Harper and Brothers, 1922.

Thompson, Ralph. "The Liberty Bell and Other Antislavery Gift Books." *New England Quarterly* 7 (1934):154-168.

Thorp, Margaret F. *Female Persuasion: Six Strong-Minded Women.* New Haven: Yale University Press, 1949.

Tyler, Alice Felt. *Freedom's Ferment: Phases of American Social History to 1860.* Minneapolis: University of Minnesota Press, 1944.

Walters, Ronald G. "The Erotic South: Civilization and Sexuality in American Abolitionism." *American Quarterly* 25 (1973):177-201.

Weisberger, Bernard A. *They Gathered at the River: The Story of the Great Revivalists and Their Impact on Religion in America.* Boston: Little, Brown, & Co., 1958.

Wilkinson, Norman B. "The Free Produce Attack on Slavery." *Pennsylvania Magazine of History and Biography* 66 (1942): 294-313.

Wolf, Hazel. *On Freedom's Altar: The Martyr Complex in the Abolition Movement.* Madison: University of Wisconsin Press, 1952.

2. Primary Sources Illustrating Women's Participation in the Antislavery Movement

Black Antislavery Writings

Mary Ann Cary's (Shadd) newspaper for free blacks, *Provincial Freeman,* is an important source for understanding the role of black women on the underground railroad. It is also a record of the dawning perception of racism in Ontario. William Craft's account of his escape to the north in the company of his wife, Ellen, *Running A Thousand Miles for Freedom; or, the Escape of William and Ellen Craft from Slavery* (1860), is a narrative which illustrates the forces that make fugitives equal and the strength of the ties of the black family. Olive Gilbert's *Narrative of Sojourner Truth; A Bondswoman of Olden Time* (1850) is a valuable source for understanding both the strength of the black religious experience and the different consciousness of black women never allowed the sanctity of the middle-class white woman's domestic sphere. Since Sojourner Truth was not literate, the reader must allow for editorial touches on the part of the transcriber of the narrative, which is nonetheless very powerful. Charlotte L. Forten, in contrast to Sojourner Truth, was the literate and privileged daughter of a prosperous free Philadelphia family. Though her journal was not written for publication, it is an important contemporary document to set beside narratives such as Craft's and Sojourner Truth's, showing as it does Forten's daily encounters with racism in the north. Such narratives and diaries are numerous, and the student may find unpublished examples of these genres in local archives.

White Antislavery Writings

Sources illustrating white women's antislavery sentiment are of three kinds. The majority are polemical writings, the polemic appearing for the first time as a genre appropriate for women. The works of Lydia Maria Child and Maria W. Chapman provide the most striking examples of such polemics based on New England culture and experience. The writing of the Grimké sisters is the most striking example of brilliant antislavery polemic based on direct southern experience. Sarah Grimké's last pamphlet, *Letters on the Equality of the Sexes* (1838), illustrates the transition from concern with slavery as an institution to a generalized concern for all forms of subordination. Frances Wright's *A Plan for the Gradual Abolition of Slavery in the United States* (1825) is the earliest such polemic derived from Wright's English radical background. A second and valuable source is the literary treatment of slavery, of which Harriet Beecher Stowe's *Uncle Tom's Cabin* (1852) and *Dred* (1856) were the most influential. Lydia Maria Child's *The Oasis* (1834) is an early fictional effort to deal with the morality of slavery which in contrast with Stowe's later work did not attract wide readership.
A third source providing valuable insight into women's involvement in the abolition movement may be found in the memoirs of women who did not participate in the polemical or literary aspects of the movement but wrote their recollections of their role in antislavery associations or the underground railroad. Laura S. Haviland's *A Woman's Life Work: Including Thirty Years' Service on the Underground Railroad and in the War* (1881) is one of the most striking of such narratives, indicating the degree to which the Methodist faith fueled abolition sentiments while retaining strict conformity to traditional views of the role of wife and mother. Elizabeth A. Roe's *Recollections of Frontier Life* (1885) and Jane G. Swisshelm's *Half A Century* (1880) are other examples which should be read in conjunction with the

polemical and literary works for a full understanding of the spectrum of opinion among women abolitionists. Unless all these sources are tapped, the historian is left puzzled by the sharp divisions within the very same religious communities on the women's rights issue and by the nature of the factions which were to emerge in the movement for women's rights.

BIBLIOGRAPHY

Black Antislavery Writings

Cary, Mary Ann (Shadd), ed. *Provincial Freeman*. Toronto weekly. March 24, 1853–September 15, 1857. During its publication life, this newspaper for free blacks in Ontario moved from Windsor to Toronto to Chatham.

Craft, William. *Running a Thousand Miles for Freedom; or, the Escape of William and Ellen Craft from Slavery*. London: W. Tweedie, 1860.

Forten, Charlotte L. Journal. With an Introduction and Notes by Ray A. Billington. New York: Dryden Press, 1953.

Gilbert, Olive. *Narrative of Sojourner Truth; A Bondswoman of Olden Time, Emancipated by the New York Legislature in the Early Part of the Present Century*. Boston: For the Author, 1850.

White Antislavery Writings

Chapman, Maria W. *Right and Wrong in Massachusetts*. Boston: Dow & Jackson's Anti-Slavery Press, 1839.

Chapman, Maria W. *Ten Years of Experience*. c. 1842.

Child, Lydia Maria. *An Appeal in Favor of That Class of Americans Called Africans*. Boston: Allen & Ticknor, 1833.

Child, Lydia Maria. *Authentic Anecdotes of American Slavery, No. 1, 2*. Newburyport, Mass.: C. Whipple, 1833–35.

Child, Lydia Maria. *The Oasis*. Boston: Allen & Ticknor, 1834.

Child, Lydia Maria. *Anti-slavery Catechism*. Newburyport, Mass.: C. Whipple, 1836.

Follen, Eliza Lee. *To Mothers in the Free States.* New York: American Anti-Slavery Society, 1855.

Grimké, Angelina. *Appeal to the Christian Women of the South.* New York: American Anti-Slavery Society, 1836.

Grimké, Angelina. *An Appeal to the Women of the Nominally Free States Issued by an Anti-slavery Convention of American Women.* New York: W.S. Dorr, 1837.

Grimké, Angelina. *Letters to Catharine E. Beecher in Reply to an Essay on Slavery and Abolitionism.* Boston: I. Knapp, 1838.

Grimké, Sarah M. *An Epistle to the Clergy of the Southern States.* New York: Bailey pamphlets, 1836.

Grimké, Sarah M. *Letters on the Equality of the Sexes, and the Condition of Women.* Boston: I. Knapp, 1838.

Haviland, Laura S. *A Women's Life Work: Including Thirty Years' Service on the Underground Railroad and in the War.* 5th ed. Grand Rapids, Mich.: S.B. Shaw, 1881.

Roe, Elizabeth A. *Recollections of Frontier Life.* Rockford, Ill.: Gazette Publishing House, 1885.

Stowe, Harriet Beecher. *Uncle Tom's Cabin.* Boston: J.P. Jewett & Co., 1852.

Stowe, Harriet Beecher. *A Key to Uncle Tom's Cabin.* Boston: J.P. Jewett & Co., 1853.

Stowe, Harriet Beecher. *Dred: A Tale of the Great Dismal Swamp.* Boston: Phillips, Sampson & Co., 1856.

Swisshelm, Jane G. *Half A Century.* Chicago: J.G. Swisshelm, 1880.

Wright, Frances (D'Arusmont). *A Plan for the Gradual Abolition of Slavery in the United States.* c. 1825.

C.   Reform Communities

1. General Works

The foundation of a community as a strategy for reform was
of interest to American historians in the twilight of the
communitarian years in the 1870s. It provoked historical
comment and analysis in the early twentieth century along
with the upsurge of American socialism, was of brief interest to sociologists in the 1940s, to historians of religion
in the 1950s, and once again to historians of American culture during the revival of a "counterculture" in the late
1960s and early 1970s. The essence of communitarian reform
was the restructuring of property relations and human relations through new approaches to production, family, and
child rearing. The availability of free land made the United
States a magnet for European groups inspired by religious or
secular visions of the ideal society. The location of such
communities in the path of the advancing frontier seemed attractive since their potential for shaping the emerging society appeared thereby enlarged, although in fact the future
lineaments of American society were forming in urban rather
than rural terms. Because the intersection of work, property,
and family was the key junction of human relationships that
all secular or sacred communities wanted to restructure, they
were of great importance in defining the mainstream and the
radical view of the potential for change in women's status.
Although, as we see from the writings of John Humphrey Noyes,
Charles Nordhoff, and William A. Hinds, the nineteenth-century
reform communities loomed large in the popular mind, they
have received only passing attention from historians of American society. The writers of the forties and fifties who
studied the utopian communities wrote from the standpoint of
the Cold War and assumed that it was self-evident that the
communities would founder on the rock of mistaken economic
assumptions and that their social impact was marginal. The
historian might by contrast argue that it is remarkable that
American society had the longest unbroken tradition of widely
publicized communitarian experimentation of any Western industrial society. One consequence of this experience was
that nineteenth-century Americans did not regard debates
about changing the sphere and position of women as matters
of abstract speculation. They had before them actual working
models of alternative arrangements that were widely commented
on in the popular press. While Victoria Woodhull and Tenney
Claflin have been credited with linking the movement for
women's rights to "free love," contemporaries merely had to
read journalist Charles Nordhoff's reports of his visits to

utopian communities and the writings of a Noyes or a Robert
Owen to know that the existing efforts to change women's position did involve abandoning the traditional Christian view of
marriage. We are in danger of underestimating the extent and
range of opposition to the movement to expand women's rights
if we attribute it only to isolated events such as the much
publicized liaisons of the Woodhull sisters. (See introduction to Section V) The communitarian experiments placed
squarely before the public the logical implications of change
and served as a focus for mobilizing opposition to change.

V.F. Calverton's *Where Angels Dared to Tread* (1941) and
Henrik Infield's *Utopia and Experiment: Essays in the Sociology of Cooperation* (1955) analyze, from the sociological
point of view, societies where cooperation rather than competition is the underlying economic principle. Mark Holloway
in *Heavens on Earth* (1951) and Whitney Cross in *The Burned-
Over District: The Social and Intellectual History of Enthusiastic Religion in Western New York, 1800-1850* (1950)
trace the relationship between religious zeal and the formation of the perfected communities treating the states of
mind and the actions of the community builders and their
recruits as deviant.

Raymond L. Muncy's *Sex and Marriage in Utopian Communities* (1973) is less judgmental. Muncy wrote when there were
an estimated two thousand communes operating in thirty-four
states, so that the communitarian method of reform seemed more
a constant than a nineteenth-century aberration in American
history. Muncy concludes that celibacy and community of
property were social arrangements which produced enduring communities, but that alternative social structures to support
the sexual urge and human generativity were difficult to
develop and sustain within a larger society profoundly hostile to such efforts. Muncy's retrospect on the nineteenth-
century communities was written before the revolution in sexual mores of the seventies was clearly established. Had he
taken into account that change in behavior, it would be difficult to reach his conclusions. The question that remains
to be answered is what impact such communitarian models have
had on the behavior and attitudes of the majority of society,
and whether behavior may change noticeably while professed
ideology of family life may remain unchanged.

BIBLIOGRAPHY

Calverton, Victor Francis. *Where Angels Dared to Tread*.
    New York: Bobbs-Merrill Co., 1941.

Cross, Whitney R. *The Burned-Over District: The Social and Intellectual History of Enthusiastic Religion in Western New York, 1800-1850.* Ithaca, N.Y.: Cornell University Press, 1950.

Hinds, William A. *American Communities.* Oneida, N.Y.: Office of the American Socialist, 1878. Reprint. New York: Corinth Books, 1961.

Hinds, William A. *American Communities and Cooperative Colonies.* Chicago: Charles H. Kerr & Co., 1908.

Holloway, Mark. *Heavens on Earth: Utopian Communities in America, 1680-1880.* New York: Library Publishers, 1951.

Infield, Henrik. *Utopia and Experiment: Essays in the Sociology of Cooperation.* New York: F.A. Praeger, 1955.

Muncy, Raymond Lee. *Sex and Marriage in Utopian Communities: Nineteenth Century America.* Bloomington: Indiana University Press, 1973.

Nordhoff, Charles. *The Communistic Societies of the United States; from Personal Visit and Observation.* New York: Harper & Brothers, 1874.

Noyes, John Humphrey. *History of American Socialisms.* Philadelphia: J.B. Lippincott & Co., 1870.

Webber, Everett. *Escape to Utopia: The Communal Movement in America.* New York: Hastings House Publishers, 1959.

2. Millennial Communities

As Raymond Muncy pointed out in his study of the sexual customs and marriage practices of the utopian communities, those communities that experienced the least hostility from the external society and faced the least internal stress were celibate communities which held property in common. Of these the Shakers were the most widely studied and reported upon by contemporaries. Charles Edson Robinson's *A Concise History of the United Society of Believers Called Shakers* (1893) is an account of the society prepared by a member of the faith. It is an invaluable source for a sympathetic account of the states of mind and perceptions of those converting to the faith. A similarly sympathetic account is given in Anna White and Leila S. Taylor, *Shakerism, Its Meaning and Message* (1904). Thomas Brown, *Account of the People Called*

Shakers: Their Faith, Doctrines and Practices (1812) is a
hostile report from a member of a Shaker community who published his narrative to justify leaving the faith. Brown's
stories of sexual repression and illicit sex do not seem to
be supported by other contemporary sources.
Marguerite Melcher's general history, *The Shaker Adventure* (1941), is a scholarly attempt to describe the appeal of
Shakerism for converts and the pattern of life within Shaker
communities. However, Melcher neither puts the formation and
growth of the society in any comparative context nor attempts
to assess the broader social forces it represented. Edward D.
Andrews' *The People Called Shakers: A Search for the Perfect
Society* (1953) does analyze forces in revival culture that led
men and women to abandon the world and begin to prepare for
the second coming, but once again the work does not give the
reader a comparative perspective to place the Shakers within
an American utopian context or to interpret the American
phenomenon in terms of millennial movements in the western
tradition.
The same may be said of the historical treatment of the
Rappite and Amana communities and the extraordinary phenomenon
of Millerism. Karl J. Arndt's *George Rapp's Harmony Society,
1785-1847* (1965) is a scholarly work which covers the printed
sources on the foundation and development of the Rappite communities but does not help the reader understand the larger
social forces that convinced the Rappites to prepare for the
second coming. For the historian of women these societies
are of unusual interest because societies organized to prepare for the second coming could ignore human generativity
and the family and thereby pass over many of the contemporary
reasons for limiting women's position.

BIBLIOGRAPHY

Andrews, Edward D. *The People Called Shakers: A Search for
the Perfect Society*. New York: Oxford University
Press, 1953.

Arndt, Karl J. *George Rapp's Harmony Society, 1785-1847*.
Philadelphia: University of Pennsylvania Press, 1965.

Brown, Thomas. *An Account of the People Called Shakers:
Their Faith, Doctrines, and Practices, Exemplified in
the Life, Conversations and Experience of the Author
during the Time He Belonged to the Society*. Troy, N.Y.:
printed by Parker & Bliss, 1812.

Cole, Marley. *Jehovah's Witnesses: The New World Society*. New York: Vantage Press, 1955.

Duss, John S. *The Harmonists, A Personal History*. Harrisburg, Pa.: Pennsylvania Book Service, 1943.

Mayer, Frederick E. *"Jehovah's Witnesses."* St. Louis, Mo.: Concordia Publishing House, 1942.

Melcher, Marguerite. *The Shaker Adventure*. Princeton, N.J.: Princeton University Press, 1941.

Robinson, Charles Edson. *A Concise History of the United Society of Believers Called Shakers*. East Canterbury, N.H.: Robinson, 1893.

Shambaugh, Bertha M. Horack. *Amana, The Community of True Inspiration*. Iowa City, Iowa: The State Historical Society of Iowa, 1908.

Spaulding, W.W. *A History of Seventh Day Adventists*. Washington, D.C.: Review and Herald Publishing Association, 1949.

White, Anna, and Taylor, Leila S. *Shakerism: Its Meaning and Message; Embracing an Historial Accounts Statement of Belief and Spiritual Experience of the Church from Its Rise to the Present Day*. Columbus, Ohio: Press of F.J. Heer, 1904.

Wisbey, Herbert A. *Pioneer Prophetess: Jemima Wilkinson, the Publick Universal Friend*. Ithaca, N.Y.: Cornell University Press, 1964.

3. Perfected Societies on Earth

Communities which were founded on the presupposition that by divine inspiration or correct economic and social theory the perfect society could be built on earth could not overlook human generativity and the responsibility to raise and educate each new generation. One of the best documented efforts to free women from dependence through community responsibility for children was the Oneida community, an early expression of nineteenth-century interest in separating sexuality from procreation. We have many male accounts of the Oneida community, a society that gave up the traditional family but retained its charismatic father figure and a strong pattern of male authority. Corinna Ackley Noyes' *The Days of My Youth*

(1960) is a memoir of life in the community written by a female member, and Ely Van de Warker reported on the health of the female population at Oneida in "A Gynecological Experiment" (1884). Pierrepont Noyes' *My Father's House: An Oneida Boyhood* (1937) is a valuable source for the pattern of child rearing and education at the Oneida community as is Allan Eastlake's *The Oneida Community* (1900). The popular hostility to Oneida is documented in John B. Ellis, *Free Love and Its Votaries* (1870). Maren L. Carden's *Oneida: Utopian Community to Modern Corporation* (1969) assumes the inevitability of the community's collapse and despite an attempt at scholarly detachment is at best ambiguous about the values enshrined in "complex marriage." Robert A. Parker's *A Yankee Saint: John Humphrey Noyes and the Oneida Community* (1935) is a sympathetic account, while John Humphrey Noyes' *History of American Socialisms* (1870) contains his own account of complex marriage.

The two fullest expressions of transcendental social sentiment, Brook Farm and Fruitlands, have attracted historical comment more because of the cluster of brilliant intellects associated with the communities than for the actual experiments. Edith R. Curtis, *A Season in Utopia: The Story of Brook Farm* (1961) is based on wide historical research, whereas Clara Endicott Sears, *Bronson Alcott's Fruitlands* (1915) is a clearly partisan account.

Paul K. Conkin's *Two Paths to Utopia: The Hutterites and the Llano Colony* (1964) is the most comprehensive study of the Mennonite communities in the United States and Canada, and this work along with J.F.C. Harrison's *Robert Owen and the Owenites in Britain and America: The Quest for the New Moral World* (1969) give readers a broad comparative framework of interpretation into which they can fit the religious and secular faith in perfectibility. William E. Wilson's *The Angel and the Serpent: The Story of New Harmony* (1964) is less satisfying since it is written from the assumption that all collectivist experiments will ultimately fail in the United States.

One does not have to be a doctrinaire Marxist to observe the intimate link between the attempt to introduce a new moral order based on cooperation rather than individualism and the need to restructure family relationships and the social institutions responsible for the rearing of the young. Community of property was acceptable in celibate communities, and indeed the Shakers were admired and respected by contemporaries. Sharing of sexual favors and community responsibility for the young excited intense hostility, but the Oneida example seems to confirm the Marxist notion that the link between monogamous family, private property, and inheritance is a profound one at both the economic and psychological level, for once Oneida abandoned group marriage, the path to the modern joint stock company was rapidly traversed. Reform communities attempted to alter many aspects of domestic life, dress, diet, child rearing, and sexual customs, and to use the domestic sphere to create the psychological makeup appropriate to the cooperative, as opposed to competitive, world. In so doing they stated that there was in fact no nonpolitical, non-competitive sphere which women and children could inhabit, and that all human relationships have political and economic sig-nificance. This was the most subversive aspect of the com-munitarian tradition, for it asserted that there could be no separate sphere for women that was exempt from economic and political motivations and could serve as a moderating force or social counterweight against the dynamic but impersonal forces of American capitalism. The student of women's role in nineteenth-century American society can deduce much from studying the tensions between the collectivist communities and the larger society because they throw light on often un-stated assumptions about the relationship between domestic, economic, and political institutions.

BIBLIOGRAPHY

Oneida

Archorn, Erik. "Mary Cragin, Perfectionist Saint: Noyes' Theory and Experiments." *New England Quarterly* 28 (1955): 490-518.

Carden, Maren L. *Oneida: Utopian Community to Modern Corporation*. Baltimore: Johns Hopkins Press, 1969.

Eastlake, Allan. *The Oneida Community: A Record of an At-tempt to Carry out the Principles of Christian Unsel-fishness and Scientific Race-Improvement*. London: G. Redway, 1900.

Ellis, John B. *Free Love and Its Votaries; or, American Socialism Unmasked*. New York: United States Publishing Co., 1870.

Noyes, Corinna Ackley. *The Days of My Youth*. 1960.

Noyes, John Humphrey. *History of American Socialisms*. Philadelphia: J.B. Lippincott & Co., 1870.

Noyes, Pierrepont. *My Father's House: An Oneida Boyhood*. New York: Farrar & Rinehart, 1937.

Parker, Robert A. *A Yankee Saint; John Humphrey Noyes and the Oneida Community.* New York: G.P. Putnam's Sons, 1935.

Van de Warker, Ely. "A Gynecological Experiment." *American Journal of Obstetrics* 17:785.

Worden, Harriet M. *Old Mansion House Memories, by One Brought Up in It.* Oneida, N.Y., 1950.

Brook Farm

Curtis, Edith R. *A Season in Utopia; The Story of Brook Farm.* New York: Nelson, 1961.

Reed, Amy L., ed. *Letters from Brook Farm, 1844-1847.* Poughkeepsie, N.Y.: Vassar College, 1928.

Sams, Henry W., ed. *Autobiography of Brook Farm.* Englewood Cliffs, N.J.: Prentice-Hall, 1958.

Swift, Lindsay. *Brook Farm; Its Members, Scholars and Visitors.* New York: Macmillan Co., 1900.

Fruitlands

Francis, Richard. "Circumstances and Salvation: The Ideology of the Fruitlands Utopia." *American Quarterly* 25 (1973): 202-234.

Sears, Clara Endicott. *Bronson Alcott's Fruitlands.* Boston: Houghton Mifflin Co., 1915.

Hutterites

Conkin, Paul Keith. *Two Paths to Utopia: The Hutterites and the Llano Colony.* Lincoln: University of Nebraska Press, 1964.

Bestor, Arthur E. *Backwoods Utopias: The Sectarian and Owenite Phases of Communitarian Socialism in America, 1663-1829.* Philadelphia: University of Pennsylvania Press, 1950.

Bestor, Arthur E., ed. *Education and Reform at New Harmony: Correspondence of William Maclure and Marie Duclos Fretageot, 1820-1833.* Indianapolis: Indiana Historical Society, 1948.

Cole, Margaret. *Robert Owen of New Lanark.* London: Batchworth Press, 1953.

Harrison, John Fletcher Clews. *Robert Owen and the Owenites in Britain and America: The Quest for the New Moral World.* London: Routledge & Kegan Paul, 1969.

Lockwood, George B. *The New Harmony Movement.* New York: D. Appleton & Co., 1905.

Owen, Robert Dale. *Twenty-seven Years of Autobiography. Threading My Way.* New York: G.W. Carleton & Co., 1874.

Pears, Sarah. *New Harmony, An Adventure in Happiness; Papers of Thomas and Sarah Pears.* Edited by Thomas Clinton Pears. Indianapolis: Indiana Historical Society, 1933.

Wilson, William E. *The Angel and the Serpent: The Story of New Harmony.* Bloomington: Indiana University Press, 1964.

4. Mormonism

At the other end of the spectrum of social experimentation from Oneida and New Harmony was the practice of polygamy and the Mormon faith. Mormonism must be understood as a sect embracing a set of beliefs which grew out of the tensions of life on the frontier, one of which was the recurring disruption of the balance of the sexes, a second of which was perpetual speculation about the possibility of perfecting inherited social institutions in new forms, and a third of which was the urge to experiment with communitarian reform especially with respect to property. Oneida was such an experiment in the direction of blending the male and female sphere and releasing women from unwanted childbearing. Mormonism moved in the other direction and solved the problem of imbalance in the number of males and females through the practice of polygamy. Much has been made of the sexual exploitation involved in the practice of polygamy, and little attention has been paid to the reports of Mormon women about the experience of a faith which continues to be a major proselytising twentieth-century religion converting males and females at approximately the same rate. Polygamy was an addition to the early Mormon teaching, and its abandonment in 1896 does not, as with complex marriage at Oneida, seem to have undermined the viability of a faith which officially saw childbearing and the domestic sphere as women's only lot. In practice the institution of polygamy increased the number of female-headed households, since a man could not be everywhere at once, and, given the differential life expectancy of males and females and the spread of ages between husband

and youngest wife, increased the number of independent widows
who had to set up in business to support their offspring. Historians of the Mormons have tended frequently to rely on the
writings of external critics of the faith rather than on the
testimony of Mormon women about the nature of their experience.
   Some typical examples of such biased outside reporting are
Frances B.H. Stenhouse, *"Tell It All": The Story of a Life's
Experience in Mormonism* (1874), A.E.W. Young, *Wife No. 19:
or The Story of Life in Bondage, Being a Complete Expose of
Mormonism, and Revealing the Sorrows, Sacrifices and Sufferings of Women in Polygamy* (1876), and Kimball Young, *Isn't
One Wife Enough?* (1954). These propaganda pieces, composed
mainly as part of the campaign against the admission of Utah
to the Union, are uniformly hostile in tone. More objective
records may be found in William Mulder and A. R. Mortenson,
*Among the Mormons: Historic Accounts by Contemporary Ob-
servers* (1958) and in Vicky Burgess-Olson's *Sister Saints*
(1978) and Claudia L. Bushman's *Mormon Sisters: Women in
Early Utah* (1980), which are excellent collections of narratives by Mormon women reporting the degree to which Mormon
women supported one another, shared household responsibili-
ties, and eased the burdens of childcare. The character of
Joseph Smith and the story of the dramatic Mormon journey to
the desert have attracted the attention of historians, though
there are no general histories treating family life and the
role of Mormon women. Fawn M. Brodie's *No Man Knows My History: The Life of Joseph Smith, the Mormon Prophet* (1945) is
a sensitive and sympathetic biography that may be supplemented
by Thomas O'Dea's objective and balanced general history *The
Mormons* (1957). Social historians have been interested in
the social background of converts to Mormonism and the situations which fostered conversion. Two valuable introductions
to this question are David Brion Davis, "The New England Origins of Mormonism" (1953) and Mario S. De Pillis, "The Social
Sources of Mormonism" (1968). There has been no systematic
effort to analyze the writing of Mormon women, though there
is a substantial body of archival material. Historians of
the suffrage movement have been puzzled by the early date at
which women were granted the suffrage in Utah and have construed this event as a tactic in the battle for statehood.
We have yet to investigate the subject of women's political
participation and consciousness in Utah on its own terms,
just as we have yet to hear women's own voices about why the
faith was attractive to converts. It is interesting to note
that while opponents of the suffrage based their opposition
on the separation between domestic life and the political
sphere, opponents of the admission of Utah to the union made
explicit connections between polygamy and political life.

BIBLIOGRAPHY

Bailey, Florence A. (Merriam). *My Summer in a Mormon Village*. Boston: Houghton Mifflin Co., 1894.

Brodie, Fawn M. *No Man Knows My History: The Life of Joseph Smith, The Mormon Prophet*. New York: Alfred A. Knopf, 1945.

Burgess-Olson, Vicky. *Sister Saints*. Provo, Utah: Brigham Young University Press, 1978.

Bushman, Claudia L., ed. *Mormon Sisters: Women in Early Utah*. Salt Lake City, Utah: Olympus Publishing Co., 1980.

Comstock, Sarah. "The Mormon Woman." *Colliers*, 2 October 1909.

Davis, David B. "The New England Origins of Mormonism." *New England Quarterly* 26 (1953):147-168.

De Pillis, Mario S. "The Social Sources of Mormonism." *Church History* 37 (1968):50-79.

Flanders, Robert B. *Nauvoo: Kingdom on the Mississippi*. Urbana: University of Illinois Press, 1965.

Froiseth, Jenny Anderson. *The Women of Mormonism; or, The Story of Polygamy As Told by The Victims Themselves*. Chicago: A.G. Nettleton, 1882.

[Green, Nelson Winch.] *Fifteen Years Among the Mormons, Being the Narrative of Mrs. Mary Ettie V. Smith*. New York: Charles Scribner, 1858.

[Green, Nelson Winch.] *Fifteen Years Residence with the Mormons. With Startling Disclosures of the Mysteries of Polygamy. By a Sister of One of the High Priests*. Chicago: n.p., 1876.

Mulder, William, and Mortenson, A. R., eds. *Among the Mormons: Historic Accounts by Contemporary Observers*. New York: Alfred A. Knopf, 1958.

O'Dea, Thomas. *The Mormons*. Chicago: University of Chicago Press, 1957.

Stegner, Wallace. *The Gathering of Zion: The Story of the Mormon Trail.* New York: McGraw-Hill, 1964.

Stenhouse, Frances B.H. *"Tell It All": The Story of a Life's Experience in Mormonism.* Hartford, Conn.: A.D. Worthington, 1874.

Victor, Metta Victoria (Fuller). *Lives of Female Mormons, A Narrative of Facts Stranger than Fiction.* Philadelphia: G.G. Evans, 1860.

Ward, Maria. *Female Life Among the Mormons, A Narrative of Many Years' Personal Experience.* London: G. Routledge, 1855.

Young, Ann Eliza Webb. *Wife No. 19: or, the Story of a Life in Bondage, Being a Complete Expose of Mormonism, and Revealing the Sorrows, Sacrifices and Sufferings of Women in Polygamy.* Hartford, Conn.: Dustin, Gilman & Co., 1876.

Young, Kimball. *Isn't One Wife Enough?* New York: Holt, 1954.

D. Unitarianism

Unitarianism, confined as it was to the educated elites, encouraged belief in the perfectibility of society and the responsibility of the individual to act immediately to secure social betterment. Like all forms of perfectionism, Unitarianism had to come to terms with the subordination of women and with some formulation of her position other than that supposed to endure perpetually as a result of Eve's sin. Theodore Parker's *A Sermon on the Public Function of Women* (1853) is the fullest Unitarian statement on this point. It draws attention to the feminine virtues which are close to those attributed to Jesus the great teacher and Redeemer and urges the expression of those virtues to perfect society. Julia Ward Howe's *Reminiscences, 1819-1899* (1899) illustrates the response of one of Boston's leading women civic reformers to Parker's ideas, and Caroline Dall (Mrs. Charles H.A. Dall) in her *Memorial to Charles H.A. Dall* (1902) provides another perspective on Unitarianism as an inspiration for women reformers. Nina M. Tiffany's *Pathbreakers* (1949) is a brief general account of Unitarian reform, while Conrad Wright, *The Beginnings of Unitarianism in America* (1955)

traces the intellectual and social roots of Unitarian beliefs
and attitudes.

BIBLIOGRAPHY

Channing, William Ellery. *Works*. London: E. Rainford, 1829.

Dall, Caroline Wells (Healey). *Memorial to Charles H.A. Dall*.
    Boston: Beacon Press, 1902.

Howe, Julia Ward. *Reminiscences, 1819-1899*. Boston:
    Houghton Mifflin Co., 1899.

Parker, Theodore. *A Sermon on the Public Function of Women*.
    Boston: R.F. Walcutt, 1853.

Parker, Theodore. *Autobiography, Poems and Prayers*. Boston:
    American Unitarian Association, 1911.

Tiffany, Nina M. *Pathbreakers*. Boston: Beacon Press, 1949.

Wright, Conrad. *The Beginnings of Unitarianism in America*.
    Boston: Starr King Press, 1955.

If we ask with Turner what was the significance of the frontier
in the history of American women, the answer must be worked
out in terms of frontier religious culture, perfectionism,
communitarian reform, the wide variety of attempts to find
new forms for institutions such as the family, and new institutions to give social form to the expression of sexuality.
The growing urban culture of the nineteenth century provided
a range of expressions for women's religious sentiment from
the Methodist circles of evangelists like Mrs. Phoebe Palmer
to the Unitarian meetings of Mrs. Howe. The intersection of
women's religious consciousness with the economic and political realities of slavery was at its most dramatic in urban
settings such as Philadelphia or Boston, and it was from the
city that women's antislavery polemical writing emerged, a
development which gave women a new voice, not merely in fiction and verse, but in social analysis of a different kind,
concerned with power and subordination. We need to assess
that voice in concert with other rural and small-town voices
concerned with the morality of slavery, acting on that concern but not carried beyond it to other forms of social analysis. Only by examining the entire spectrum of participation
in the abolition movement can we discover what led some women
to generalize from their concern with slavery to other social

and political institutions, and to see as the communitarian
reformers did that politics and family were part of one polity,
and what led others to remain comfortably concerned with abolition work and the support of the underground railroad as
simply a form of Christian good works. Because the history
of the suffrage movement has prompted biographies of the major
suffrage leaders but not of antisuffragists, we tend to place
mistaken emphasis on religious motives and the abolition movement as a source of feminist perceptions, and to make gender
an explanatory concept when in fact women as a gender group
held views on the slavery question covering the spectrum of
possible positions from radical abolitionist to conservative
opponent of slavery in the north. The history of southern
Methodism and the spectrum of southern views on the question
remains to be written, though we know that the raw materials
for such a history exist in countless narratives of frontier
life such as the memoirs of Mrs. Roe, written for family and
friends, but nonetheless important historical records.

SECTION V

WOMEN AND POLITICS, 1776-1930

Western political theory, whether classical, medieval,
early modern, or modern, has taken no cognizance of women.
Politics has been thought of as part only of the public
sphere of life, a sphere separate from the domestic world of
women and slaves. Only very recently have historians of the
transition from medieval to modern society broadened the
definition of political behavior to include all forms of collective action directed toward conserving or altering power
relationships, whether these fit the conventional modes of
dispute about public authority or not. Thus we see historians of early modern Europe interested in the behavior of
the crowd, in the symbolism of bread riots, in the language
of popular processions and rites even though the actors were
illiterate and not participants in the formal polity. Before
the interest of social historians in the study of popular
political behavior, the family, though seen as the basic
social unit, was not thought of as a political institution,
either congruent with or in conflict with the formal political institutions of society. Indeed, most political theorists
have been happily able to posit the rule of force, of en-
lightened self-interest, or of naked individualism within the
public sphere while accepting without examination the notion
of the domestic or family sphere as one governed by altruism
and self-denial. Thus it has been possible for historians
and political theorists to assume that the rise of universal
male suffrage and the democratic polity led in due course to
universal adult suffrage, and to ignore the obvious fact that
the suffrage for women did not result in the styles of political participation and power associated with male access to
the vote.

Historians of American women's political participation
confined their attention to the formal institutions of public authority until the feminist writings of the 1970s. Because of the assumption that only the exercise of the vote
indicated political behavior, they ignored the powerful political movements concerned with opposition to the suffrage and

the expansion of women's rights. While this approach has
given center stage to the suffrage agitation, it has ignored
the bitter and far more significant struggles of the nineteenth
and early twentieth century related to women's participation
in the organization of trades unions, the socialist and anarchist movements, the temperance movement, and the struggle
for legal access to birth-control information. These struggles were fought between groups and movements operating from
two virtually unreconcilable views of women's place in society and of the basis of her political participation. These
were the ideology of equal rights and equal participation in
all sectors of society with men and the ideology of women's
sacred mission to guard and protect the functions associated
with her role within the family and domestic life, the non-
acquisitive, altruistic sphere of society.

Because little attention has been paid to women's political behavior and ideologies, most writing about women in
politics has been either biographical, focusing on the woman
leader but not upon the social dynamics of the movement she
led, or concerned with the analysis of the strategy and tactics of isolated movements to the neglect of larger questions
customarily raised about the nature of political participation
by men. We know, for instance, that class perspective did
not change women's view of the home and the domestic sphere,
although it is almost axiomatic that class position affected
men's view of the economic institutions within which they
were lodged. We have no theoretical grasp of the process of
radicalization for women, though this is a standard formulation for writing about the recruitment of men into reform
organizations. Many women's movements such as the temperance
movement do not fit into the chronological scheme used to
characterize American politics in the nineteenth and twentieth
century. Prohibition and the suffrage for women are seen as
Progressive reforms, though the women's organizations which
launched these reforms took shape during and just after the
Civil War. The antisuffrage movement represents an important predecessor of the opposition to the equal rights amendments of the 1920s and the 1970s, though both are treated entirely in terms of the political currents of the decade in
question.

If we examine the entire spectrum of women's political
actions and trace the roots of the ideologies that gave rise
to them, we see in the Revolutionary period the definition of
a polity excluding women from formal political participation
specifically on grounds of gender. We may then view the period from 1800 to the 1930s as one in which new styles of political action were developed congruent with the role assigned
the family within that newly formed polity. A long chapter

in this history concerns the movement for equal rights, a
movement launched in the 1840s and decisively defeated in
favor of participation linked to gender and a special sphere
for women by the 1920s and '30s.

A.   Women in the American Revolution

1. Women as Patriots and Military Figures

Although the participation of women in the Paris mob and
in the political debates of Revolutionary Paris has long excited the attention of historians, little has been written
about women's collective action in the War for Independence
or in the classic mob actions against unpopular colonial officials. Colonial society was sufficiently unmodernized for
us to expect women's participation in street crowds, in wartime bread riots, and in patriotic associations. We know
from the press, from contemporary depictions of the Boston
Massacre and the tarring and feathering of customs officials,
that women were participants in colonial mobs. We know that
they adopted the colonial homespun as a political comment on
the Stamp Act controversy, and that they were active participants in the popular rite of dancing round the Liberty tree.
However, with only one or two notable exceptions, writing
about women in the Revolutionary era concentrates on the
occasional military figure and on the spouses of leaders of
Patriot or Loyalist factions.

Elizabeth Cometti's "Women in the American Revolution"
(1947) describes women's participation in bread riots during
the Revolutionary War and indicates the range of sources
from the press and contemporary letters which document this
type of political activity. A variety of eulogistic accounts
describe the military exploits of the one isolated woman figure known to have participated as a regular combatant in the
war. These are summarized in H. Mann's *The Female Review,
Life of Deborah Sampson, The Female Soldier in the War of
Revolution* (1866). The contributions of women participants
to the battle of Fort Washington are reviewed in Edward H.
Hall's *Margaret Corbin, Heroine of the Battle of Fort Washington, 16 November 1776* (1932).

BIBLIOGRAPHY

Cometti, Elizabeth. "Women in the American Revolution."
    New England Quarterly 20 (1947):329-346.

Hall, Edward H. *Margaret Corbin, Heroine of the Battle of
    Fort Washington, 16 November 1776.* New York: American
    Scenic and Historic Preservation Society, 1932.

Kerber, Linda. *Women of the Republic: Intellectual and
    Ideology in Revolutionary America.* Chapel Hill:
    University of North Carolina Press, for the Institute
    of Early American History and Culture, 1980.

Mann, Herman. *The Female Review, Life of Deborah Sampson,
    The Female Soldier in the War of Revolution.* Boston:
    J.K. Wiggin & W.P. Lunt, 1866.

Myers, Albert C., ed. *Sally Wister's Journal, a True Narra-
    tive; Being a Quaker Maiden's Account of Her Experiences
    with Officers of the Continental Army, 1777-1778.*
    Philadelphia: Ferris & Leach, 1902.

Perrine, William D. *Molly Pitcher of Monmouth County, N.J.
    and Captain Molly of Fort Washington, N.Y., 1778-1937.*
    Princeton Junction, N.J.: n.p., 1938.

Wing, C.P. "Moll Pitcher." *Pennsylvania Magazine of
    Biography and History* 3 (1879):109-110.

2. "First Ladies"

The sources and secondary accounts of the lives of women
related to revolutionary leaders highlight what were to become two separate and important themes with respect to
women's political position in the Republic.   Charles Francis
Adams' two-volume edition of the letters of Abigail Adams,
Letters of Mrs. Adams (1848, fourth edition), Lyman H. Butterfield's *Adams Family Correspondence* (1963), and Katherine
Anthony's *First Lady of the Revolution: The Life of Mercy
Otis Warren* (1958) show the two women closest to the leaders
of the struggle in Massachusetts moved by the discussion of
sovereignty to consider the position of women and to argue
for an enlargement of their rights within the new political
system.   By contrast the biographies of Martha Washington,
whether eulogistic nineteenth-century accounts such as Anne
Hollingsworth Wharton's *Martha Washington* (1897) or Elswyth
Thane's somewhat more objective *Washington's Lady* (1960),

describe a woman who resolutely refused to enter her husband's
sphere of public affairs and was idolized as the embodiment
of feminine virtue precisely because of this refusal.

BIBLIOGRAPHY

Adams, Charles Francis, ed. *Letters of Mrs. Adams, the Wife
of John Adams.* 2 vols. 4th rev. ed. Boston: Wilkins,
Carter, & Co., 1848.

Adams, Charles Francis, ed. *Familiar Letters of John Adams
and His Wife Abigail Adams during the Revolution.*
New York: Hurd & Houghton, 1876.

Anthony, Katherine. *First Lady of the Revolution: The Life
of Mercy Otis Warren.* Garden City, N.Y.: Doubleday, 1958.

Bobbé, Dorothie. *Abigail Adams, the Second First Lady.*
New York: Minton, Balch, & Co., 1929.

Butterfield, Lyman H., ed. *Adams Family Correspondence.*
Cambridge, Mass.: Harvard University Press, Belknap
Press, 1963.

Desmond, Alice Curtis. *Martha Washington, Our First Lady.*
New York: Dodd, Mead, 1942.

Thane, Elswyth. *Washington's Lady.* New York: Dodd, Mead,
1960.

Wharton, Anne Hollingsworth. *Martha Washington.* New York:
Charles Scribner's Sons, 1897.

Whitney, Janet P. *Abigail Adams.* Boston: Little, Brown, &
Co., 1947.

3. Loyalist Women

Loyalist women, by virtue of their links to transatlantic
society and an aristocratic tradition of women's political
participation at court and in the salon, were more likely to
leave diaries and letters of acute political insight. Ann
Hulton's *Letters of a Loyalist Lady* (1927) and *The Diary of
Grace Growden Galloway* (1971) reveal the acute woman observer
of political events, and Louisa Hall Tharp's *The Baroness and
the General* (1962) gives a clear account of the life of the
wife of a German mercenary in the British service. The
letters and diaries of the Baroness in question have been

published as *Baroness von Riedesel and the American Revolution,*
eds. Marvin L. Brown and Martha Huth (1965). All these sources
indicate the easy assumption that women of high status should
be involved in common political cause with husbands and male
members of their circle. This is an attitude to politics rejected by the Founding Fathers, who saw it as a product of
the corrupt morals of European aristocratic society.

While Loyalist or Patriot women of the Revolutionary era
have not been well served by biographers, the popular biographer, such as Janet Whitney, tends to turn biography into
fiction to make the eighteenth-century mind and manners of an
Abigail Adams seem familiar. The same may be said for the
lives of Loyalist women. They are not seen in the round as
political and social beings, but as spectators of history.
Fortunately the growing volume of published diaries and
letters from the period invites fresh historical attention.

BIBLIOGRAPHY

Aikman, Louisa Susannah (Wells). *The Journal of a Voyage
    from Charleston to London.* 1906. Reprint. New York:
    New York Times, 1968.

Brown, Marvin L., and Huth, Martha, eds. *Baroness Von
    Riedesel and the American Revolution: Journal and Cor-
    respondence of a Tour of Duty, 1776-1783.* Chapel Hill:
    University of North Carolina Press, 1965.

Galloway, Grace Growden. *Diary of Grace Growden Galloway.*
    Edited by Raymond C. Warner. New York: New York Times,
    1971.

Hulton, Ann. *Letters of a Loyalist Lady.* Cambridge, Mass.:
    Harvard University Press, 1927.

Tharp, Louise Hall. *The Baroness and the General.* Boston:
    Little, Brown, & Co., 1962.

4. Women as Citizens: The New Jersey Case

Much attention has been paid by historians to the developing concepts of representation and consent as they were
understood by the Revolutionary generation. However, virtually no attention has been paid to the development of these
concepts with respect to women. There is, in the debates on
representation and the franchise in New Jersey, an archive
which can illuminate this question. Sophie H. Drinker has
drawn attention in her "Votes for Women in Eighteenth Century

New Jersey" (1962) that single or widowed women of property voted in New Jersey until the franchise was specifically removed from them in 1807. The debates on this legislative action have been treated by historians as revealing discussions of the way in which the Founding Fathers thought about the relationship between property and the right to vote. They are also important documents setting out the way in which this generation thought about the relationship between gender and the right to vote and Sophie Drinker's pioneering essay deserves further elaboration.

BIBLIOGRAPHY

Drinker, Sophie H. "Votes for Women in Eighteenth Century New Jersey," *Proceedings of New Jersey Historical Society* 80 (1962):87-98.

It is important to see the literary, political, and intellectual trends of the Federal period in the round. When we reflect that the source of Hannah Foster's Coquette's downfall is her interest in politics and life outside the home, that Benjamin Rush thought his women patients cured from hysteria by the Revolution because their wombs could resume the right physical location under a correct political system, and that by 1807 there was a definitive statement that gender was a characteristic that governed fitness for the franchise, we see clearly that the change in sovereignty did bring with it the need to rethink the relationship of women and the family to public authority. In his essays on the forms of education appropriate to republican societies, Benjamin Rush gave the clearest statement of the reasons for the direction of change. The Founding Fathers feared, with all the weight of colonial experience of eighteenth-century political patronage, the voter who could be manipulated for the purpose of faction. Because of the dispersion of property, economic status could not be made the qualification for voting, and in its place was enshrined the concept of the "independent voter" who was free of dependent relationships. Hence Rush assumed that there would be no male servants, or indeed a servant class, in the Republic, and therefore women must be educated to manage the household and the care of young children entirely on their own while men concentrated their energies on economic and political tasks. To ensure that independence and freedom from subordinate relationships did characterize the voter, it became increasingly necessary to segregate domestic life from the arena of politics, since eighteenth-century theories of the psyche could

not comprehend the concept of multivariate human relationships. This set of assumptions undergirds the discussion on
women's voting capacity in New Jersey as it did the acceler-
ating trend to segregate the social territory of the sexes.
The student of women's political life in the United States
cannot afford to ignore the Revolutionary and Federal period
and date the beginning of thought about women and politics
from the Jacksonian period, for in doing so he or she will
fail to understand the unstated assumptions that were being
affirmed or challenged by opponents and supporters of the
vote for women in the 1840s and thereafter.

B. Feminism

One of the problems which dogs all discussion of the
history of the movement for women's rights in the nineteenth
and twentieth century is the vagueness of the label words,
"feminist," "suffragist," and "radical," and the incomplete
grasp of most historians on the total context of thought
about women's position in society and its intellectual roots.
Much writing does not even take into account the fact that
there were two general varieties of feminism involved in
the debates about women's position in the nineteenth century. The first was concerned with increasing the importance and status of women within their separate sphere, and
the second with dismantling the boundaries of the separate
sphere so that women might mingle on equal terms with men
throughout the realm of social, political, and economic activity. In opposition to these two broad streams of thought
about women's position were those who saw the vote as undermining the integrity of women's separate and altruistic
sphere of competence and those who, on philosophical and
religious terms, were opposed to women's equality with men
in access to divorce, property rights, and the custody of
children. Later in the century this group was joined by
opponents of access to birth-control information who were
opposed to any separation of female sexuality from procreation. Because historians have tended to confuse the two
broad streams of thought about improving women's position,
they have not been able to understand the political and
social forces that made the antifeminist and antisuffrage
arguments so powerful, and they have tended to ignore the
intellectual seriousness and the range of social perceptions
from which these views were advanced.

If we take as feminists both those concerned to elevate
women's status within their sphere and those working to

secure women's equality with men, we need to develop some
terminology which will enable us to distinguish between the
two. For the purposes of this essay, they are divided into
the categories of equal-rights feminists and enhanced-
authority feminists. Historians have, on the whole, only
paid attention to the equal-rights variety of feminist since
they preempted the ground by producing the multivolume *History
of Woman Suffrage,* edited by Susan B. Anthony and Elizabeth
Cady Stanton with the assistance of numerous colleagues and
published between 1881 and 1920. Ida Husted Harper also
wrote a eulogistic biography of Anthony in 1899, which has
shaped all subsequent accounts. Stanton's *Eighty Years and
More* (1898) defined her form of feminism as the dominant form
of her era. Stanton and Anthony may be seen as first-generation equal-rights feminists who came to their sweeping assessment of the subordination of women through participation
in the abolition and temperance movements respectively. As
social types they are middle-class, educated, and brought to
their demand for equality with men from the experience of
expressing moral concerns that could not be acted upon without legislative and judicial change. Their inability to
bring about change led to the search for a constituency or
group to support change, the first such constituency being
black, the second working-class, and the final one middle-
class women interested only in the suffrage. Along the path
to the final constituency, Stanton and Anthony were radicalized by the rejection of the women's cause by black men and
fellow white male reformers, by their encounters with the
trades-union movement, and with nineteenth-century sexual
radicals such as Victoria Woodhull. Their history of the
suffrage movement does not, however, reveal a clear understanding of the nature of the opposition to broadening
women's rights. They attribute the delays in securing the
suffrage to male politicians, afraid of the female vote, and
to the liquor industry which feared that enfranchised women
would impose prohibition. They thus subscribe to a plot
theory of history and ignore the very large body of female
opinion mobilized in the antisuffrage movement.

Frances E. Willard, in her autobiography *Glimpses of
Fifty Years* (1889), provides the fullest possible account of
the development of the first-generation enhanced-authority
feminist. As social type, Willard came from a more impover-
ished and isolated rural background than Stanton or Anthony.
She found her constituency immediately in western Methodist
women, who were easily mobilized around a movement Willard
styled as seeking temperance reform to protect home and
country. Willard's *Portraits and Biographies of Prominent
American Women* (1901), written with Mary A. Livermore, is a

collective biography of the leaders of the first generation
of enhanced-authority feminists. The work reveals a clear
understanding of the dynamics of enhanced-authority feminism.
She stresses its religious roots, its link to preserving and
purifying the separate woman's sphere of the home, and its
deliberate rejection of all varieties of reform sentiment
linked to sexual or economic freedom for women. It is noteworthy that Willard and her brand of feminism have not attracted the continuing attention of historians, though the
forces mobilized by Willard for the temperance movement were
deployed by later generations in opposition to constitutional
amendments in favor of equal rights.

In the 1920s and early thirties a number of historical
accounts of the leadership of the movement for the suffrage
were written in the wake of the Suffrage Amendment. Rheta C.
Dorr's *Susan B. Anthony, The Woman Who Changed the Mind of a
Nation* (1928) is written from a "great woman" theory of history and ignores the division between equal-rights and enhanced-authority feminists by implying that all suffrage
supporters were eventually converted to Anthony's brand of
feminism. Alice Stone Blackwell's *Lucy Stone, Pioneer of
Woman's Rights* (1930) is written from the same point of view.
Sophonisba Breckinridge's *Women in the Twentieth Century:
A Study of Their Political, Social and Economic Activities*
(1933) is more detached but underplays the significance of the
differences of opinion between equal-rights and enhanced-
authority feminists. Otelia Cromwell's life of Lucretia
Mott, written by one of the first black graduates of Smith
College as part of a doctoral dissertation, links Mott's
espousal of equal rights to her Quaker background, her experiences as a woman preacher, and the radicalizing encounters with male abolitionists who were opposed to women speaking at abolition meetings.

Charlotte Perkins Gilman (1860-1935) was the only theorist
of equal-rights feminism. A transitional figure whose work
began to capture attention in the 1930s, Gilman articulated
with great clarity the full implications of the changes in
society necessary to secure the goal of equal rights with
men. *Women and Economics,* first published in 1898, linked
women's subordination to the cult of domesticity and women's
confinement to the domestic sphere. Women could only manage
the psychological autonomy and the economic independence
that were preconditions to equal rights if the home were
collectivized and most household needs were met by cen-
tralized service organizations. Gilman was the only critic
of the supposedly morally enriching pattern of domestic work
and child care developing in her generation, and her views
were anathema to the feminists in search of enhanced authority.

Her autobiography, *The Living of Charlotte Perkins Gilman* (1935), confirmed the worst fears of supporters of domesticity about the decline of maternal instincts and the breakup of the family, for Gilman voluntarily surrendered custody of her child to her husband and his second wife in order to secure more freedom to pursue her own career. Gilman's correct perception that equality was only possible in a social order which did not confine altruism to the female role in the home and was willing to surrender much of the bourgeois ethos of the privacy of family life, links her on one hand to the utopian communitarians and on the other to the believers in planned communities and public utilities of the New Deal. Gilman's autobiography gained in popularity during the 1930s, but we have had to wait for the 1980s for a full-length biography. Mary A. Hill's *Charlotte Perkins Gilman: The Making of a Radical Feminist, 1860-1896* (1980) is the first volume of a full-length study of Gilman which meets the most demanding standards of objectivity and places Gilman correctly in the contradictions between her collectivism and her drive to secure the liberated life for herself. Alma Lutz's biography of Stanton, *Created Equal: A Biography of Elizabeth Cady Stanton* (1940), and Mary E. Dillon's *Frances Willard: From Prayers to Politics* (1944) share the assumptions of the forties that the work of the feminist movement was completed, a view shortly to be confronted by Gunnar Myrdal's *An American Dilemma* (1944) analyzing discrimination on the basis of race and sex in America. Lutz and Dillon are clearly hesitant to discuss the sexual orientation of their subjects and skate lightly over the psychological sources of their rebellion, sources which Gilman, shaped in a pre-Freudian era, felt perfectly free to discuss.

Prompted by Myrdal's careful documentation of discrimination against women in post-World War II America, students of feminism in the fifties approached the subject with a different set of questions and a clearer generational perspective. Katherine Anthony approached her biography of Anthony, *Susan B. Anthony: Her Personal History and Her Era* (1954), from the point of view of Anthony's capacities as a leader, assessing her tactics from the point of view of a struggle still to be completed. Carl Degler in "Charlotte Perkins Gilman on the Theory and Practice of Feminism" (1956) and in a long essay introducing a re-issue of *Women and Economics* (1966) drew attention to the revival of the cult of domesticity in the 1950s and the power of Gilman's critique. When Alma Lutz published her second biographical study of the team who led the radical wing of the suffrage struggle, she gave it the title *Susan B. Anthony: Rebel, Crusader, Humanitarian* (1959) and discussed Anthony's career from the

perspective of the major nineteenth-century movements for
human rights. Yuri Suhl's study of Ernestine Rose, published
the same year, linked her feminism to a worldwide, unfinished
movement for human rights, and Eleanor Flexner's history of
the feminist movement, given the title *Century of Struggle*
(1959), concluded with some pithy analysis of the relatively
modest gains of a century of agitation for women's rights.
Flexner, Degler, Suhl, and Anthony all agreed that the major
feminist phenomenon of the century from 1850 to 1950 had been
the movement for equal rights, and overlooked the strength
of the opposition and the large and readily mobilized constituency of those who drew their authority from women's exclusive sphere in society such as Willard.

The dominant observation of historians of feminism writing
in the sixties was the failure of the broad movement for equal
rights and the apparent emptiness of the victory won for the
suffrage in 1919. Robert E. Riegel in *American Feminists* (1963)
and Christopher Lasch in *The New Radicalism in America, 1889-
1963* (1965) focused on the failures of adjustment and the ambiguity about sexuality of the leaders of the movement for equal
rights, implying that the failure to understand or analyze
the problem of sexuality left the leaders of the movement unable to advance consistent strategies for psychological as
well as political equality. Andrew Sinclair and Aileen
Kraditor focused attention on the narrow range of issues on
which feminists had been able to unite, so that the suffrage
struggle alone, devoid of a program for reform, was bound to
be self-defeating, while William O'Neill published *Everyone
was Brave: The Rise and Fall of Feminism in America* (1969)
analyzing the reasons for the collapse of most feminist organizations in the decade of the 1920s. O'Neill, Sinclair,
and Kraditor wrote after the publication of Betty Friedan's
The Feminine Mystique (1963), a forceful and unequivocal
statement that the legal fictions of equal political rights
masked a culture which still assigned women to the separate
social territory of domesticity. The seventies thus saw an
outburst of research on the history of American feminism,
much of it episodic and much of it focused as in the past
on the movement for equal rights to the neglect of analysis
of the social basis and intellectual justification for opposition to equal rights.

BIBLIOGRAPHY

Anthony, Katherine. *Susan B. Anthony: Her Personal History
    and Her Era*. Garden City, N.Y.: Doubleday, 1954.

Berg, Barbara. *The Remembered Gate. Origins of American Feminism: The Women and the City, 1800-1860.* New York: Oxford University Press, 1978.

Blackwell, Alice S. *Lucy Stone, Pioneer of Woman's Rights.* Boston: Little, Brown, & Co., 1930.

Breckinridge, Sophonisba. *Women in the Twentieth Century: A Study of Their Political, Social and Economic Activities.* New York: McGraw-Hill, 1933.

Cromwell, Otelia. *Lucretia Mott.* Cambridge, Mass.: Harvard University Press, 1958.

Degler, Carl N. "Charlotte Perkins Gilman on the Theory and Practice of Feminism." *American Quarterly* 8 (1956): 21-39.

Dillon, Mary Earhart. *Frances Willard: From Prayers to Politics.* Chicago: University of Chicago Press, 1944.

Dorr, Rheta C. *Susan B. Anthony, The Woman Who Changed the Mind of a Nation.* New York: Frederick A. Stokes Co., 1928.

Flexner, Eleanor. *Century of Struggle: The Woman's Rights Movement in the United States.* Cambridge, Mass.: Harvard University Press, Belknap Press, 1959.

Freedman, Estelle. *Their Sisters' Keepers: Women's Prison Reform in America, 1830-1938.* Ann Arbor: University of Michigan Press, 1981.

Friedan, Betty. *The Feminine Mystique.* New York: Norton, 1963.

Gilman, Charlotte Perkins. *Women and Economics: A Study of the Economic Relation between Men and Women as a Factor in Social Evolution.* Boston: Small, Maynard & Co., 1898.

Gilman, Charlotte Perkins. *The Living of Charlotte Perkins Gilman, An Autobiography.* New York: D. Appleton Co., 1935.

Gilman, Charlotte Perkins. *Women and Economics: A Study of the Economic Relation between Men and Women as a Factor in Social Evolution.* Reprint. Edited by Carl N. Degler. New York: Harper & Row, 1966.

Harper, Ida Husted. *The Life and Work of Susan B. Anthony;
    including Public Addresses, Her Own Letters and Many from
    Her Contemporaries during Fifty Years.* 3 vols. Indianap-
    olis: Bowen-Merrill Co., 1898-1908.

Hill, Mary A. *Charlotte Perkins Gilman: The Making of a
    Radical Feminist, 1860-1896.* Philadelphia: Temple
    University Press, 1980.

Kraditor, Aileen, ed. *Up From the Pedestal: Selected
    Writings in the History of Feminism.* Chicago:
    Quadrangle Books, 1968.

Johnston, Johanna. *Mrs. Satan: The Incredible Saga of
    Victoria C. Woodhull.* New York: G.P. Putnam's Sons,
    1967.

Lasch, Christopher. *The New Radicalism in America, 1889-1963;
    The Intellectual as a Social Type.* New York: Knopf, 1965.

Lutz, Alma. *Created Equal: A Biography of Elizabeth Cady
    Stanton.* New York: The John Day Co., 1940.

Lutz, Alma. *Susan B. Anthony: Rebel, Crusader, Humanitarian.*
    Boston: Beacon Press, 1959.

Myrdal, Gunnar. *An American Dilemma: The Negro Problem and
    Modern Democracy.* New York: Harper & Brothers, 1944.

O'Neill, William L. *Everyone Was Brave: The Rise and Fall
    of Feminism in America.* Chicago: Quadrangle Books, 1969.

Riegel, Robert E. *American Feminists.* Lawrence: University
    of Kansas, 1963.

Scott, Anne F. *The Southern Lady: From Pedestal to Politics,
    1830-1930.* Chicago: University of Chicago Press, 1970.

Sinclair, Andrew. *The Emancipation of the American Woman.*
    New York: Harper & Row, 1966.

Stanton, Elizabeth Cady. *Eighty Years and More (1815-1897).
    Reminiscences of Elizabeth Cady Stanton.* New York:
    European Publishing Co., 1898.

Stanton, Elizabeth Cady, et al., eds. *History of Woman
    Suffrage.* 6 vols. New York: Fowler & Wells, 1881-1920.

Stern, Madeleine B. *We the Women: Career Firsts of Nineteenth-
    Century America.* New York: Schulte Publishing Co., 1963.

Suhl, Yuri. *Ernestine L. Rose and the Battle for Human Rights.* New York: Reynal, 1959.

Willard, Frances E. *Glimpses of Fifty Years: The Autobiography of an American Woman.* Boston: G.M. Smith & Co., 1889.

Willard, Frances E., and Livermore, Mary A. *Portraits and Biographies of Prominent American Women: A Comprehensive Encyclopedia of the Lives and Achievements of American Women during the Nineteenth Century.* New York: Crowell & Kirkpatrick Co., 1901.

C. Sources for the Analysis of Antifeminism

1. Nineteenth- and Twentieth-Century Women Antifeminists

When we ask why women and men were opposed to the equal-rights version of feminist thought, we ask a question which can only be answered in the total context of American society in the nineteenth and twentieth century. Most historians have considered the questions only from the perspective of the suffrage agitation, a perspective that obscures the broader social issues which moved opponents of equal status for women and of a blending of the male and female social spheres. Opponents of equal-rights feminism were drawn from a broad social spectrum ranging from the predominating Protestant denomination of Methodism with its strong western base to New England Unitarians concerned with the elevation of mankind. Male and female antisuffrage arguments departed from the same assumptions, though women and men antisuffrage writers tended to structure their arguments somewhat differently. Whether male or female, antifeminists had a stronger perception of the competitive character of American society than feminists, and as a consequence of that perception placed greater store on the supposedly altruistic sphere of the home and domestic life. Although troubled by the emerging character of American capitalism, they were staunch supporters of private property and the Protestant religion, profoundly aware of the growth and development of the socialist, communitarian experiments that represented one strand of criticism of capitalist values. Because of their wish to mitigate the consequences of unbridled economic competition, they were obliged to find some class or group within society that could be the agent of restraints of a nonsocialistic kind, and lacking the recourse of the European Tory to church and aristocracy for such a set of interests, they turned to women. Once women

were identified as the moderating force on economic individualism, it became logical to oppose the granting of equal
status with men to them, because to do so would be to put an
end to the set of social arrangements that made it possible
for women to develop perceptions and values other than those
adopted to function within the competitive world of business,
the professions, and politics. The individual of wealth and
status troubled by the emerging class divisions of nineteenth-
century America and the growth of urban poverty could reap
the benefits of the economic system, while resting assured
that altruism and concern for the victims of the system were
safely institutionalized within the female sphere of society.
Women opponents of feminism who were members of or identified
with eastern elites and who exercised influence through women's
supposed responsibility for social uplift had some political
insight through their experience of influence and opposed the
suffrage from the correct perception that the vote alone was
not the key to political power. Thus a Dorothea Dix or a
Sarah Josepha Hale, whose careers were built out of the exploitation of women's separate sphere, could argue that women
would lose power through insisting on equal political rights
with men. A broader segment of society fell within the evangelical culture opposed to change in the nature of the family
and its links to other social or political institutions. The
drive to segregate the home from corrupting economic or political forces was linked to a conservative version of Methodist
perfectionism stressing the Christian home as the source of
conversion and moral perfection. This large constituency
could be mobilized to protect the home and counter the equal-
rights variant of feminism because of the well-founded perception that equality meant abandonment of the double standard in sexual morality and equal access to divorce for
women. Women who were opposed to equal-rights feminism could
be in favor of enhanced authority for women within their
sphere and might support the suffrage on this ground. However, they assumed that the differences between male and
female which were of importance went far beyond biology, and
that these differences in temperament and morality, far from
being gender-linked, were the product of different social
function and separate social territory. Some anti-equal-
rights women could see merit in expressing those social differences within the polity, so that the perceptions of women
derived from their separate sphere could affect legislation,
while others with a vested interest in women's use of "influence" were opposed to the vote.
     Women's polemical writing opposed to equal-rights feminism
was reactive in character and basically repetitive in every
period of opposition to new facets of the movement for women's

rights. Thus we may see in Hannah Mather Crocker's *Observations on the Real Rights of Women, with Their Appropriate
Duties, Agreeable to Scripture, Reason and Common Sense* (1818)
a polemic prompted by the French Revolutionary debate about
the rights of women and the dissemination of Mary Wollstonecraft's writing in the United States. Crocker's argument
links scriptural justification for women's subordination with
natural law and exhibits the distrust of European aristocratic
mores characteristic of the early national period. Crocker
saw the family as the key institution for maintaining Republican values and clearly expected women to exercise greater
social influence from within it. Catharine Beecher's pamphlets
opposing the role assumed by women within the antislavery
movement and drawing attention to the declining health of
American women may be seen as polemics designed to assert the
importance of the family and the domestic sphere and to improve
women's position for influence within their appropriate
sphere. Lydia Sigourney's *Letters to Mothers* (1838) illustrates the same stress on the sacredness of the family as
the source of saving grace for the young, while Mrs. Little's
essay in the second volume of *The Ladies Wreath* (1848-1849)
was prompted by the plans for and the publicity provoked by
the first women's-rights convention at Seneca Falls. Crocker,
Beecher, Sigourney, and Little all stressed the importance of
women's separate sphere, predicted serious social problems if
it were not maintained as a vital and effective part of the
social system, and opposed the idea of equal rights for women
on the ground that women's special characteristics would dis-
appear were they to enter the world on equal terms with men.
The next stage in the argument was prompted by the movement
for easier divorce for women, a movement which, as William L.
O'Neill has pointed out in his *Divorce in the Progressive
Era* (1967), drew on the ideas of European marriage reformers
rather than on the native American impulses fostering Progressivism. Margaret Lee's novel *Divorce* (1882) and her essay
of 1890 published in the *North American Review* suggest that
the female capacity for self-sacrifice and altruism would
be totally eroded were women to seek individual happiness
and sexual fulfillment in marriage on the same terms as
men. Lee's novel introduces a theme frequently used by
male antifeminist writers but rarely by women, suggesting
that men will be unsexed by women who claim the rights of
equal partners. The final torrent of anti-equal-rights-
feminist writing was prompted by the last phase of the suffrage agitation when the press was systematically exploited
as a vehicle for the national suffrage movement. The case
made against the suffrage by writers such as Mariana Van
Rensselaer in *Should We Ask for the Suffrage?* (1895), Grace

Goodwin in *Anti-Suffrage: Ten Good Reasons* (1912), and Helen
Kendrick Johnson in her *Woman and the Republic* (1909) was
that women possessed greater power to affect society through
influence, that participation in politics on the same terms
as men would deprive women of their special talent to criticize
and improve a selfish and highly acquisitive society, and
that women being inferior to men in strength could not participate in police and military service without being unsexed.
By 1917 Mrs. James Wadsworth, President of the National Association Opposed to Woman Suffrage, was carrying arguments
about military service and loyalty to the state further by
impugning the loyalty of feminists who opposed Wilson's entry
into World War I. There has been only one book-length study
of the antisuffrage movement devoted to the analysis of the
Massachusetts Association Opposed to Women's Suffrage. Jane
Camhi, in *Women Against Women: American Antisuffragism 1880-
1920* (1974), draws attention to a high proportion of Catholic
women in the Association and to the direct encouragement given
by the Catholic hierarchy to women's participation in organizations opposed to the suffrage. While this was true of the
urban northeast, the participation of equally high concentra-
tions of Methodist women in antisuffrage activities may be
documented in the midwest. Camhi concludes that the movement
was well organized, effectively led and possibly more consistent in argumentation than the suffrage movement. Unlike the
suffrage forces, the antisuffrage movement could link up with
a strong working-class constituency through the Catholic and
Methodist organizations for women which could disseminate
anti-equal-rights opinions. Thus it is not difficult to
understand why the suffrage amendment was so long delayed and
the equal-rights movement of the 1920s was unsuccessful.

There are many unanswered questions about the nature of
opposition to the equal-rights feminists. We do not know
the exact social profile of persons who saw the need for
restraints on acquisitiveness built into the social structure. We do not know why the equal-rights feminists utterly
failed to address the problem which prompted opposition to
the equal-rights position. Because we have no collective
biography of male or female, anti-equal-rights feminists, we
do not know what the gender groups had in common besides this
political stance.

BIBLIOGRAPHY

Nineteenth Century

Beecher, Catharine E. *An Essay on Slavery and Abolitionism,
    with Reference to the Duty of American Females.* Boston:
    Perkins & Marvin, 1837.

Beecher, Catharine E. *The Evils Suffered by American Women and American Children: The Causes and the Remedy.* New York: Harper & Brothers, 1846.

Crocker, Hannah Mather. *Observations on the Real Rights of Women, with Their Appropriate Duties, Agreeable to Scripture, Reason and Common Sense.* Boston: printed for the author, 1818.

Hale, Sarah Josepha. *Woman's Record: Or, Sketches of All Distinguished Women From the Beginning till A.D. 1850.* New York: Harper & Brothers, 1853.

Lee, Margaret. *Divorce.* New York: J.W. Lovell Co., 1882.

Lee, Margaret. "Final Words on Divorce." *North American Review* 150 (1890):236-264.

Little, Mrs. E. "What are the Rights of Women?" *Ladies Wreath* 2 (1848-1849):133-138.

Sigourney, Lydia H. *Letters to Mothers.* Hartford, Conn.: Hudson & Skinner, 1838.

Van Rensselaer, Mariana (Griswold). *Should We Ask for the Suffrage?* New York: De Vinne Press, 1895.

Twentieth Century

Camhi, Jane. *Women Against Women: American Antisuffragism 1880-1920.* Medford, Mass.: Tufts University, 1974.

Goodwin, Grace. *Anti-Suffrage: Ten Good Reasons.* New York: Duddfield & Co., 1913.

Haien, J.A., ed. *Anti-Suffrage Essays, by Massachusetts Women.* Boston: Forum Publications of Boston, 1916.

Johnson, Helen K. *Woman and the Republic: A Survey of the Woman-Suffrage Movement in the United States and a Discussion of the Claims and Arguments of its Foremost Advocates.* New York: National League for the Civic Education of Women, 1909.

Johnson, Rossiter. *Helen Kendrick Johnson, the Story of Her Varied Activities.* New York: Publishers Printing Co., 1917.

Massachusetts Association Opposed to the Further Extension of
    Suffrage to Women. *Why Women Do Not Want the Ballot.*
    3 vols. Massachusetts State Library, 1900-1914.

O'Neill, William. *Divorce in the Progressive Era.* New Haven:
    Yale University Press, 1967.

"Suffrage Appeals to Lawless and Hysterical Women." An inter-
    view with Helen K. Johnson in the *New York Times,*
    30 March 1913.

Wadsworth, Mrs. James W., Jr. "Case Against Suffrage,"
    New York Times Magazine, 9 September 1917.

2. Male Antisuffragist Writing

The male opponents of equal-rights feminism showed the
same concern with competition and the need to control acquisitive drives as women opposed to equal-rights feminism. However, male polemicists certainly placed greater stress on
gender-linked characteristics than did women antifeminists.
Thus they worried on one hand about women going into labor
while making political speeches and on the other about
whether gender characteristics might be undermined by equal
rights, so that a society which accorded men and women the
same rights within political and economic spheres might lose
the heterosexual bonding which established the family in the
domestic sphere. These worries were expressed by Joel Foster
in *The Duties of a Conjugal State* (1800), Thomas R. Dew in
his "Dissertation on the Characteristic Differences Between
the Sexes, and on the Position and Influence of Women in Society" (1835), Daniel Smith in his collection of essays on moral
and ethical questions relating to marriage entitled *Lectures on
Domestic Duties* (1837), and in the speeches and essays of
Daniel Webster (see especially "Remarks to the Ladies of
Richmond," October 5, 1840 in *The Writings and Speeches of
Daniel Webster,* Vol. 3 (1903) and Noah Webster's writing on
morals and politics (see Noah Webster, *A Collection of Papers
on Political, Literary and Moral Subjects* (1843). Before
the publication of Darwin's *Origin of Species* (1859),* concerns about the variability of gender characteristics were
based upon notions of environmentalism and natural law, but
after the systematic explanation of variability as essential

*Charles Darwin. *On the Origin of Species by Means of Natural
    Selection* (London: J. Murray, 1859).

to natural selection and the positive direction of variation as a function of mate selection, gender and mating came to have a new and emotion-laden significance for male critics of equal-rights feminism.

We may see the different tone and structure of argumentation used by antifeminists as a result of Darwin's influence by comparing Thomas Wentworth Higginson's *Woman and Her Wishes, an Essay: Inscribed to the Massachusetts Constitutional Convention* (1853) and the same author's *Common Sense About Women* in its 1882 version. While the first work argued that women could not discharge both domestic and political duties without reduced efficiency in both, the second argued that progress would be endangered to the degree that women left their biologically ordained sphere. Horace Bushnell's influential writing on the home and women's function as the agent of salvation within it are fine examples of the blending of evangelical ideas about the home as the source of Christian conversion and evolutionary ideas about the significance of gender. In *Christian Nurture* (1861) Bushnell explains the importance of home and maternal influence on the development of the child's moral and spiritual character. By 1869, when Bushnell wrote his specific critique of the movement for women's rights, he called it *Women's Suffrage: The Reform Against Nature* and based his opposition to the suffrage for women on the grounds that men and women possessed distinct mental and moral characteristics based upon their physiological differences. These could be ignored only at the peril of social chaos, for it was through subordination that women acquired the traits necessary to make them self-sacrificing and altruistic mothers. Horace Greeley's views on the indissolubility of marriage likewise rest on the belief that the two sexes are biologically different in mental and moral qualities so that their mutual dependence will provide the stable family unit necessary for social order.

Goldwin Smith's "Woman Suffrage" in *Essays on Questions of the Day* (1893) anticipates most of the male antifeminist views of the twentieth century. Thus Smith argues for a privileged position for women to protect them from the pressures of economic competition and political life in order that they may exercise a civilizing influence on society through the family. Smith suggests in his argument that women in fact like their subordination and would not be psychologically fulfilled by equality. These two themes, the need to protect women in the interests of the family and the supposed psychological need of a woman to bond with a dominant male, are further developed in the writing of Lyman Abbott, Richard Barry, and James M. Buckley. In *The Wrong*

and Peril of Woman Suffrage (1909), Buckley suggests that
women who want the vote and equality with men may be frigid
sexually and unable to gain psychological satisfaction from
"normal" sex roles. Benjamin V. Hubbard revealed the oppo-
site pole of this view in *Socialism, Feminism and Suffragism,
The Terrible Triplet, Connected by the Same Umbilical Cord,
and Fed from the Same Nursing Bottle* (1915) by arguing that
women interested in equality with men were only interested in
equality for sexual freedom and escape from the monogamous
family. These male depictions of the equal-rights feminist
as sexually deviant were reinforced by the popularization of
Freudian thought after 1909 and male critiques of feminism
became progressively more Freudian thereafter. When it is
clear that the two major intellectual influences of late nine-
teenth- and early twentieth-century America, Darwin and Freud,
were appropriated as authorities for the anti-equal-rights
position, why this appropriation was not challenged by equal-
rights feminists becomes of particular interest. We need to
understand better why proponents of the equal-rights position
structured their arguments the way they did and why they did
not tackle the opposition on its own ground. We shall see
later that proponents of the enhanced-authority view of the
woman question did argue from a Darwinian standpoint, though
they also ignored the dangers of the reductive view of the
female popularized by Freud's American followers.

BIBLIOGRAPHY

Abbott, Lyman. "Why Women Do Not Wish the Suffrage." *Atlantic
Monthly,* September 1903, 289-296.

Barry, Richard. "Why Women Oppose Woman's Suffrage." *Pearson's Magazine,* February-March 1903.

Bernbaum, E., ed. *Anti-Suffrage Essays, by Massachusetts
Women.* Boston: J.A. Haien, 1916.

Buckley, James M. *The Wrong and Peril of Woman Suffrage.*
New York: F.H. Revell Co., 1909.

Bushnell, Horace. *Christian Nurture.* New York: Charles
Scribner, 1861.

Bushnell, Horace. *Women's Suffrage; The Reform Against
Nature.* New York: Charles Scribner, 1869.

Dew, Thomas R. "Dissertation on the Characteristic Differences Between the Sexes, and on the Position and Influence of Women in Society." *Southern Literary Messenger*
1 (1835):493-512.

Foster, Joel. *The Duties of a Conjugal State.* Stonington-
     Port, Conn.: printed by Samuel Trumbull, 1800.

Greeley, Horace. "Marriage and Divorce. A Discussion be-
     tween Horace Greeley and Robert Dale Owen." Greeley,
     Horace. *Recollections of a Busy Life.* New York:
     J.B. Ford & Co., 1868.

Higginson, Thomas W. *Woman and Her Wishes, an Essay: In-
     scribed to the Massachusetts Constitutional Convention.*
     Boston: R.F. Wallcut, 1853.

Higginson, Thomas W. *Common Sense About Women.* Boston:
     Lee & Shephard, 1882.

Hubbard, Benjamin V. *Socialism, Feminism and Suffragism,
     The Terrible Triplets, Connected by the Same Umbilical
     Cord, and Fed From the Same Nursing Bottle.* Chicago:
     American Publishing Co., 1915.

Price, Eli K. *Discourse on the Family as an Element of
     Government.* Philadelphia: Caxton Press of C. Sherman
     Son & Co., 1864.

Smith, Daniel D. *Lectures on Domestic Duties.* Portland:
     S.H. Colesworthy, 1837.

Smith, Goldwin. "Woman Suffrage." *Essays on Questions of
     the Day, Political and Social.* New York: Macmillan Co.,
     1893.

Webster, Daniel. "Remarks to the Ladies of Richmond, Octo-
     ber 5, 1840." In *The Writings and Speeches of Daniel
     Webster.* 18 vols. Boston: Little, Brown, & Co., 1903.

Webster, Noah. *A Collection of Papers on Political, Literary
     and Moral Subjects.* New York: Webster & Clark, 1843.

D. The Battle for the Vote:
Sources and Historical Analysis

The volume of the sources on the battle for the suffrage
explains why the suffrage movement has taken center stage in
the history of American women's political life, though an
equally powerful political movement organized by women opponents of the suffrage was extremely effective for more
than forty years. The leaders of the prosuffrage forces

knew they were making history and left an unusually rich crop
of autobiographies after them. Many were the subject of biographies written by associates who had begun collecting biographical material while the movement was under their leadership. Thus it is not surprising that their point of view on
the reasons why the battle was prolonged and the nature of
the forces ranged against them should have been enshrined in
history. The annual ritual of the Senate hearings on women
suffrage provided a rich record of testimony on the issue, and
this is supplemented by the four histories of the movement
written by participants.

By contrast there are no scholarly biographies of the
leading women opponents of the suffrage, though we do have
several short eulogistic accounts of their work written by
family members. Even a standard historical work concerned
with the rise and decline of feminist sentiments in early
twentieth-century America, William L. O'Neill's *Everyone Was
Brave: The Rise and Fall of Feminism in America* (1969), concentrates on analyzing the nature and leadership of feminist
organizations, although the collapse of the movement might
well be analyzed in terms of its organized opposition. Until
this oversight is corrected and we know as much about the
leadership, support and tactics of the antisuffrage forces as
we now do about the National American Women Suffrage Association and the American Woman Suffrage Association, we will not
understand the nature of the "victory" they won. Historians
have long puzzled about the collapse of most equal-rights
feminist organizations in the aftermath of the suffrage victory. In order to understand why this happened, we need to
know whether the forces opposed to equal-rights feminism
merely changed tactics and shifted their attention to other
types of opposition to equal rights in the period from 1915
to 1919. We have no clear idea of the directions taken by
antisuffrage organizations after 1919 except for the successful D.A.R. attempt to brand leading feminists as unpatriotic
tools of Bolshevism. In short, we should not assume that the
successful passage of the suffrage amendment represented the
defeat of the opponents on more than a small tactical front.

The autobiographies of the prosuffrage leaders illustrate
the movement's leadership at every stage in the development
of the organization. Harriot K. Hunt's memoir *Glances and
Glimpses* (1856) is an excellent source for understanding the
early stages of the movement and the shaping influence of the
abolition movement on early ideas about women's political
rights in America. Dexter C. Bloomer's *Life and Writings of
Amelia Bloomer* (1895) contains sufficient material of an
autobiographical nature to establish why dress reform seemed
such an important component of the movement in its early

stages. It is also an invaluable source illustrating the inability of the early suffrage leaders to anticipate how their
actions would be perceived by the general public and represented by their opponents. Mary A. Livermore, *The Story of
My Life* (1897) and Belle Kearney, *A Slaveholder's Daughter*
(1900) are excellent sources for the growth of the suffrage
movement outside New England.

Jane Addams' two volumes of autobiography, *Twenty Years
at Hull House* (1910) and *The Second Twenty Years at Hull
House* (1930), introduce the reader to a second generation of
women concerned about the suffrage for reasons quite different from those originally prompted by the abolition movement.
Born during and just after the Civil War, this generation
sought political rights in order to act effectively on women's
perceptions of the problems of the city and industrial society, and most of them lacked the passionate commitment to
equality for the freed Negro that had inspired their predecessors. Olympia Brown Willis' *Acquaintances Old and New,
Among Reformers* (1911) provides valuable insight into the
interlocking network of women's reform organizations that
virtually offered career paths to those ready to commit their
life to staff roles within the reform movement. Anna Howard
Shaw's *The Story of a Pioneer* (1915) documents the process by
which the vote for women became an end in itself, and the victorious suffrage organization was built without reference to
an agreement about a program to be sought by women voters.
Doris Stevens' *Jailed for Freedom* (1920) offers the best insight available in published form to the thinking of women
who became radical suffragists and became proponents of
direct action to secure the vote. Charlotte Perkins Gilman's
The Living of Charlotte Perkins Gilman (1935) documents the
development of a feminist analysis of the range of political
and economic change which must accompany the vote if the
social goals of feminist reformers were to be achieved.

The tone and structure of these autobiographies is so
similar that they become almost a genre of their own. The
standard form of the suffrage autobiography describes the
influences of childhood and the events leading to an awakening about the limitations placed on women as citizens; involvement in prosuffrage organizations follows the awakening,
and the remainder of the autobiography describes the joys and
disappointments of campaigning, the in-fighting of various
wings of the suffrage movement, the hecklers silenced, and
the progress made in the span of a single lifetime. In most
instances the narratives are remarkable for their lack of
analysis of the full extent of the "woman problem" and hence
show little comprehension of the barriers to political participation still to be surmounted after the suffrage was won.

Two notable exceptions to this pattern are the narratives of
Jane Addams and Charlotte Perkins Gilman. Addams understood
the extent of class and ethnic conflict in the United States
and appreciated the complicated workings of the urban political machine; she had experienced for herself the bitter
hostility directed toward women who were active in politics
as well as in good works. When writing the first volume of
her autobiography, she believed that enfranchised women would
be the political constituency which would support the woman
reformer in politics. By 1930 she had experienced a decade
of intense criticism of her pacifism, much of it voiced by
the same women's organizations with which she had worked on
urban reform. This led her to a troubled but unfocused recognition of the effectiveness with which opponents of women's
political participation could use the Freudian critique of
the woman in search of power. Gilman, because of her understanding of the relationships between economic and psychological dependence, recognized the difference between political
rights and the inner capacity to use them effectively within
the framework of elective politics.

The twenties saw the first biographies of suffrage leaders,
though this was not a subject for the popular reader or the
scholarly historian. Sophonisba P. Breckinridge, herself an
ardent supporter of the franchise for women, wrote a biography
of a family member recording Madeline McDowell Breckenridge's
attempts to support the franchise for women in the hostile
environment of the south. This volume, part of the general
interest in the modernizing south, *Madeline McDowell Breckinridge: A Leader in the New South* (1921), is a scholarly work
by an able social scientist on the faculty of the University
of Chicago's School of Social Service Administration. The
same cannot be said of the other major biography of the twenties, Emanie Sachs' *"The Terrible Siren," Victoria Woodhull
(1838-1927)* (1928), published the year after Woodhull's death.
The sensational aspects of Woodhull's career and much of the
myth surrounding a born publicist are recounted, and the pro-
suffragist belief that Woodhull's celebrated avowal of belief
in free love discredited the suffrage movement is given full
credence. While this assessment has been repeated by later
biographers of Woodhull, its acceptance must be taken as indicative of the inability of prosuffrage writers to understand the extent to which religious and social Darwinist
ideas lent support to the anti-position. In the 1940s
two long studies of the major leaders of the winning phase
of the suffrage movement were published. Katherine Devereux
Blake, in her study of her mother, *Champion of Women: The
Life of Lillie Devereux Blake* (1943), inevitably finds it
difficult to strike a balance between family pride and

assessment of Blake's leadership. Mary Gray Peck's *Carrie Chapman Catt* (1944), while crammed with detail and firsthand information, is inevitably partisan since Peck began collecting papers and letters from Catt some three decades before the work was published in order to do justice to her life.
    Clavia Goodman's *Bitter Harvest: Laura Clay's Suffrage Work* (1946) may be seen as the first work of relative historical detachment chronicling the life of a suffrage leader and attempting to weigh the relative contributions of different figures to the cause. Edith Finch's *Carey Thomas of Bryn Mawr* (1947) and Madeline B. Stern's *Purple Passage: The Life of Mrs. Frank Leslie* (1953) are similar works which attempt some criticism and analysis of the role of their subjects in the suffrage movement. 1967 saw the publication of two studies of Victoria Woodhull, both responsive to the new wave of feminism and the claims of the movement for women's liberation. M.M. Marberry's *Vicky: A Biography of Victoria C. Woodhull* (1967) attempts to fathom the character and intellectual development of Woodhull, while Johanna Johnston's *Mrs. Satan: The Incredible Saga of Victoria C. Woodhull* (1967) directs more attention to public perceptions of Woodhull's career.
    None of the biographies pays serious attention to theoretical considerations, such as where the subject might be placed in a typology of women reformers or what family and social forces may be identified as radicalizing for a Woodhull but not present in the melioristic career of a Carrie Chapman Catt. Links to international reform forces are frequently recounted but without reference to mobility and the experience of travel in raising consciousness. Clearly prosopographical studies of both pro- and antifeminist leaders are needed before we can make further advances in analysis of the movement, its outcome, and the nature of its leadership.
    The contemporary chroniclers of the movement displayed much the same inability to understand its opponents as did its leaders in writing their autobiographies. Paulina Wright Davis' *A History of the National Women's Rights Movement for Twenty Years, from 1850 to 1870* (1871) is valuable for its description of early recruitment into the movement and early assumptions about the need for the suffrage to affect change. Elizabeth Cady Stanton's major six-volume history, completed over several decades with the assistance of all the major figures in the movement, suffers in focus from the multiple authorship and repeats the suffrage leaders' perception that their opponents were wicked plotters rather than representatives of an opposing ideology and accompanying political program. Frances M. Bjorkman's *Woman Suffrage: History, Arguments and Results* (1913) is more of a campaign document designed to refute antisuffrage views of the consequences of

votes for women than a reasoned and detached history, but it
is nonetheless valuable for its conciseness and accuracy
about the struggle to that date. Floyd Dell's *Women as World
Builders: Studies in Modern Feminism* (1913) is a paean to the
social benefits to be anticipated as a consequence of women's
equal participation in politics with men. It has the tone of
the zealous convert, and it is noteworthy as one of the few
outspoken works favoring equal-rights feminism written by a
male. Dell's involvement in radical circles in New York was
shortly to lead him into psychoanalysis and antifeminist
views, but though brief, his period of support for the goals
of feminism is important, and his 1913 essays are an admirable
summary of the ideas that made men like Dell and Max Eastman
feminists.

After this initial wave of historical writing, the subject
attracted little attention until the 1950s when the high point
was reached in American confidence that the United States
model was the path along which all developing societies would
move until they reached the relatively perfected democracy to
be found in an economically expansive and politically stable
United States. The foundation of the United Nations gave an
international perspective to questions about the status of
women and prompted the research reported in Maurice Duverger's
The Political Role of Women sponsored by UNESCO and published
in 1955. Duverger's work was the first to attempt to analyze
in comparative terms what use women actually made of the right
to vote. His conclusions drew attention to the relatively
modest political participation of American women compared with
the British, European, or Asian counterparts who possessed
the suffrage. Marion K. Sanders' *The Lady and the Vote* (1956)
attempted to analyze the voting behavior of American women
since 1919 and raised important questions about whether women
behave differently or comparably with males of the same class
and economic background. Duverger and Sanders drew attention
to the modest, if not lackluster, success of women in participation beyond the level of the polling booth, and their
work was followed by studies of the ideas which eventually
proved persuasive in the suffrage movement. Both Aileen
Kraditor's *The Ideas of the Woman Suffrage Movement* (1965)
and Alan P. Grimes' *The Puritan Ethic and Woman Suffrage*
(1967) drew attention to the illiberal and expedient arguments that finally won support for votes for women. Kraditor's collection of documents illustrating the change
from the early argument for rights for women as human beings, arguments inherited from the eighteenth century, to
the successful propaganda arguing for votes for women to
counteract the influence of blacks and immigrants in the
polity is accompanied by incisive comment on the progression

from natural-rights ideology to valueless pragmatism. William
L. O'Neill's *Everyone Was Brave: The Rise and Fall of Feminism
in America* (1969) directed further attention to the failure
of American women to make use of the political rights so ener-
getically sought and to the decline of most feminist organizations in both impact and membership in the 1920s. O'Neill
attributed some of this decline to styles of leadership and
to the self-defeating terms on which the vote had been sought.
His distinction between suffragists for whom the vote was
paramount and social feminists for whom the vote was secondary
to a wide range of social-reform goals drew attention to an
important division within the suffrage ranks, but his analysis
did not go beyond the prosuffrage forces to consider the styles
of leadership and power to draw members of antisuffrage organizations. Kirsten Amundsen's *The Silenced Majority: Women
and American Democracy* (1971) continued the analysis of voting behavior begun by Duverger and Sanders and documented
more fully the extent to which women experienced difficulty
in rising within the ranks of party organizations or in securing backing for political campaigns. William Chafe's *The
American Woman: Her Changing Social, Economic and Political
Roles, 1920-1970* (1972) supplied the context of social attitude, access to work, and experience of discrimination through
which to interpret the trends in political behavior produced
by the analysis of women's voting patterns since 1919. Chafe's
1978 extended essay *Women and Equality* analyzed for the first
time the ramifications of the problem of equality as a goal
for women and pointed out the degree of interaction between
economic, political, and social spheres within the social
system so that equal rights in one sphere may be negated in
another. Maren L. Carden's *The Feminist Movement* (1974)
traced the stages by which the resurgent feminist movement
of the 1970s developed, and the new sophistication of its
position on the interaction of social and political institutions.
Susan and Martin Tolchin's *Clout: Womanpower and Politics*
(1974) corrected the balance of earlier writing by identifying some of the successes of women's political action beyond
the suffrage movement and the national impact of the lobbying
efforts of the feminist social reformers. Ellen Carol DuBois'
*Feminism and Suffrage: The Emergence of an Independent Women's
Movement in America, 1848-1869* (1978) attempts to put the
early defeats and the divisions within the suffrage movement
into context. In DuBois' view the experience of organizing
and directing a political movement led by women with goals
of exclusive concern to women was in itself a transforming
experience giving to leaders and followers alike the awareness that women could act to change their position. This she
sees as more important than the normal factionalism of reform

movements that the suffrage movement like any other possessed
in good measure. Sandra Baxter and Marjorie Lansing in *Women
and Politics: The Invisible Majority* (1980) review the literature on the study of women's political behavior written
since 1919 and raise important theoretical questions about
the way we build theories concerning woman as a political
animal. In particular, they cite Susan Bourque and Jean
Grossholtz, "Politics as an Unnatural Practice: Political
Science Looks at Female Participation" (1974), which identifies some key assumptions of modern political science that
tend to make studies of women's political organizations identify women's political functioning as defective because the
assumed norm of such behavior is the standard male pattern.
Susan Moller Okin discusses this problem with respect to the
history of political theory in a provocative introduction
and conclusion to a book of selected readings in political
theory entitled *Women in Western Political Thought* (1979).
The question with which she opens and concludes her discussion is whether we may simply add women to the sum total of
"mankind" dealt with in classical political theory when almost every such theory from Aristotle up to the feminist
John Stuart Mill was built upon the assumption of female
subordination.

     Such questions make it all the more important to return
to the basic documents written by women about their view of
politics as a sphere of action for women, and in the absence
of clear statements of abstract theory from our sources, attempt to deduce the theoretical models of the political process with which the early feminists and suffragists worked.
In this respect, Lillie Devereux Blake's *Woman's Place To-day*
(1883) and *A Daring Experiment, and Other Stories* (1892), Jane
Addams' *The Modern City and the Municipal Franchise* (1906),
Elizabeth Cady Stanton et al., *History of Woman Suffrage*
(1881-1920), Stanton et al., *The Woman's Bible* (1895-1898),
and Julia Jessie Taft's *The Woman Movement from the Point of
View of Social Consciousness* (1915) are invaluable starting
points. Carrie Chapman Catt and Nettie Rogers Shuler's
Woman Suffrage and Politics (1923) is also an important
source. Catt does not have the sense of politics as a con-
test in which two contending teams vie for the prize. She
could only discern dishonest and evil motives in her opponents,
and she could never have seen politics as the avocation of
homo ludens.* Only further research will clarify her view of
woman as a political animal. Many suffrage workers did see

*See Johan Huizuiga. *Homo Ludens: A Study of the Play Element
    in Culture* (London: Routledge & Kegan Paul, 1949).

the addition of women to the voting population as merely incremental to the sum of male voters, but others, such as Jane Addams, had a vision of a new kind of urban *polis* in which the woman voter would play a new and different role from men. The student would do well to begin with the writing of Addams on the municipal franchise since she and other urban reformers did not hark back to the Declaration of Independence and the Revolution for their claim to the vote for women in urban politics, but looked forward to the new kind of urban polity they could see developing in the modern American city. The theme of the municipal franchise was treated mainly in the press and contemporary periodicals, and the significant publications on this subject are cited in Albert Krichmar, *The Women's Rights Movement in the United States, 1848-1970: A Bibliography and Sourcebook* (1972). The subject is also fully discussed in Mary Jo Buhle and Paul Buhle's *The Concise History of Women's Suffrage* (1974).

BIBLIOGRAPHY

Addams, Jane. *The Modern City and the Municipal Franchise for Women*. Warren, Ohio: National American Woman Suffrage Association, 1906.

Addams, Jane. *Twenty Years at Hull House*. New York: Macmillan Co., 1910.

Addams, Jane. *The Second Twenty Years at Hull House*. New York: Macmillan Co., 1930.

Addams, Jane. *Jane Addams: A Centennial Reader*. New York: Macmillan Co., 1960.

Amundsen, Kirsten. *The Silenced Majority: Women and American Democracy*. Englewood Cliffs, N.J.: Prentice-Hall, 1971.

Annals of the American Academy of Political and Social Science: Significance of the Woman Suffrage Movement. Supplement. Philadelphia: American Academy of Political and Social Science, 1910.

Baxter, Sandra, and Lansing, Marjorie. *Women and Politics: The Invisible Majority*. Ann Arbor: University of Michigan Press, 1980.

Bjorkman, Frances M., ed. *Woman Suffrage; History, Arguments and Results*. New York: National American Woman Suffrage Association, 1913.

Blake, Katherine Devereux. *Champion of Women: The Life of Lillie Devereux Blake*. New York: Fleming H. Revell Co., 1943.

Blake, Lillie Devereux. *Fettered for Life; or, Lord and Master*. New York: Sheldon & Co., 1874.

Blake, Lillie Devereux. *Woman's Place To-day*. New York: J.W. Lovell Co., 1883.

Blake, Lillie Devereux. *A Daring Experiment, and Other Stories*. New York: Lovell, Coryell & Co., 1892.

Blatch, Harriet Stanton, and Lutz, Alma. *Challenging Years: The Memoirs of Harriet Stanton Blatch*. New York: G.P. Putnam's Sons, 1940.

Bloomer, Dexter C. *Life and Writings of Amelia Bloomer*. Boston: Arena Publishing Co., 1895.

Bourque, Susan, and Grosshaltz, Jean. "Politics as an Unnatural Practice: Political Science Looks at Female Participation." *Politics and Society* 4 (1974):255-266.

Breckinridge, Sophonisba P. *Madeline McDowell Breckinridge: A Leader in the New South*. Chicago: University of Chicago Press, 1921.

Buhle, Mary Jo, and Buhle, Paul. *The Concise History of Women's Suffrage*. New York: Russell Sage Foundation, 1974.

Carden, Maren L. *The Feminist Movement*. Urbana: University of Illinois Press, 1974.

Catt, Carrie Chapman, and Shuler, Nettie Rogers. *Woman Suffrage and Politics: The Inner Story of the Suffrage Movement*. New York: Charles Scribner's Sons, 1923.

Chafe, William. *The American Woman: Her Changing Social, Economic and Political Roles, 1920-1970*. New York: Oxford University Press, 1972.

Chafe, William. *Women and Equality: Changing Patterns in American Culture*. New York: Oxford University Press, 1978.

Cheney, Ednah Dow. *Reminiscences of Ednah Dow Cheney.* Boston: Lee & Shepard, 1902.

Davis, Paulina Wright. *A History of the National Women's Rights Movement for Twenty Years, from 1850-1870.* New York: Journeymen Printers' Co-operative Association, 1871.

Dell, Floyd. *Women as World Builders: Studies in Modern Feminism.* Chicago: Forbes & Co., 1913.

Duniway, Abigail Scott. *Path Breaking: An Autobiographical History of the Equal Suffrage Movement in Pacific Coast States.* Portland, Ore.: James, Kerns, & Abbot Co., 1914.

DuBois, Ellen Carol. *Feminism and Suffrage: The Emergence of an Independent Women's Movement in America, 1848-1869.* Ithaca, N.Y.: Cornell University Press, 1978.

Duverger, Maurice. *The Political Role of Women.* Paris: UNESCO, 1955.

Finch, Edith. *Carey Thomas of Bryn Mawr.* New York: Harper, 1947.

Gambone, Joseph G. "The Forgotten Feminist of Kansas: The Papers of Clarina I.H. Nichols, 1854-1885," *Kansas Historical Quarterly 39 (1973):12-57.*

Gilman, Charlotte Perkins. *The Living of Charlotte Perkins Gilman, An Autobiography.* New York: D. Appleton-Century Co., Inc., 1935.

Goodman, Clavia. *Bitter Harvest: Laura Clay's Suffrage Work.* Lexington, Ky.: Bur Press, 1946.

Grimes, Alan P. *The Puritan Ethic and Woman Suffrage.* New York: Oxford University Press, 1967.

Harper, Ida H. *The Life and Work of Susan B. Anthony.* 3 vols. Indianapolis and Kansas City: Bowen-Merrill Co., 1898-1908.

Havemeyer, Louisine W. *Sixteen to Sixty: Memoirs of a Collector.* New York: Metropolitan Museum of Art, 1961.

Hunt, Harriot K. *Glances and Glimpses; or, Fifty Years Social, including Twenty Years of Professional Life.* New York: Sheldon, Lamport & Blakeman, 1856.

Johnson, Kenneth R. "Kate Gordon and the Woman Suffrage Movement in the South," *Journal of Southern History* 38 (1972):365-392.

Johnston, Johanna. *Mrs. Satan: The Incredible Saga of Victoria C. Woodhull.* New York: G.P. Putnam's Sons, 1967.

Kearney, Belle. *A Slaveholder's Daughter.* New York: The Abbey Press, 1900.

Kraditor, Aileen. *The Ideas of the Woman Suffrage Movement, 1890-1920.* New York: Columbia University Press, 1965.

Kraditor, Aileen. *Up From the Pedestal: Selected Writings in the History of American Feminism.* Chicago: Quadrangle Books, 1968.

Krichmar, Albert. *The Women's Rights Movement in the United States, 1848-1970: A Bibliography and Sourcebook.* Metuchen, N.J.: Scarecrow Press, 1972.

Lasch, Christopher. *The New Radicalism in America, 1889-1963: The Intellectual as a Social Type.* New York: Alfred A. Knopf, 1965.

Livermore, Mary A. *The Story of My Life; or, The Sunshine and Shadow of Seventy Years.* Hartford, Conn.: Worthington, 1897.

Mann, Arthur. *Yankee Reformers in the Urban Age.* Cambridge, Mass.: Harvard University Press, Belknap Press, 1954.

Marberry, M.M. *Vicky: A Biography of Victoria C. Woodhull.* New York: Funk & Wagnalls, 1967.

Nathan, Maude. *Once Upon a Time and Today.* New York: G.P. Putnam's Sons, 1933.

Okin, Susan Moller. *Women in Western Political Thought.* Princeton, N.J.: Princeton University Press, 1979.

O'Neill, William L. *Everyone Was Brave: The Rise and Fall of Feminism in America.* Chicago: Quadrangle Books, 1969.

Peck, Mary Gray. *Carrie Chapman Catt: A Biography*. New York: H. Wilson Co., 1944.

Sachs, Emanie. *"The Terrible Siren," Victoria Woodhull (1838-1927)*. New York: Harper & Brothers, 1924.

Sanders, Marion K. *The Lady and The Vote*. Boston: Houghton Mifflin Co., 1956.

Scott, Anne Firor. *The Southern Lady: From Pedestal to Politics, 1830-1930*. Chicago: University of Chicago Press, 1970.

Shaw, Anna Howard, with Jordan, Elizabeth. *The Story of a Pioneer*. New York: Harper & Brothers, 1915.

Spencer, Anna Garlin. *Woman's Share in Social Culture*. New York: M. Kennerley, 1913.

Stanton, Elizabeth Cady, et al., eds. *History of Woman Suffrage*. 6 vols. New York: Fowler & Wells, 1881-1920.

Stanton, Elizabeth Cady, et al. *The Woman's Bible*. 2 vols. New York: European Publishing Co., 1895-98.

Stern, Madeleine B. *Purple Passage: The Life of Mrs. Frank Leslie*. Norman: University of Oklahoma Press, 1953.

Stevens, Doris. *Jailed for Freedom*. New York: Boni & Liveright, 1920.

Taft, Julia Jessie. *The Woman Movement from the Point of View of Social Consciousness*. Chicago: University of Chicago Press, 1915.

Tolchin, Susan, and Tolchin, Martin. *Clout: Womanpower and Politics*. New York: Coward, McCann & Geoghegan, 1974.

U.S. Congress, Senate, Committee on Woman Suffrage, *A joint resolution proposing an amendment to the Constitution of the United States, extending the right of suffrage to women*. 63rd Congress, 1st Session, 19-26 April 1913.

U.S. Congress, Senate, Committee on Woman Suffrage, *Reports of the Committee on Woman Suffrage, U.S. Senate, from the organization of the Committee, December 5, 1882, to the close of the Forty-ninth Congress, 1887*. 49th Congress, 2nd Session, 25 January 1887.

Willis, Olympia Brown. *Acquaintances Old and New, Among Reformers*. Milwaukee: S.E. Tate Printing Co., 1911.

E. Trades-Union Women

The suffrage movement intersected with the popular protest of the working woman through the interests of the second generation of feminists, concerned with the nature of the modern city and the social problems of industrial society. The popular protest itself first found expression in the New England textile towns of the 1840s when women's protests erupted over the fight for the ten-hour day and over wages and working conditions. The leaders of this protest were native-born American women, and they may be thought of as the first generation of women workers engaging in mass demonstrations and the standard forms of working-class protest. The second generation of women seeking improved working conditions and struggling to organize to exert pressure on employers were not native born, typically the children of Irish or Jewish immigrants. They have not attracted the attention of biographers, and there are few secondary sources to introduce the student to them except the excellent brief biographies of women labor leaders included in volumes 1 through 4 of *Notable American Women: A Dictionary of Biography* (1974-80), edited by Edward T. James.

Because the woman industrial worker was of immigrant background and because she was entering a labor market where unskilled female labor was in oversupply, there was little interest on the part of native American labor leaders in supporting women's labor organizations. Attention in the male labor movement was focused on organizing and developing the negotiating ability of skilled male workers. Thus the early organization of women workers was supported by the link between the unskilled textile worker, sweated clothing laborer, domestic servant, or service worker and the consumer of her product, usually a middle-class native American woman. This intersection of economic need and social conscience took place initially through the medium of the settlement house, and the history of social settlements and early women's labor organizations is closely intertwined. The sources illustrating this history must be carefully analyzed from the point of view of the class status of both author and intended audience for the document in question. Many labor historians have concluded that the necessary reliance on the support of middle-class women reformers slowed down the pace of women's labor organization and deflected it from militancy. Others have seen the embourgeoisement of the young woman radical through her contact with affluent women reformers and the educational opportunities provided by them. While this may be true of the working-class women involved in the leadership of the Women's Trades Union League, it is certainly not correct for the majority of second-generation woman labor organizers,

whose grinding poverty and homes in ugly industrial towns
kept them well insulated from the chance of embourgeoisement.
   Before we can usefully review the sources and secondary
writing on the history of women's organized labor, some important theoretical baselines must be drawn. We need to
establish what we understand as the nature of women's work,
and we must come to some conclusion as to the long-term significance of industrialization for that work. Much history
of women's labor has been written with the unstated assumption that women's "real" work is in the home, and that her
outside "paid work" is merely an avocation pursued to provide
pin money or a higher standard of family consumption. Much
labor history has been written assuming that women's recruitment into the textile industry represented their first opportunity for nondomestic work or paid labor, and thus this
opportunity, no matter how grueling, represented an improvement in status. This view must be discounted as ahistorical
since women's work outside the home as agricultural laborer
or as self-employed textile worker is a well documented pre-
industrial phenomenon. There is, furthermore, a debate among
economists as to the economic significance of bias in employ-·
ment, and whether women's lack of skilled training produces
the differential in their wages compared to those of men or
whether discrimination produces a secondary labor market with
depressed wages regardless of the skill level of women workers.
Fortunately there are some excellent theoretical discussions
of the meaning of work in women's lives, drawn mainly from
European studies, but nonetheless applicable to the analysis
of American labor history. There is also a small but growing
body of analysis of secondary labor markets and the significance of skill level versus discrimination in wages. Because
of the discontinuity of married women's work arising from their
unshared responsibility for child care, there are other factors which may separate a female working career from that of
an equally skilled male and may affect peak earning capacity.
With one or two exceptions there has been little discussion
of what the sociability of the work place might mean to working women compared with the opportunity to stay home and de-
vote time to domestic tasks and child care. Yet some understanding of this contrast is essential if we are to explain
why most women labor organizers gave up the cause on marriage
while other working women clung to the friendliness of peers
on the job.
   The student of women's work and industrial society may
best begin with Louise A. Tilly and Joan W. Scott's *Women,
Work and Family* (1978)*. Although this work treats

*Tilly, Louise A., and Joan W. Scott. *Women, Work and Family*.
   New York: Holt, Rinehart, and Winston, 1978.

industrialization in England and Europe, it is the best concise theoretical discussion of the impact of industrialization on women's work. Scott and Tilly, in their introduction
and conclusion, dispose quickly of the myth that women were
not laborers before the industrial revolution and introduce
the reader to the concept of the family economy, the sum of
the productive labors of all household members under the
domestic system of production. The consequence of the industrial revolution, they point out, was not to alter the
sum total of work performed by males, females, and children
within a household, but rather to substitute a family wage
economy for the previous family economy based on domestic
production. What changed with the separation of production
from the household was the ease and rapidity with which married women could contribute to the family wage economy. Alva
Myrdal and Viola Klein in *Women's Two Roles, Home and Work*
(1956) described the tension between unpaid domestic work and
paid industrial work in contemporary society. Scott and
Tilly's study provides an historical context from which to
view this tension.

Mark Aldrich and Randy Albelda, in "Determinants of Working
Women's Wages During the Progressive Era" (1980), have analyzed the literature on the subject of discrimination, skill
levels, and returns on the work of groups whose members are
the objects of discrimination. They conclude that based on
the evidence of wage patterns within nineteenth-century
American industry and service occupations, there was indeed
a secondary labor market for women's labor in which levels
of skill and training did not bear the same relationship to
earnings as levels of skill did for the compensation of male
workers. Tamara K. Hareven and Randolph Langenbach in
Amoskeag: Life and Work in an American Factory-City (1978)
have tried to record through the oral history of surviving
workers from the Amoskeag Mills in Manchester, New Hampshire,
answers to the question of what workplace sociability meant
to women who were regular industrial workers. These reports
show a level of sociability in a mill town quite different
from that experienced by the middle-class family, and the
evidence Hareven has collected suggests that women enjoyed
the opportunity to leave home for work, although they did
this intermittently because tradition required a woman to
stay home unless extreme economic pressures made her earnings
necessary for family survival.

Thus we may see women's industrial work as an important
part of the family wage economy, even though that work might
be intermittent during the peak years of childbearing. Its
returns may be seen as a function of a secondary market for
female labor in which the earnings curve and the returns for

age and experience were flatter than for her male counterpart.
Thus the incentives for gaining skills were less or alterna-
tively the penalties for intermittent work were reduced, while
the psychic returns of sociability and escape from the crowded
family tenement were valued by women even though disapproved
by husbands and families.

We may usefully divide the study of the labor movement in
the United States and of women's place within that movement
into three periods. The first from 1910 through the early
1920s coincided with the rise and rapid growth of the socialist movement in the United States. Along with this early
utopian phase of the movement went the strong interest of
socialist reformers in women's position. August Bebel's
Woman and Socialism (1910) was more widely read than Marx and
Engels on this subject, though it is important to remember
that one of the key settlement leaders concerned with the
position of working women in industrial America, Florence
Kelley, was also the translator of Engels' *Condition of the
Working Class in England in 1844*. The second period may be
characterized as a period of reflection on the growth and
institutional stabilization of organized labor in the 1930s
produced by scholars writing in the 1940s and '50s. In this
period the focus of attention was much less on the woman
worker because of the dominant ideology of the period which
located Mom in a sentimentalized home. The third period
represents an entirely new phase in the writing of the history of the working class in which working-class culture and
the meaning of work for both men and women has been the center of attention. Major questions concerning the social
mobility of workers, the rich ethnic heritage of working-class
culture, the functioning of different family systems within
the structure of industrial society have once again focused
attention on the woman worker, her contribution to the family
economy, and the meaning of work outside the home for her.

General studies of the industrial work force and the
growth of organized labor within it have varied widely in the
degree of attention given to the woman worker. Edith Abbott's
Women in Industry (1910) is still an invaluable source of information about women's recruitment into the work force, the
wage levels of women workers and their relative position in
different industries vis-a-vis male workers. John B. Andrews
and W.D.P. Bliss, *History of Women in Trades Unions* (1911),
is part of a larger federal investigative report entitled
Women and Child Wage Earners in the U.S. Andrews and Bliss
are strongly paternalistic in their attitudes to the woman
worker and divide her participation in the labor movement into
four stages: the organization of cotton-mill operatives, 1825-
40; the establishment of labor reform associations among

textile workers, cap makers, boot and shoe workers, and
tailoresses, 1840-60; the establishment of genuine unions
organized by trade, 1860-80; and the participation of women's
trades unions in the Knights of Labor and the American Federation of Labor, 1881-1911. The authors note the reliance of
women trades unionists on external leadership, the defection
of women union members on marriage and regard women's labor
organizations as simply less well developed versions of male
craft unions. John R. Commons' massive *History of Labor in
the United States* (1918-35) and Paul F. Brissenden's *The
I.W.W.: A Study in American Syndicalism* (1919) document carefully the participation of women radicals in labor organization but show limited understanding of the extent to which
male craft unions worked to exclude women from skill training.
Alice Henry's *The Trade Union Woman* (1918) and *Women and the
Labor Movement* (1923) are invaluable sources written by an
actual participant in the organization of working women in the
textile and clothing industry, and one of the key strategists
for the building of women's unions.

Gladys Boone's *The Women's Trade Union Leagues in Great
Britain and the U.S.A.* (1942) brings the comparative perspective of British socialism to bear on American developments
and provides a detailed account of the organizational history
of the Women's Trades Union League, founded in 1903. Boone
documents clearly the lack of interest in organizing women
displayed by the American Federation of Labor and highlights
the importance of the alliance of feminists, settlement-house
workers, and working-class women that brought the League into
being. The League's funds for strike support, effective
lobbying and public-relations work, and its training school
for the woman trades unionist made it a key factor in the
growth of women's unions. However, Boone rightly raises but
does not answer the question of whether or not the participation of middle-class women reformers did not slow down the
development of working-class leadership and objectives for
the movement. Howard Quint's *The Forging of American Socialism* (1953) takes up the same question with respect to
women's labor organization. Robert Smuts, on the other hand,
treats women's participation in the work force from a consensus point of view, characterizing the woman worker as
working for "extras" and basically concerned with home and
family. David Herreshoff in *American Disciples of Marx: From
the Age of Jackson to the Progressive Era* (1967) and James J.
Kenneally in "Women and Trades Unions 1870-1920: The Quandary
of the Reformer" (1973) also treat the tactical problem that
faced organizers of female labor, who had to contend with an
oversupply of unskilled women workers and a discriminatory
system of skill training which prevented the development of
an elite of highly conscious women workers.

Individual accounts of union organizing and histories of notable strikes give us an episodic picture of the movement, but much work remains to be done to provide a detailed understanding of the events that fueled women's militance. Three autobiographies are extremely helpful in establishing the profile of the strong woman union leader. Alice Henry's *Memoirs of Alice Henry* (1944), Agnes Nestor's *Woman's Labor Leader, An Autobiography* (1954), and Rose Schneiderman's *All for One* (1967) are revealing accounts of the lives of important organizers. *Autobiography of Mother Jones* (1925), edited by Mary F. Parton, is less useful because of the great labor heroine's penchant for embroidering a good story. Dale Fetherling's *Mother Jones, The Miners' Angel* (1974) sees Jones as a mixture of primitive folk rebel and utopian builder of an industrial democracy. It is notable for its attempt to separate fact from myth in the Jones' life and to place her efforts in the context of the larger labor movement.

Lewis L. Lorwin's *The Women's Garment Workers: A History of the International Ladies' Garment Workers' Union* (1924) recounts the most successful organizing effort of the movement, while Hannah Josephson's *The Golden Threads: New England's Mill Girls and Magnates* (1949) and Caroline Ware's *The Early New England Cotton Manufacture* (1931) chronicle the organizing efforts of the earliest phase of the movement. Daniel J. Walkowitz's essay on the nature of protest by women workers in a late nineteenth-century New York mill town, "Working Class Women in the Gilded Age: Factory, Community and Family Life Among Cohoes, New York, Cotton Workers" *Workers in the Industrial Revolution,* eds. Peter N. Stearns and Daniel J. Walkowitz (1974)), shows the changed meaning of factory and community for immigrant mill workers as opposed to the native-born textile workers of the early cotton industry. Violent protest for women mill workers in Walkowitz's view was prompted by threats to the modicum of status and economic well being so marginally gained by mill workers rather than the total alienation of labor in Marxist theory.

A biased but valuable source of information on women workers and labor organization may be found in the autobiographical and biographical writing that chronicles the lives of middle-class women reformers who took up the working woman's cause. Howard E. Wilson's biography, *Mary McDowell, Neighbor* (1928), describes the founder and leader of a settlement noted for its systematic support of labor protest. Maude Nathan's autobiography, *Once Upon a Time and Today* (1933), describes the awakening of one of New York's rich Jewish communities to the abuses of the sweated clothing trades and her long-time support of what was to become the International Ladies' Garment Workers' Union. Mary K. Simkhovitch's *Neighborhood: My Story of*

Greenwich House (1938) records the founding years of one of
New York's most successful settlement houses and the circle
of radical critics of capitalism who frequented it. Mary E.
Dreier's biography of her sister, *Margaret Dreier Robins:
Her Life, Letters and Work* (1950), is a record drawn from
family papers of one of the most effective middle-class reformers responsible for supporting and publicizing the pioneering efforts of the Women's Trades Union League and for attempting to build a broader organization of working women
through the establishment of an international congress for
working women. Dorothy Rose Blumberg's biography of Florence
Kelley, translator of Marx and Engels, executive director of
the National Consumers' League, and skillful strategist and
exposer of working conditions hazardous to the lives of working women, chronicles an extraordinary reformer's career that
illustrates vividly why youthful radicals became meliorist
reformers in the context of American capital and labor relations. Kelley's early Marxism and her passionate commitment
to a more just industrial society were moderated by the apparent impossibility of organizing both skilled and unskilled
labor and by the problems posed through the effort to run
union meetings in a babble of different tongues. Kelley's
efforts to organize consumers and to exploit the social conscience of the middle class represent the archetypal response
of the educated middle-class radical to late nineteenth-
century American industrial capitalism.

BIBLIOGRAPHY

Abbott, Edith. *Women in Industry: A Study in American
    Economic History.* New York: D. Appleton & Co., 1910.

Aldrich, Mark, and Albelda, Randy. "Determinants of Working
    Women's Wages During the Progressive Era." *Explorations
    in Economic History* 17 (1980):323-341.

Andrews, John B., and Bliss, W.D.P. *History of Women in
    Trade Unions.* 61 Cong., 2nd Session, Senate Document
    No. 645, 1911.

Bebel, August. *Woman and Socialism.* Translated by Meta L.
    Stern. New York: Socialist Literature Co., 1910.

Bloor, Ella R. *We Are Many: An Autobiography.* New York:
    International Publishers, 1940.

Blumberg, Dorothy Rose. "Dear Mr. Engels: Unpublished Letters,
    1884-1894, of Florence Kelley to Frederick Engels,"
    Labor History 5 (1964):103-133.

Blumberg, Dorothy Rose. *Florence Kelley: The Making of a Social Pioneer*. New York: A.M. Kelley, 1966.

Boone, Gladys. *The Women's Trade Union Leagues in Great Britain and the U.S.A.* New York: Columbia University Press, 1942.

Brissenden, Paul F. *The I.W.W.: A Study of American Syndicalism*. New York: Columbia University Press, 1919.

Campbell, Helen S. *Women Wage Earners: Their Past, Their Present and Their Future*. Boston: Roberts Brothers, 1893.

Carsel, Wilfred. *A History of the Chicago Ladies' Garment Workers' Union*. Chicago: Normandie House, 1940.

Commons, John R., et al. *History of Labor in the United States*. 4 vols. New York: Macmillan Co., 1918-35.

Cornell, Robert J. *The Anthracite Coal Strike of 1902*. Washington, D.C.: Catholic University of America Press, 1957.

Davis, Allen F. "The Women's Trade Union League: Origins and Organization." *Labor History* 5 (1964):3-17.

Dreier, Mary E. *Margaret Dreier Robins, Her Life, Letters and Work*. New York: Island Cooperative Press, 1950.

Fetherling, Dale. *Mother Jones, The Miners' Angel: A Portrait*. Carbondale: Southern Illinois University Press, 1974.

Fox, Genevieve M. *The Industrial Awakening and the Y.W.C.A.* New York: Y.W.C.A., 1919.

Glück, Elsie. *John Mitchell, Miner: Labor's Bargain with the Gilded Age*. New York: John Day Co., 1929.

Hareven, Tamara K., and Langenbach, Randolph. *Amoskeag: Life and Work in an American Factory-City*. New York: Pantheon Books, 1978.

Henry, Alice. *The Trade Union Woman*. New York: D. Appleton & Co., 1918.

Henry, Alice. *Women and the Labor Movement*. New York: George H. Doran Co., 1923.

Henry, Alice. *Memoirs of Alice Henry*. Edited with postscript
    by Nettie Palmer. Reproduced from typewritten copy.
    Melbourne: n.p., 1944.

Herreshoff, David. *American Disciples of Marx: From the Age
    of Jackson to the Progressive Era*. Detroit: Wayne State
    University Press, 1967.

James, Edward T., ed. *Notable American Women, a Biographical
    Dictionary*. 3 vols. Cambridge, Mass.: Harvard Univer-
    sity Press, Belknap Press, 1971.

Jones, Mary. *Autobiography of Mother Jones*. Edited by
    Mary F. Parton. Chicago: C.H. Kerr & Co., 1925.

Josephson, Hannah. *The Golden Threads: New England's Mill
    Girls and Magnates*. New York: Duell, Sloan & Pearce,
    1949.

Josephson, Matthew. *Sidney Hillman, Statesman of American
    Labor*. Garden City, N.Y.: Doubleday, 1952.

Kenneally, James J. "Women and Trade Unions 1870-1920: The
    Quandary of the Reformer." *Labor History* 14 (1973):
    42-55.

Kennedy, Kate. *Doctor Paley's Foolish Pigeons, and Short
    Sermons to Workingmen*. San Francisco: Cubery & Co., 1906.

Kugler, Israel. "The Trade Union Career of Susan B. Anthony."
    Labor History 2 (1961):90-100.

Lorwin, Lewis Levitzki. *The Women's Garment Workers: A His-
    tory of the International Ladies' Garment Workers' Union*.
    New York: B.W. Huesch, 1924.

Lynch, Alice Clare. *The Kennedy Clan and Tierra Redonda*.
    San Francisco: Marnell & Co., 1935.

Marot, Helen. *A Handbook of Labor Literature*. Philadelphia:
    Free Library of Economics and Political Science, 1899.

Marot, Helen. *Creative Impulse in Industry: A Proposition
    for Educators*. New York: E.P. Dutton & Co., 1918.

Myrdal, Alva, and Klein, Viola. *Women's Two Roles, Home and
    Work*. London: Routledge and Kegan Paul, 1956.

Nathan, Maude. *Once Upon a Time and Today*. New York: G.P. Putnam's Sons, 1933.

Nestor, Agnes. *Woman's Labor Leader, An Autobiography*. Rockford, Ill.: Bellevue Books Publishing Co., 1954.

Oppenheimer, Valerie Kincade. *The Female Labor Force in the United States: Demographic and Economic Factors Governing Its Growth and Changing Composition*. Berkeley: Institute of International Studies, University of California, 1970.

Pesotta, Rose. *Bread Upon the Waters*. New York: Dodd, Mead & Co., 1944.

Quint, Howard. *The Forging of American Socialism: Origins of the Modern Movement*. Columbia: University of South Carolina Press, 1953.

Rayback, Joseph G. *A History of American Labor*. New York: Macmillan Co., 1959.

Schneiderman, Rose. *All for One*. New York: P.S. Erikson, 1967.

Simkhovitch, Mary K. *Neighborhood: My Story of Greenwich House*. New York: W.W. Norton & Co., 1938.

Smuts, Robert W. *Women and Work in America*. New York: Columbia University Press, 1959.

Stearns, Peter N., and Walkowitz, Daniel J., eds. *Workers in the Industrial Revolution: Recent Studies in the United States and Europe*. New Brunswick, N.J.: Transaction Books, 1974.

Steel, Edward M. "Mother Jones in the Fairmont Field, 1902." *Journal of American History* 57 (1970):290-307.

Stern, Madeleine B. *We the Women: Career Firsts of Nineteenth-Century America*. New York: Schulte Publishing Co., 1963.

Ware, Caroline F. *The Early New England Cotton Manufacture: A Study in Industrial Beginnings*. Boston: Houghton Mifflin Co., 1931.

Ware, Norman. *The Industrial Worker, 1840-1860: The Reaction of American Industrial Society to the Advance of the Industrial Revolution*. Boston: Houghton Mifflin Co., 1924.

Wilson, Howard E. *Mary McDowell, Neighbor.* Chicago: University of Chicago Press, 1928.

Carola Woerishoffer, Her Life and Work. Bryn Mawr, Pa.:
published by the Class of 1907, Bryn Mawr College, 1912.

Wolman, Leo. *The Growth of American Trade Unions, 1880-1923.*
Ch. 5. New York: National Bureau of Economic Research,
1924.

Younger, Maud. "Diary of an Amateur Waitress," *McClure's
Magazine*, March-April, 1907.

Younger, Maud. "Revelations of a Woman Lobbyist," *McCall's
Magazine*, September-October-November, 1919.

F. Radicals and Anarchists

While the group of reformers around the Women's Trades
Union League had serious criticisms of industrial capitalism,
they remained content to work for change in the system of
production and distribution through existing structures of
authority. Most of the working women and all of the middle-
class reformers were models of Victorian circumspection in
their sexual lives. Some were motivated by Christianity,
like Margaret Dreier Robins; by Jewish ideals of philanthropy,
like Maude Nathan; or by Quakerism, like Florence Kelley. A
few like Mary Kingsbury Simkhovitch linked the Judeo-Christian
tradition with the subordination of women, but none were sufficiently critical of the state and of contemporary culture
to seek its overthrow. The small group of women who became
radical critics of American society arrived at their radical
perspective by three typical routes. Sexual radicals such as
Margaret Sanger or Mabel Dodge arrived at their break with
inherited values through their sense of outrage at male
dominance and their pursuit of greater sexual liberty for
women. Anarchists like Emma Goldman began their alienation
against authority in Europe and found their inspiration in
the immigrant ghetto among the small groups of anarchist
émigrés who drew their inspiration from the European anarchist tradition. Women of the radical left who were converts
to either the Soviet or the Chinese version of communism made
their way through relative privilege, higher education, and
contact with the radicalism of the western miners and long-
shoreman's unions.
Christopher Lasch in *The New Radicalism in America* (1965)
sets out to explain why there was such a powerful rebellion

against the philistine materialism of the Gilded Age on the
part of the educated and privileged young. This rebellion
took educated women into social settlements and social work,
it took young men into crusading reform as muckraking journalists or municipal reformers, but in general this revolt
stopped short of real alienation and fitted easily into the
American reform tradition inherited from nineteenth-century
evangelical culture. The exceptions did not rest in that
reforming stance and became committed to values genuinely
opposed to those of the melioristic reformers. The reasons
why are not easily determined. The process of radicalization
is generally understood in psychodynamic or social structural
terms. If authority is corrupt and exploiting during the early
stages of individual development, then the resulting rage may
be unleashed on social institutions and values by the adult.
The privileged young trained to fill elite roles in society
may be radicalized by the discovery that such opportunities
are not there in the social structure entered as an adult.
For women there clearly was another factor in sexual exploitation and the perception that established social institutions
and values stood in the way of sexual fulfillment. There was
clearly another variant of the social structural explanation
in the career of Mother Jones, whose Catholic education trained
her to prepare for marriage and maternity and whose rage at
economic exploitation and fearless confrontation of police
and Pinkerton guards came after she had lost a husband and all
her children to yellow fever, a tragedy which left her at 37
without family or traditional roles to play. We have yet to
see adequate theoretical models for the process of radicalization for women and the mainstream of writing about radicalism
in America has been concerned with male anarchists and intellectuals on the left.

Since ideology shapes perception and requires the recast-
ing of events, the autobiographical writings of great radical
figures are always adapted to political positions. The clas-
sics of the genre are Emma Goldman's *Living My Life* (1931),
Margaret Sanger's *Margaret Sanger: An Autobiography* (1938),
and Anna Louise Strong's *I Change Worlds: The Remaking of an
American* (1935). Goldman and Strong both describe an historical process of political radicalization and cumulative disenchantment with American economic and political institutions.
Sanger, who had become a pillar of the progressive reform establishment by the time she wrote her autobiography, had more
difficulty describing the process. Richard Drinnon's biography of Goldman is sensitive, filled with insight but careful to point out where Goldman invented her past or inflated
her political role. Peter G. Filene's *Americans and the
Soviet Experiment, 1917-1933* (1967) provides a clear picture

of the intellectual context in which the U.S.S.R. seemed to promise the fulfillment of ideals not realized in the United States. This was particularly the case for women who were early rebels against what Betty Friedan was later to name the feminine mystique. Anna Louise Strong relished the Soviet notion of marriage as a union to be undertaken to serve the party and the state rather than the romanticized "love match" she had been taught to seek in her childhood. She saw in Soviet commitment to child care and work for women the institutions which could offer the equality that seemed only talk to her in America. Mabel Dodge Luhan's *Intimate Memories* (1933-1937) recounts a different path toward rejection of conventional American sentimental ideas of male-female relationships, Luhan's being toward idealization of more "authentic" Indian culture.

Agnes Smedley and Kate Richards O'Hare Cunningham represent two variants of the path to radicalism followed by midwestern women in the closing decades of the nineteenth century. O'Hare's stint in prison following her pacifist speeches in 1919 produced one of the classic feminist critiques of American capitalism, while Agnes Smedley's *Battle Hymn of China* (1943) contains a biographical sketch that is a moving account of the process of alienation from the United States and from western capitalism and her deep commitment to the Chinese revolution. What is striking about all these variants of the radical rejection of American culture and values is that each woman's psychological development released in her the springs of anger that women's socialization is and was designed to suppress. Psychohistorians write the history of "what may be thought and felt" in any given period and the historian of the woman radical must understand in those ways that the pattern of individual development in her life intersected with social structures to produce ways of thinking and feeling so different from those that the general social system operated to produce. O'Hare, Smedley, Goldman, and Strong are all case studies of the process of radicalization as yet little understood in women's lives.

BIBLIOGRAPHY

Drinnon, Richard. *Rebel in Paradise: A Biography of Emma Goldman.* Chicago: University of Chicago Press, 1961.

Filene, Peter G. *Americans and the Soviet Experiment, 1917-1933.* Cambridge, Mass.: Harvard University Press, 1967.

Flynn, Elizabeth Gurley. *I Speak My Own Piece: Autobiography of "The Rebel Girl."* New York: Masses & Mainstream, 1955.

Fryer, Peter. *The Birth Controllers*. New York: Stein & Day, 1966.

Goldman, Emma. *Anarchism and Other Essays*. New York: Mother Earth Pub. Association, 1910.

Goldman, Emma. *Living My Life*. 2 vols. New York: Alfred A. Knopf, 1931.

Herreshoff, David. *American Disciples of Marx: From the Age of Jackson to the Progressive Era*. Detroit: Wayne State University Press, 1967.

Howe, Frances. "Leonora O'Reilly, Socialist and Reformer." Honors Thesis, Radcliffe College, 1952.

Kennedy, David M. *Birth Control in America: The Career of Margaret Sanger*. New Haven: Yale University Press, 1970.

Lasch, Christopher. *The New Radicalism in America, 1889-1963: The Intellectual as a Social Type*. New York: Alfred A. Knopf, 1965.

Luhan, Mabel Dodge. *Intimate Memories*. New York: Harcourt & Brace & Co., 1933-37.

Nearing, Scott. *Woman and Social Progress: A Discussion of the Biologic, Domestic, Industrial and Social Possibilities of American Women*. New York: Macmillan Co., 1912.

O'Hare, Kate Richards. *The Sorrows of Cupid*. Rev. and enl. St. Louis, Missouri: The National Rip-Saw Pub. Co., 1912.

O'Hare, Kate Richards. *Kate O'Hare's Prison Letters*. 3rd ed. Girard, Kansas: People's Pocket Series, 1919.

O'Hare, Kate Richards. *In Prison*. New York: Alfred A. Knopf, 1923.

Sanger, Margaret. *My Fight for Birth Control*. New York: Farrar & Rinehart, 1931.

Sanger, Margaret. *Margaret Sanger: An Autobiography*. New York: W.W. Norton & Co., 1938.

Schuster, Eunice Minetta. "Native American Anarchism." *Smith College. Studies in History* 17 (1932):5-202.

Simons, May Wood. *Woman and the Social Problem*. Chicago:
     C.H. Kerr & Co., 1899.

Smedley, Agnes. *Daughter of Earth*. New York: Coward-McCann,
     1929.

Smedley, Agnes. *China Fights Back: An American Woman with
     the Eighth Route Army*. New York: Vanguard Press, 1938.

Smedley, Agnes. *Battle Hymn of China*. New York: Alfred A.
     Knopf, 1943.

Spargo, John. *Socialism and Motherhood*. New York: B.W.
     Huebsch, 1914.

Strong, Anna Louise. *I Change Worlds: The Remaking of an
     American*. New York: H. Holt and Co., 1935.

G. The Temperance Movement

The temperance movement represents one of the most successful political initiatives of enhanced-authority feminists.
The argument for the control or elimination of the sale of alcohol was made in the name of preserving the sanctity of the
home and preserving the welfare of dependent mothers and
children. Thus even though the tactics of the movement often
involved a variety of forms of direct action, sit-downs in
saloons, the smashing up of barrels, and parades which required the facing down of hostile crowds, the participants
in the movement were never perceived as unwomanly or as seeking power for other than disinterested reasons.

The fact that the goals of the movement coincided with
the attitudes of the Methodist and Baptist churches on the
consumption of alcohol meant that temperance leaders had a
ready-made constituency and a national network at their dis-
posal almost immediately. Many revival techniques were bor-
rowed by the movement, and its use of slogans, songs, and
symbols such as the white ribbon represented an inspired adaptation of religious culture for secular purposes. The autobiographical writing of the leaders indicates the religious
attitudes with which they approached their work and the formidable energies released by the cause. Eliza Daniel Stewart's
Memories of the Crusade (1888) show the local grass-roots
origins of the movement. "Mother Stewart," as she came to be
known, began her work by aiding a wife in a court case against
her drunken husband. The publicity surrounding the case led
to a flood of similar requests and Stewart found her cause.

She became known throughout the midwest as a leader of demonstrations and prayer meetings, events which served to mobilize
one district after another. Stewart's memoirs emphasize the
intellectual and spiritual development which came from working
for the cause and the importance of the movement as a source
of education for women.

Frances E. Willard, the organizational mastermind of the
movement, recorded her own experience in the process of describing the other leaders of the Women's Christian Temperance
Union in *Woman and Temperance: or, The Work and Workers of
the Woman's Christian Temperance Union* (1883). Willard's
organizational talents are well displayed in her famous *Do
Everything: A Handbook for the World's White Ribboners* (1895).
Although her own writing does not reveal it, Willard also was
educated by the movement and by the opportunities it gave her
to travel and move in reform circles in the United States and
England. Anna Adams Gordon's *The Beautiful Life of Frances
Willard* (1898) is a saccharine account by a devoted secretary
who wipes out all the strength and the contradictions of
Willard's personality. Mary E. Dillon's *Frances Willard:
From Prayers to Politics* (1944) shows "Frank" Willard more in
the round and gives some sense of the broadening of perspective and social concern that accompanied Willard's travel for
the cause. Several autobiographies and briefer sketches illustrate the spiritual flavor of the movement. Eliza J. Thompson et al., *Hillsboro Crusade Sketches and Family Records*
(1896), Hannah Whitall Smith, *The Unselfishness of God and
How I Discovered It: A Spiritual Autobiography* (1903), and
Carry A. Nation, *The Use and Need of the Life of Carry A.
Nation* (1904) are vivid examples of the sense of calling
which inspired the movement's leadership and incidentally
clear accounts of the dimensions of the problem of alcohol
abuse against which it was directed.

The history of the movement has not attracted the attention of scholars until very recently. Annie T. Wittenmyer's
History of the Woman's Temperance Crusade (1878) is a partisan, eyewitness account. B.F. Austin's *The Prohibition
Leaders of America* (1895) and Mary H. Hunt's two works, *An
Epoch of the Nineteenth Century* (1897) and *A History of the
First Decade of the Department of Scientific Temperance Instruction in Schools and Colleges* (1891) are laudatory accounts written by participants. Gertrude Stevens Leavitt
and M.L. Sargent, *Lillian M.N. Stevens, A Life Sketch* (1921)
is a sympathetic biography of a major temperance leader.
Elizabeth Putnam Gordon's *Women Torch-Bearers: The Story of
the W.C.T.U.* (1924) begins a slightly more objective narra-
tion of the history of the W.C.T.U.'s foundation and leadership.
Gordon has a great-woman view of history and devotes most of

her attention to leadership, though the grass-roots nature of
the movement and the breadth of participation were obviously
key factors in its success. Margaret Farrand Thorp's *Female
Persuasion* (1949) devotes more attention to the movement qua
movement, as does Helen E. Tyler in *Where Prayer and Purpose
Meet* (1949). Logan Pearsall Smith, in his edition of family
letters, *Philadelphia Quaker: The Letters of Hannah Whitall
Smith* (1950), raises new questions about the psychology of
participants and the relationship of the temperance movement
to other religious and reform drives in American culture.
More recently Janet Zollinger Giele has brought the techniques
of the modern social sciences to bear on the analysis of
women's roles as reformers and their varying styles of action.
Giele's "Centuries of Womanhood: An Evolutionary Perspective
on the Feminine Role" (1972), and her essay in *Women: Roles
and Status in Eight Countries* (1977), edited by Janet Z. Giele
and A.C. Smock, raises questions about the structural pressures
in American society that prompted various styles of female reform and comments on the way these movements were perceived.
However, Giele's work merely raises some of the questions necessary for the analysis of the temperance movement. These are
of two types. First, why was there such a difference in response to women as political beings in the suffrage and temperance campaigns? What can role theory provide by way of explanation of the differential response? What was the consciousness of the typical temperance reformer compared with her
suffragist counterpart? A second set of questions relates to
the types of social protest expressed through the temperance
movement. What kinds of discontent prompted participation
and how well did the movement and its outcome respond to those
discontents?

A further set of questions may be added to Giele's as a
basis for further research. In many respects the temperance
movement represented a rural variant of the typical early
modern style of political protest by the urban crowd. In the
early modern city we see many such protests led and supported
by women who saw collective action as expressing an unstated
but widely understood moral consensus about economic matters
and relationships between rulers and ruled. In rural America
a new style of direct action by women evolved akin to the
early modern crowd action, and from this rural phenomenon a
new kind of pressure group emerged which by a process of accommodation to American political realities became a national
lobby. We need to understand why the political action of
women drawing on this early modern political role was so effective while the claim to modern-style participation in the
American polity evoked such hostility. In this respect the
study of women's political activity may throw revealing light

on the lineaments of American society in the second half of
the nineteenth century and the stages of its modernization.

BIBLIOGRAPHY

Austin, Benjamin Fish, ed. *The Prohibition Leaders of
America*. 2 vols. Toronto: n.p., 1895.

Bordin, Ruth. *Woman and Temperance: The Quest for Power and
Liberty, 1873-1900*. Philadelphia: Temple University
Press, 1981.

Caldwell, Dorothy J. "Carrie Nation, A Missouri Girl, Won
Fame As a Kansas Crusader." *Missouri Historical Review*
63 (1969):461-488.

Dillon, Mary Earhart. *Frances Willard: From Prayers to
Politics*. Chicago: University of Chicago Press, 1944.

Giele, Janet Z. "Social Change in the Feminine Role: A
Comparison of Woman's Suffrage and Woman's Temperance,
1870-1920." Ph.D. Dissertation, Radcliffe, 1961.

Giele, Janet Z. "Centuries of Womanhood: An Evolutionary
Perspective on the Feminine Role." *Women's Studies* 1
(1972):97-110.

Giele, Janet Z., and Smock, Audrey C., eds. *Women: Roles
and Status in Eight Countries*. New York: John Wiley &
Sons, 1977.

Gordon, Anna Adams. *The Beautiful Life of Frances E. Willard*.
Chicago: Women's Temperance Publishing Association, 1898.

Gordon, Elizabeth Putnam. *Women Torch-Bearers: The Story of
the W.C.T.U.* Evanston, Ill.: National Woman's Christian
Temperance Union Publishing House, 1924.

Hunt, Mary H. *An Epoch of the Nineteenth Century*. Boston:
P.H. Foster & Co., 1897.

Hunt, Mary H. *A History of the First Decade of the Department of Scientific Temperance Instruction in Schools and
Colleges*. 2nd ed. Boston: Washington Press, 1891.

Leavitt, Gertrude Stevens, and Sargent, M.L. *Lillian M.N.
Stevens, A Life Sketch*. n.p., 1921.

Nation, Carry A. *The Use and Need of the Life of Carry A. Nation.* Topeka, Kans.: F.M. Steves & Sons, 1904.

Smith, Hannah Whitall. *The Unselfishness of God and How I Discovered It: A Spiritual Autobiography.* New York: F.H. Revell Co., 1903.

Smith, Logan Pearsall. *Philadelphia Quaker: The Letters of Hannah Whitall Smith.* New York: Harcourt, Brace, 1950.

Stewart, Eliza Daniel. *Memoirs of the Crusade.* Columbus, Ohio: W.J. Hubbard & Co., 1888.

Thompson, Eliza J., et al. *Hillsboro Crusade Sketches and Family Records.* Cincinnati: Cranston & Curts, 1896.

Thorp, Margaret Farrand. *Female Persuasion: Six Strong-minded Women.* New Haven: Yale University Press, 1949.

Tyler, Helen E. *Where Prayer and Purpose Meet: The W.C.T.U. Story, 1874-1949.* Evanston, Ill.: Signal Press, 1949.

Unger, Samuel. "A History of the National Woman's Christian Temperance Union." Ph.D. Dissertation, Ohio State University, 1933.

Willard, Frances E. *Woman and Temperance: or, The Work and Workers of the Woman's Christian Temperance Union.* Chicago: J.S. Goodman & Co., 1883.

Willard, Frances E. *Do Everything: A Handbook for the World's White Ribboners.* Chicago: Woman's Temperance Publishing Association, 1895.

Wittenmyer, Annie T. *History of the Woman's Temperance Crusade.* Philadelphia: Published at the office, the Christian Woman, 1878.

H. Women Seekers of Elective Office:
The First Generation

Women's participation in electoral politics, whether municipal, state or federal, has been little analyzed until the 1960s and '70s when surveys of voter participation and attitudes to women candidates began to analyze why fifty years after the granting of the suffrage so few women had gained elective office. Chapter Seven, "Participatory

"Politics," in Sandra Baxter and Marjorie Lansing's *Women and Politics: The Invisible Majority* (1980), summarizes the current theoretical understanding of why women tend to be found as elected officials at the municipal level more often than in state and federal elective office, and why they are to be found in greater numbers in state legislatures where the role of the state government is least prestigious. This study is supplemented in detail by Marilyn Johnson and Kathy Stanwick, eds., *Women in Public Office: A Biographical Directory and Statistical Analysis* (1978). Marianne Githens and Jewel L. Prestage, *A Portrait of Marginality* (1977) analyzes why women have remained in marginal positions in the standard political party structures and why so few enter the elite of elected state or federal office. Hope Chamberlin's study of women in the U.S. Congress, *A Minority of Members: Women in the U.S. Congress* (1977), documents the slow evolution from three members in 1925 to the standard twelve of the late sixties and early seventies. Paula J. Dubeck's "Women's Access to Political Office: A Comparison of Female and Male State Legislators" (1976) provides a clear comparative perspective on sources of support and access to party organizations. Marjorie Lansing's "The American Woman: Voter and Activist," in Jane S. Jaquette, ed., *Women in Politics* (1974) is a useful source of historical perspective. Political scientists have yet to examine the history of the League of Women Voters from its inception in 1919 to the present. In 1919 the founders of the League saw its future work as the systematic removal of all barriers to women's full participation in society, although within a year the League was split over whether to pursue the goal of supporting women for elective office within the existing party structure or to direct the League's influence toward the goal of securing social-welfare legislation. This basic split was healed by the adoption of new goals for the League focused on the education of the electorate, goals which required a nonpartisan stance and placed League members at the margins of the established party system for securing office. J. Stanley Lemons' *The Woman Citizen: Social Feminism in the 1920's* (1973) analyzes this development and introduces the reader to a large and valuable archive on the history of women's political activity following the securing of the franchise. Sandra Baxter's unpublished Ph.D. dissertation, "Women and Politics: The Parties, The League of Women Voters and the Electorate" (University of Michigan, 1974), is a recent study of the papers and publications of the National League of Women Voters, but further study of the League at the national and state level is clearly necessary.

Carrie Chapman Catt's "Woman Suffrage: Only an Episode in
an Age-Old Movement" (1927) is a revealing statement of the
expectations of suffragists on the question of political participation. Charlotte Perkins Gilman's "Woman's Achievements
since the Franchise" (1927) is more cautious and reveals an
understanding of the problem of entry into established party
structures. Only the Socialist party, intent on building its
constituency and feminist on ideological grounds, made serious
effort to include women within its local and national structure. Mary Jo Buhle's "Women and the Socialist Party, 1901-
14" in Edith Altbach, ed., *From Feminism to Liberation* (1971)
documents the high point of participation in the party in
1912 and the split which occurred at that point on whether
women's struggle for liberation and the class struggle were
identical or required separate goals and separate organizations.

The history of the Woman's Party and its early efforts
for a constitutional guarantee of equal rights for women is
told with clarity and passion in Inez Haynes Irwin's *The Story
of the Woman's Party* (1921), but this early effort at establishing a separate political structure has not received the
study it warrants. A few biographical or autobiographical
accounts of early women members of state and national legislatures can be gleaned from contemporary periodicals of which
Winnifred S. Huck's "What Happened to Me in Congress" (*Women's
Home Companion,* July 1923) and Hazel Canning's "She Represents
New York" (*Independent Woman,* December 1934) are the most revealing. They demonstrate clearly what may also be gleaned
from the papers of the National League of Women Voters that
the suffrage movement's pragmatic approach to securing the
vote left individual women without party structure or plat-
form when the opportunity to seek office was finally secured.
Much more needs to be done to establish the collective profile of the woman who was successful in running for political office and the reasons why she did gain a foothold within
the party structure.

BIBLIOGRAPHY

Altbach, Edith, ed. *From Feminism to Liberation.* Cambridge,
    Mass.: Schenkman Publishing Co., 1971.

Baxter, Sandra. "Women and Politics: The Parties, The
    League of Women Voters and the Electorate." Ph.D.
    Dissertation, University of Michigan, 1974.

Baxter, Sandra, and Lansing, Marjorie. *Women and Politics:
    The Invisible Majority.* Ann Arbor: University of
    Michigan Press, 1980.

Buhle, Mary Jo. "Women and the Socialist Party, 1901-1914."
In *From Feminism to Liberation,* edited by Edith Altbach.
Cambridge, Mass.: Schenkman Publishing Co., 1971.

Canning, Hazel. "She Represents New York." *Independent
Woman,* December 1934.

Catt, Carrie Chapman. "Woman Suffrage: Only an Episode in
an Age-Old Movement." *Current History* 27 (1927):1-6.

Chamberlin, Hope. *A Minority of Members: Women in the U.S.
Congress.* New York: Praeger Publishers, 1977.

Diggs, Annie L. "Women in the Alliance Movement." *Arena* 4.

Dubeck, Paula J. "Women's Access to Political Office: A
Comparison of Female and Male State Legislators."
Sociological Quarterly 17 (1976):45-52.

Felton, Rebecca Ann. *My Memoirs of Georgia Politics.*
Atlanta: Index Printing Co., 1911.

Felton, Rebecca Ann. *The Romantic Story of Georgia's Women.*
Atlanta: Atlanta Georgia and Sunday American, 1930.

Gilman, Charlotte Perkins. "Women's Achievements Since the
Franchise." *Current History* 27 (1927):7-14.

Githens, Marianne, and Prestage, Jewel L. *A Portrait of
Marginality: The Political Behavior of the American
Woman.* New York: Longman, 1977.

Huck, Winnifred S. "What Happened to Me in Congress."
Woman's Home Companion, July 1923.

Irwin, Inez Haynes. *The Story of the Woman's Party.*
New York: Harcourt, Brace & Co., 1921.

Jaquette, Jane S., ed. *Women in Politics.* New York:
John Wiley & Sons, 1974.

Johnson, Marilyn, and Stanwick, Kathy, eds. *Women in Public
Office: A Biographical Dictionary and Statistical Analysis.* Metuchen, N.J.: Scarecrow Press, 1978.

Landes, Bertha K. "Does Politics Make Women Crooked?"
Colliers, 16 March 1929.

Lansing, Marjorie. "The American Woman: Voter and Activist."
    In *Women in Politics*, edited by Jane S. Jaquette. New
    York: John Wiley & Sons, 1974.

Lease, Mary Elizabeth. *The Problem of Civilization Solved*.
    Chicago: Laird & Lee, 1895.

Lemons, J. Stanley. *The Woman Citizen: Social Feminism in the
    1920's*. Urbana: University of Illinois Press, 1973.

Lockwood, Belva. "How I Ran for the Presidency." *National
    Magazine,* March 1903.

Paxton, Annabel. *Women in Congress*. Richmond: The Dietz
    Press, Inc., 1945.

Spaulding, Joe Powell. "The Life of Alice Mary Robertson."
    Ph.D. Dissertation, University of Oklahoma, 1959.

Stern, Madeleine. *We the Women: Career Firsts of Nineteenth-
    Century America*. New York: Schulte Publishing Co., 1963.
    Chapter on Belva Lockwood.

Van Kleeck, Mary. *Suffragist and Industrial Democracy*.
    New York: National Woman's Suffrage Publishing Co., 1919.

SECTION VI

BIOLOGY AND DOMESTIC LIFE:
EVOLUTIONARY THOUGHT AND
ITS IMPACT, 1830-1900

For the eighteenth century it was most important to understand theological views of women and their function in society. For the revolutionary period it was important to grasp the underlying assumptions about women which shaped political ideas. For the period 1830-1900 the focus of attention shifted to scientific and romantic culture which combined to make biology the basis of a woman's destiny. Biology shaped what was believed about women's mental health, and the question of mind-body relationships suffused professional medical writing, as it did the doctrines of popular scientific cults like phrenology or Christian Science or the diet and health fads such as vegetarianism or the vogue for water cures. We do not know why mind-body relationships were of such concern at both the popular and learned cultural level, but the change of emphasis is obviously one aspect of secularization in both learned and professional culture, while the new religions of phrenology or Christian Science were popular reactions to new scientific ideas. We may thus see the period in which the literary concern with the romantic female and an idealized nature, and the growing concern with science and technology after 1830 combined to produce cultural forces which worked together to evolve new definitions of the female. Science and the romantic mentality might be at odds in other areas of society, but with respect to femininity, maternal needs and drives, and the nature of family life, the scientific and literary imagination worked in harmony.

Where writers of the eighteenth century had seen women's sphere as divinely ordained, and the founding fathers had seen the separate sphere of the female as a countervailing force in the polity, the new view of the female which took shape in the mid-nineteenth century made biological forces the key to her need for a separate social territory. Official

science and the phrenologist both had roughly the same thing
to say about woman's nature. When the ideas of Johan Gaspar
Spurzheim and Franz Joseph Gall began to attract popular attention in the United States in the 1830s, the key attraction
of the new "science" of phrenology was the idea that human
beings were born with basically good moral natures which were
distorted by social constraints to produce mental and physical problems. The wise parent or teacher had only to understand the thirty-seven faculties of the brain and through the
study of the cranium their relative development in the young
to devise the system of education most likely to lead to a
happy, satisfied, and fruitful life. This formulation of the
problem of human nature and the role of the environment in
moral development may be seen as a comfortable secularization
of the ideas embodied in evangelical teaching about Christian
nurture. The emphasis placed by phrenologists on sound education for the proper development of inherited mental ability
made them particularly interested in the role of women. Since
they also believed that sound physical bodies housed sound
minds, they gave particular attention to the health of women
and to sound mental hygiene about matters sexual. Thus under
the auspices of the science of phrenology, it became possible
to write and speak about female physiology and gynecological
matters hitherto never discussed in respectable society. What
was preached, however, was a clear and unequivocal statement
that biology was destiny and that women's education, dress,
and physical regimen should be directed toward supporting
their reproductive functions in the most healthful way.

Where phrenology left off official science took over. In
1869 Dr. George H. Napheys began to publish his medical texts
on female physiology and psychology, all of which claimed to
state the laws of women's physical life and the way her physical nature shaped her destiny. Napheys' work drew on the increasing knowledge of the female reproductive system, the result of the developing field of obstetrics in the nineteenth
century, and he was a pioneer in his wish to make that knowledge freely available to women through the writing of simple
and easily understood texts.

The definition of the female in terms of her reproductive
system and its interactions with mental states could have
both positive and negative consequences depending on whether
the popularizer of medical knowledge focused attention on the
healthily functioning female body or upon the possible diseases and malfunctions of the reproductive system. Thus the
new biological definition could stress the recognition of
women's sexual appetites and the importance of a healthful
physical regimen, or it could lead to a negative obsession
with female masturbation and its supposed consequences in

hysteria and emotional illness. Those whose concern was with
the diseases of the female generally tended to stress the importance of keeping women within their sphere in the interests
of their health, while those holding positive views of female
sexuality could proceed to argue for new sets of economic and
social arrangements so that the normal biological drives of
male and female need not be distorted by women's need to use
their sexual attractiveness to compensate for economic and
psychological dependence. Thus the popularizers of medicine
and the health writers of the water-cure movement might lace
their books of advice on matters of exercise, rest, and mental hygiene with injunctions to women to seek economic independence and to value practical work.

Whether they construed biology to dictate the limitation
or the expansion of women's sphere, it is clear that the medical writers of the second half of the century had a new view
of the human body as a system of interrelating parts and as
a system for the generation and expenditure of energy.* In
this context puberty for both males and females involved obvious threats to the conservation of energy. Menstruation
was seen as a recurring drain on the female system, the more
threatening because of its involuntary nature and its unpre-
dictability. Since the body was not viewed as an energy-
maximizing system, it followed that energy drained away in
menstruation was not available for intellectual or physical
work and that the emotional balance of the female was seen
as particularly at hazard with the onset of puberty. Once
again a radical wing of the popular writers on health for
women maintained that sound diet, adequate rest, and appropriate dress made menstruation a natural and normal process,
and that care in limiting conception could make pregnancy
likewise a healthy and natural state.

We must thus examine with care the full spectrum of opinion and interpretation resulting from the biological definition of male and female roles before coming to conclusions as
to the direction of change in women's social position it represents. A partial reading of the sources will certainly suggest that the rise of modern obstetrics imposed new restraints
on female roles. On the other hand, the new biological view
of women brought eventual acceptance of the need for dress
reform and physical exercise no matter what set of social attitudes medical writers might otherwise express. We may thus

*Nowhere is this view more concisely expressed than in the
    writing of Darwin's and Huxley's pupil, Patrick Geddes,
    whose *The Evolution of Sex* (London: W. Scott, 1889) was
    required reading for all American nineteenth-century
    social theorists.

view this period as one in which the popularization of evolutionary biology and the development of modern medicine carried
contradictory tendencies toward the recognition of female sexuality on the one hand and the acceptance of a biologically
determined sphere for women on the other. This acceptance was
universal before the popularization of Freudian ideas in the
United States. Indeed, we see from consulting the medical
literature of the second half of the nineteenth century that,
far from shaping the view that biology was women's destiny,
as many intellectual historians have claimed, Freud and his
followers found acceptance in America because of the univer-
sality of the popular acceptance of this basic Freudian tenet.

A. Medical Views of Female Disorders:
Health Manuals and Histories of Medicine

Secondary Sources

Richard Shryock's *Medicine and Society in North America*
1660-1860 (1960), Herbert Thoms' *Chapters in American Obstet-*
rics (1933), and John S. Haller, Jr. and Robin M. Haller's
The Physician and Sexuality in Victorian America (1974) provide a chronological view of the development of knowledge of
the female reproductive system and the evolving attitudes of
the medical profession toward female sexuality. Ronald G.
Walters' *Primers for Prudery: Sexual Advice to Victorian*
America (1974) stresses the constraints against open discussion of sexual matters rather than the work of physicians like
Napheys or popular writers like Mary Sargeant Nichols. Ben
Barker Benfield, in his study of the developing practice of obstetrics and gynecology, stresses the negative attitudes toward
female sexuality apparent in medical practices such as the
cauterization or excision of the clitoris as a cure for female masturbation. Authors whose works focus on the attitudes of surgeons have so far failed to make use of a comparative perspective or to link such nineteenth-century medical
practices to sexual customs prevalent in many tribal cultures.
Much historical commentary has revolved around the question of how puberty and menopause were construed as stages
in a woman's life, and how the biological view of women became so exclusively derived from her childbearing years.
Carroll Smith-Rosenberg and Charles Rosenberg, in "The Female
Animal: Medical and Biological Views of Woman and Her Role in
Nineteenth Century America" (1973) and Carroll Smith-Rosenberg
in "Puberty to Menopause: The Cycle of Femininity in Nineteenth Century America" (1973) draw attention to the medical
writing which justified only the domestic and childbearing

roles of women and argued against education or a larger social
role for them. They cite some of the extremes of this strand
of opinion such as the physicians who argued that women were
only in a truly healthy state when pregnant. Ann Douglas
Wood in "The Fashionable Diseases: Women's Complaints and
Their Treatment in Nineteenth Century America" (1973) and
Carroll Smith-Rosenberg's "Volition, Aggression and Conflict:
Hysteria as a Female Social Role" (1973) argue that women's
fashionable ailments may have played a useful functional role
as a means of power and an avenue of escape from the duties
of the kitchen and the bedroom. While Smith-Rosenberg and
Wood conclude that women physicians and health reformers had
more liberal views about female sexuality and were untroubled
by the supposed health hazards of education for women, Regina
Morantz, in "The Perils of Feminist History" (1974), points
out that the treatment of women must be assessed in terms of
the general standards of medical practice which involved many
cruel and seemingly sadistic procedures for males also. Thus
the total context of medical practice may alter the way we
construe the treatment of women.

Primary Sources--Health Manuals

If we look at a representative sample of the manuals published on the subject of women's health from the onset of the
vogue phrenology in the 1830s to the more detailed works on
anatomy and physiology which began to appear in the 1880s, we
see that the popularity of phrenology and the water-cure movement prompted a number of works in the 1840s and '50s designed
to educate women about the female body, and that these works
in their turn evoked counterarguments from physicians and
moralists opposed to the freer expression of the female sexual appetites. A.M. Mauriceau's *The Married Woman's Private
Medical Companion* (1847) is an early example of the new freedom in discussing female medical subjects, while Mary Sargeant Nichols' *Lectures to Ladies on Anatomy and Physiology*
(1842) is one of the earliest publications by a woman health
reformer interested in both phrenology and the water-cure
movement. Nichols' later work, *Mary Lyndon; or, Revelations
of a Life. An Autobiography* (1855), describes the psychological consequences of loveless marriage and female dependency
and is a thinly fictionalized polemic urging women to take
control of their lives and develop their own medical exper-
tise. Its portraits of male doctors are uniformly negative
except for those connected with the study of phrenology and
hydropathy.

R.T. Trall's *Home Treatment for Sexual Abuses* (1853) is
the work of a sympathetic male health reformer who established

the first water-cure spa in the United States in 1844 and
eventually added the reform of dress and diet to his health
program for women. William A. Alcott's *The Young Woman's
Book of Health* (1850) is typical of the mixture of advice on
diet, dress, healthy patterns of sleep and exercise, and advice on the supposed stresses of puberty which had wide circulation in the mid-century. In opposition to such positive
books of advice for women were cautionary works on the dangers
of masturbation such as Samuel Gregory's *Facts and Important
Information for Young Women; On the Subject of Masturbation,
with Its Causes, Prevention and Cure* (1850). Gregory's main
concern was with the curbing and controlling of female appetites and with instilling fear of sexuality in his readers.

The change of attitude and the expectation that sexuality
was to be understood scientifically may be seen in the title
of Orson Fowler's *Sexual Science* (1870), which was notable
for the vividness of its descriptions and the inaccuracy of
its information. R.T. Trall's *Uterine Diseases* (1854) was
likewise specific, and its colored engravings supported the
exhortations to preserve the health of women of a noted birth-
control advocate. Eliza B. Duffey's *What Women Should Know.
A Woman's Book About Women* (1873) is a later variant of
Nichols' writing urging women to assume responsibility for
their own health. Dio Lewis' *Five Minute Chats with Young
Women and Certain Other Parties* (1874) is an outstanding example of the feminist writing produced by sympathetic male
health reformers who favored work outside the home and economic independence for women so that they could marry for love
rather than economic security. Lewis was concerned with the
genetic improvement of society and the problems of bad hered-
ity, and wanted to see marriage and reproduction dealt with
scientifically.

Eliza Barton Lyman's *The Coming Woman; or, The Royal Road
to Physical Perfection. A Series of Medical Lectures* (1880)
and Mary Virginia Hawes Terhune's *Eve's Daughers; or, Common
Sense for Maid, Wife and Mother* (1882) offered practical ad-
vise for women in each life stage and described the responsibility of women to preserve their health as a sacred duty
for the coming generations. Lyman and Terhune thought women
could safely pursue higher education if they gave careful attention to their health, but their views were strenuously
questioned by William Goodell, whose "The Dangers and the Duty
of the Hour (the Faulty System of Female Education; The Decay
of Home Life and the Unwillingness of Our Women to Become
Mothers)" (1881) threatened that the education of women in the
northeast was undermining the fertility of the better classes.

Whatever the prescriptive literature had to say, the actual medical and demographic records of the later decades of

the nineteenth century indicate that women's attitudes toward
their sexuality were changing. Both premarital and extramarital sex were increasing in the decade of the 1890s, and the
women interviewed in the ubiquitous social surveys of modern
social science indicated pleasure in and acceptance of their
sexuality not before documented. The records available are
limited, but they offer some indications about both college-
educated and working-class women. Carl Degler has reported
in "What Ought to Be and What Was: Women's Sexuality in the
Nineteenth Century" (1974) the results of a questionnaire ad-
ministered to Stanford women by Dr. Clelia Duel Mosher in the
1890s. Robert Latou Dickinson and Laura Beam report in *The
Single Woman* (1934) on the evidence available to them on the
sexual behavior of single working women in the 1890s. Both
sources suggest that the previous decades of discussion of
female sexuality in positive terms had affected attitudes and
that the ideas of William Goodell and Samuel Gregory were
definitely no longer persuasive.

Given the evidence of the prescriptive writing and the
episodic data available from early studies of sexual behavior,
one of the major questions which must concern the historian
is why contemporaries and historians writing in the first half
of the twentieth century should have dated the modern changes
in women's sexual behavior from the decade of the 1920s rather
than the 1890s, and why the phenomenon of the single working
woman should not have attracted attention before the 1920s.
One reason must certainly be the preoccupation of historians
of women's role and status with the legal battles of the movement for freely available birth-control information. A second
must be that the early twentieth-century fighters for women's
rights like Margaret Sanger had no access to this history and
unwittingly overdrew the picture of ignorance and negative
assessment of female sexuality which went before them. Certainly the dissemination of Freudian thought in the opening
decades of the twentieth century and the earliest results of
research on the endocrine system threw a different light on
the earlier writing about female sexuality and women's sex
drives. The discovery of the endocrine system made women's
sex drives seem on the one hand less under women's rational
control and more driven than the nineteenth-century writers
had thought, and on the other returned to an earlier theme
in nineteenth-century evangelical culture which had seen
women's most important emotional drive as that of maternity.

In any event we may conclude that by the close of the
decade of the 1890s the biological view of the female was fully
elaborated in both learned and popular culture. It had preempted ground formerly occupied by religious definitions of
women, and it was susceptible of both feminist and antifeminist

interpretations. The main trend of change in the later decades of the nineteenth century was toward a moderate feminist position, though conservative strands of opinion gained
high visibility in the battles about the use of the mails to
disseminate birth-control information and in the various vice
crusades which attempted to control prostitution. The question which remains unanswered is why it was that the school
of opinion represented by Nichols, Trall and Lewis was so
quickly silenced in the early years of the twentieth century.
The answers to this question must lie in the reshaping of medical education which took place in the early twentieth century
and the financial and social pressures which resulted in the
closing of most of the small and poorly financed women's medical colleges. Mary Walsh in her *"Doctors Wanted, No Women
Need Apply": Sexual Barriers in the Medical Profession, 1835-
1975* (1977) provides a guide to the available sources on this
subject which cries out for further investigation.

Health Manuals for Men

This bibliography lists only a representative sampling of
health manuals for men. The literature is vast but the
reader will find samples of most schools of opinion listed
here. Before students can interpret the significance of gender in the definition of what was appropriate for the female,
they must understand what was typical in instructions to males
about the understanding of sexuality. As Ben Barker Benfield
has pointed out in his essay, "The Spermatic Economy: A Nineteenth Century View of Sexuality" (1972), all strands of medical opinion in the mid-nineteenth century were unhesitating
in viewing the expenditure of sperm whether in intercourse or
masturbation as expenditures of vital energy which was thus
not available for intellectual or physical work. The difference between males and females in the writer's view being
that men could control such depletions of the system while
for women menstruation was involuntary. Given this general
view, the old Puritan concern with the sin of Onan was simply
replaced in nineteenth-century advice books and health manuals by alarming descriptions of the damage to health from
frequent masturbation. Medical advice varied as to the best
ways to avoid the dangers of exhaustion from such a cause depending on whether it was proffered by an enthusiast for
water cures, cold water, dietary reform, and the dangers of
meat and spices, a temperance advocate, or an opponent of the
use of tobacco.

Samuel Gregory's *Facts and Important Information for
Young Men, on the Subject of Masturbation; With Its Causes,
Prevention and Cure* (1857) is an example of the typical

cautionary work urging continence, thrift, hard work, and the
careful selection of a mate in the interest of an early escape from the dangers of masturbation. It should be contrasted with Joseph W. Howe's *Excessive Venery, Masturbation
and Continence* (1883) which is, if anything, more threatening
in its depiction of the dangers to mental health of masturbation than the earlier work. Sylvester Graham's *A Lecture to
Young Men on Chastity* (1834) and Dio Lewis in *Chats with
Young Men* (1870) express the popular view among dietary reformers that the sexual appetites could be controlled by a
diet free of stimulants or free of meat and spices. Orson S.
Fowler's *Phrenology versus Intemperance* (1841) advises that
all excesses of sexual desire are the consequences of over-
indulgence in alcohol and suggests the dangers to mental health
of drink and "self-abuse."

By contrast Robert Dale Owen, in his *Moral Physiology*
(1831), began to write in the tone of the modern sex counselor.
Owen was remarkable for his generation in encouraging his
readers to agree with him that the pleasures of the sexual
union were natural and a source of happiness to both partners.
Owen was an early public propagandist for birth control and
believed that the responsibility for limiting conception
should belong to the male partner. Conception should be limited, he thought, in the interest of the wife's health and
the health of the couple's offspring, to provide for the
couple's mutual enjoyment of one another as sexual partners,
and to limit the size of their family to one consistent with
economic mobility for the family as a unit. Even with these
advanced views, Owen thought intercourse to result in serious
depletion of the energies and advised intercourse no more frequently than once a week.

Much more radical than Owen and much more widely read was
the founder and leader of the Oneida community, John Humphrey
Noyes. Noyes was an advocate of freedom for male and female
to follow their sexual attractions provided that conception
could be planned and deliberately separated from the pursuit
of sexual pleasure. His ideas set out in his widely read
Male Continence (1866) were not widely accepted, but his
cheerful advocacy of the pursuit of sexual pleasure through
his particular variant of coitus interruptus, which favored
the enjoyment of the female partner, did circulate widely
and was unique in its advice to men about the nature of female sexual pleasure.

The student of nineteenth-century attitudes and practice
should thus be aware that men as well as women were instructed
by conduct books to see their energies as part of a single
system and, so far as the majority view went, to see the expression of sexual drives as undertaken at the expense of

intellect and physical energy. We know, of course, that conduct books bear only a very evanescent relationship to behavior as all confessional literature makes clear. However,
for our purposes it is important to realize that men as well
as women were exposed to a prescriptive literature which must
have made them perceive sexual expression as at odds with the
life of the mind or the expenditures of energy necessary for
economic success. Post-Freudian generations raised to fret
about the neurosis involved in not engaging in a regular heterosexual life will never understand the confident energy of
single women reformers and their bachelor allies in the nineteenth century until they can comprehend this difference in
attitude. Like women, men of the period from 1830 to 1900
received contradictory advice about how to understand their
sexuality, although the general trend of the advice books
during the nineteenth century is in the direction of separating procreation from sexual pleasure, as was the general
trend of advice to women. In the case of male readers the
difference was that women's sexual experience was assumed to
be linked to eventual procreation, while that of males no
longer carried this meaning. The general tone of the advice
books encouraged the young man to look for health and character in a future spouse and to consider biological fitness
as well as moral fitness in planning for married life. Advice books to young men might stress a woman's health as an
important consideration in planning for a family, but it was
in the hortatory literature addressed to females that the
health reformers had their field day.

BIBLIOGRAPHY

Secondary Sources

Bullough, Vern, and Voght, Martha. "Women, Menstruation and
    Nineteenth Century Medicine." *Bulletin of the History
    of Medicine* 47 (1973):66-82.

Conway, Jill. "Stereotypes of Femininity in a Theory of
    Sexual Evolution." *Victorian Studies* 14 (1970):47-62.

Degler, Carl N. "What Ought to Be and What Was: Women's
    Sexuality in the Nineteenth Century." *American Histori-
    cal Review* 79 (1974):1467-1490.

Ehrenreich, Barbara, and English, Deirdre. *Complaints and
    Disorders: The Sexual Politics of Sickness*. Old West-
    bury, N.Y.: Glass Mountain Pamphlet No. 2, 1973.

Haller, John S., Jr., and Haller, Robin M. *The Physician
    and Sexuality in Victorian America*. Urbana: University
    of Illinois Press, 1974.

Morantz, Regina. "The Perils of Feminist History." *Journal of Interdisciplinary History* 4 (1974):649-660.

Reed, Amy L. "Female Delicacy in the Sixties." *Century* 68 (1919):855-864.

Shryock, Richard. *Medicine and Society in North America, 1660-1860.* New York: New York University Press, 1960.

Smith-Rosenberg, Carroll. "Puberty to Menopause: The Cycle of Femininity in Nineteenth Century America." *Feminist Studies* 1 (1973):58-72.

Smith-Rosenberg, Carroll. "Volition, Aggression and Conflict: Hysteria as a Female Social Role." Paper presented at the 66th annual meeting of the Organization of American Historians, 12 April 1973, at Chicago.

Smith-Rosenberg, Carroll, and Rosenberg, Charles. "The Female Animal: Medical and Biological Views of Woman and Her Role in Nineteenth Century America." *Journal of American History* 60 (1973):332-356.

Smith, Daniel Scott. "Family Limitation, Sexual Control and Domestic Feminism in Victorian America." *Feminist Studies* 1 (1973):40-57.

Thoms, Herbert. *Chapters in American Obstetrics.* Springfield, Ill. and Baltimore: C.C. Thomas, 1933.

Walters, Ronald G. *Primers for Prudery: Sexual Advice to Victorian America.* Englewood Cliffs, N.J.: Prentice-Hall, 1974.

Wood, Ann Douglas. "The Fashionable Diseases: Women's Complaints and Their Treatment in Nineteenth Century America." *Journal of Interdisciplinary History* 4 (1973): 25-52.

Primary Sources--Health Manuals

Alcott, William A. *The Young Woman's Book of Health.* Boston: Tappan Whittemore & Mason, 1850.

Austin, George Lowell. *Perils of American Women; or a Doctor's Talk with Maiden, Wife and Mother.* Boston: Lee and Shepard, 1883.

Dickinson, Robert Latou, and Beam, Laura. *The Single Woman:
A Medical Study in Sex Education.* Baltimore: Williams &
Wilkins Co., 1934.

Duffey, Mrs. Eliza B. *What Women Should Know. A Woman's Book
About Women.* Philadelphia: J.M. Stoddart & Co., 1873.

Foote, Edward Bliss. *Plain Home Talk About the Human System-
the Habits of Men and Women..Embracing Medical Common
Sense Applied to Causes, Prevention, and Cure of Chronic
Diseases.* New York: Wells & Coffin, 1870.

Fowler, Orson. *Sexual Science: Including Manhood, Womanhood
and Their Mutual Interrelations.* New York: National Publishing Co., 1870.

Geddes, Patrick. *The Evolution of Sex.* London: W. Scott,
1889.

Goodell, William. "The Dangers and the Duty of the Hour (the
Faulty System of Female Education; the Decay of Home
Life and the Unwillingness of Our Women to Become
Mothers)." *Transactions of Medical and Chirurgical
Faculty,* Baltimore 88 (1881):71-87.

Gregory, Samuel. *Facts and Important Information for Young
Women, on the Subject of Masturbation, with Its Causes,
Prevention and Cure.* Boston: G. Gregory, 1850.

Gregory, Samuel. *Facts and Important Information for Young
Women; on the Self-Indulgence of the Sexual Appetite,
Its Destructive Effects on Health.* Boston: G. Gregory,
1857.

Lewis, Dio. *Five Minute Chats with Young Women, and Certain
Other Parties.* New York: Harper & Brothers, 1874.

Lyman, Eliza Barton. *The Coming Woman; or, The Royal Road
to Physical Perfection. A Series of Medical Lectures.*
Lansing, Mich.: W.S. George & Co., 1880.

Mauriceau, A.M. *The Married Woman's Private Medical Companion.* New York: n.p., 1847.

Moore, Madame. *The Wife's Secret of Power.* c. 1871.

Nichols, Mary Sargeant. *Lectures to Ladies on Anatomy and Physiology.* Boston: Saxton & Pierce, 1842.

Nichols, Mary Sargeant. *Mary Lyndon; or, Revelations of a Life. An Autobiography.* New York: Stringer & Townsend, 1855.

Stockham, Alice B. *Tokology. A Book for Every Woman.* 29th edition. Chicago: Sanitary Publishing Co., 1883.

Terhune, Mary Virginia Hawes. *Eve's Daughters; or, Common Sense for Maid, Wife and Mother.* New York: J.R. Anderson & H.S. Allen, 1882.

Trall, R.T. *Home Treatment for Sexual Abuses.* c. 1853.

Trall, R.T. *Uterine Diseases and Displacements; a Practical Treatise on the Various Diseases, Malpositions, and Structural Derangements of the Uterus and Its Appendages.* New York: Fowlers & Wells, 1854.

Trall, R.T. *Sexual Physiology: A Scientific and Popular Exposition of the Fundamental Problems in Sociology.* New York: Miller, Wood, 1866.

Trall, R.T. *The Mother's Hygenic Handbook; for the Normal Development and Training of Women and Children, and The Treatment of Their Diseases with Hygenic Agencies.* New York: S.R. Wells, 1874.

Walsh, Mary. *"Doctors Wanted, No Women Need Apply": Sexual Barriers in the Medical Profession, 1835-1975.* New Haven: Yale University Press, 1977.

Primary Sources--Health Manuals for Men

Benfield, Ben Barker. "The Spermatic Economy: A Nineteenth Century View of Sexuality." *Feminist Studies* 1 (1972): 49-64.

Fowler, Orson S. *Phrenology Versus Intemperance.* Philadelphia: n.p., 1841.

Graham, Sylvester. *A Lecture to Young Men on Chastity.* Providence: Weeden & Cory, 1834.

Gregory, Samuel. *Facts and Important Information for Young Men, on the Subject of Masturbation; With Its Causes, Prevention and Cure.* Boston: G. Gregory, 1857.

Howe, Joseph W. *Excessive Venery, Masturbation and Continence.* New York: Berningham & Co., 1883.

Lewis, Dio. *Chats with Young Men.* c. 1870.

Noyes, John Humphrey. *Male Continence; or, Self-control in Sexual Intercourse.* Oneida, N.Y.: Office of the Circular, 1866.

Owen, Robert Dale. *Moral Physiology.* New York: Wright & Owen, 1831.

Ware, John. *Hints to Young Men, on the True Relation of the Sexes.* Boston: Tappan, Whittemore & Mason, 1850.

B. Women and the Health-Reform Movement

There is no satisfactory published study of the movement to improve the health of women through reform in dress, physical education, and a variety of mind cures of which Mesmerism and Christian Science were outstanding examples. The movement had a variety of sources following the Civil War. Women who were gaining access to medical education through study in Europe were powerful advocates of reforms in dress to avoid the damage to the spine and ribs produced by tight lacing and the harm to the circulatory system produced by many styles which required constant pressure on the waist or the ribs. Women of feminist leanings who had struggled with varieties of emotional illness became publicists for Mesmerism, while women in rebellion against neurotic illness and the drastic remedies of professional medicine launched movements such as Christian Science.* Proponents of exercise and physical culture for women took their justification from Social Darwinism and encouraged the development of strong, healthy females for the eugenic betterment of society. All these changes were signs of the shifting of attitude brought about by the acceptance of evolutionary biology, for social progress now required health in women and the publication of popular medical texts like Dr. George H. Napheys' *The Physical Life of Women*

*See Section VII.

(1869) discussed the subject of the female body in practical and relatively matter-of-fact terms.

Harriet Martineau's *Letters on Mesmerism* (1845) should be seen as a courageous account of her recovery from crippling illness following hypnosis. These were widely read following the publication by Martineau's regular physician of his records of her case. (See Thomas Greenhow, *Medical Report of the Case of Miss H- M-* (London, 1845)). Martineau's cure and Greenhow's scornful characterization of her recovery, as long predicted by her physician who nonetheless had for years prescribed heavy doses of opiates to relieve the pain of a tumor pressing on her spine, serve as a useful vignette of the appeal of mesmerism when compared with a standard medical practice which was so accepting of female invalidism. Valerie Kossew Pichanick's *Harriet Martineau: The Woman and Her Work 1802-1876* (1980) provides a balanced discussion of Martineau's medical ills and the widespread impact of her writing on matters of illness and mesmerism. Abba Louisa Woolson, ed., *Dress-Reform; A Series of Lectures Delivered in Boston, on Dress as It Affects the Health of Women* (1874) provides a vivid sample of the new arguments for dress reform as a contributor to women's health and sound bodily functioning developed by women physicians. Particularly striking for the audiences and readers of the day were the reports of postmortems performed on females whose bones or vital organs were deformed as a result of current fashions in dress. Women were urged to wear loosely fitting clothes, supported from the shoulders rather than from the waist, and to wear warm garments covering the chest and legs effectively in the winter. The proponents of reform were careful to distinguish themselves from feminist radicals such as Mrs. Lydia Bloomer. They made clear that their goal was to improve women's health so as to improve their capacity for female functions, not to seek equality with men. Woolson was quick to point out that major changes in dress required considerable psychological adjustment, whereas she and her followers merely wanted to modify existing styles in ways conducive to women's health.

Alongside more healthful dress went a more healthful diet, for current fashions in food and clothing combined to produce problems of the digestive system. Nineteenth-century mores resulted in the definition of a "fine table" as one loaded with overcooked meats, pickles, and pies. Fresh fruit and vegetables were thought harmful to the digestion, and strong coffee had replaced the tisanes and fruit punches of the eighteenth century. Sylvester Graham's contribution to the popular health movement was to prescribe a diet of cereals, fresh vegetables, and fruits and to forbid the consumption of meat, heavy pastries and coffee or tea. Richard H. Shryock,

in his "Sylvester Graham and the Popular Health Movement,
1830-1870" (1931), traces the extent of Graham's influence
and the links which were popularly accepted between sound diet
and mental or nervous health.

Robert E. Riegel was one of the first historians to draw
attention to the links between the popularity of phrenology
and support for health reform. Riegel's "Early Phrenology in
the United States" (1930), addressed to a medical readership,
and "The Introduction of Phrenology to the United States"
(1933) stressed the role of leading phrenologists as educators of the public on healthful exercise, dress, and diet.
More recent commentary has focused attention on the eccentric-
ities of the leaders of popular phrenology than on their role
as educators. Thus John D. Davies' *Phrenology: Fad and Science*
(1955) and Madeleine B. Stern's *Heads and Headlines: The Phrenological Fowlers* (1971) give prominence to the extraordinary
Fowler family, their range of interests and the popular response to them. Karl M. Dallenbach, on the other hand, sees
in the popular response to phrenology a cultural demand for
simple psychological insight far removed from the learned
European culture that produced psychoanalysis ("Phrenology
Versus Psychoanalysis" (1955)).

William B. Walker's unpublished thesis, "The Health Reform
Movement in the U.S., 1830-1870" (Johns Hopkins University,
1955), weaves the strands of health reform together in a coherent narrative which explains both the intellectual sources
for the movement and the nature of popular response. He is
careful to point out that the new concern with physical education for women, customarily linked to the founding of colleges for women, had broader roots in the general concern with
a more healthful life for women.

We can date the more general interest in physical education from the spread of the movement for free tax-supported
public schools in mid-nineteenth-century America. This movement spawned a fierce debate as to the relative merits of
military drill or Swedish gymnastics for the health of male
students and by extension prompted an interest in the potential benefits of gymnastics for the health of women. The
pioneer founders of schools for women such as Catherine
Beecher, Emma Willard, and Mary Lyon had all favored calisthenics as a stimulus to mental alertness and the next generation of leaders in women's education expanded this interest
because of the medical theories indicating that exertions of
the mind might limit women's fertility or their mental balance. Thus the first class of women at Smith College in the
1870s were given calisthenics by instructors trained in Dio
Lewis's School of Gymnastics founded in Boston in the year
1860. By the 1890s when the first full-scale gymnasiums

for women were built, the "natural exercise theories" aimed
at developing muscular strength and lung capacity of Dr. Dudley A. Sargent, Director of the Gymnasium and Assistant Professor of Physical Training at Harvard, had become the standard program for women's colleges and for schools for women.
Meanwhile the need to provide for exercise programs for women
in the school system encouraged the admission of women to normal schools offering training in physical education. The
first normal schools were established in Boston and New York,
but their programs were quickly exported to the midwest through
the inclusion of physical education in the subjects treated at
the annual summer sessions of the Chatauqua Institution. By
1900 the first experimental studies of the effects of exercise
on women's health had been carried out at eastern women's colleges and the benefits of competition in basketball, fencing,
and gymnastics were being debated. Proponents of women's team
sports cited the value of team participation in ethical development and character building, while opponents of competitive development in women claimed that women who participated
in athletic contests were made more masculine and lost many
of the most important female virtues such as modesty and physical fragility. The debate on the value of the experience
of competition was to continue unabated through the first half
of the nineteenth century, but by 1900 there was general acceptance of the value of exercise for female health and of
the importance of outdoor play in parks and of physical exercise programs in schools.

General works on the history of physical education and
athletics in the United States date from the decade of the
1920s after the establishment of graduate physical-education
programs in both public and private universities. Emmett A.
Rice's *A Brief History of Physical Education* (1926), Fred Eugene Leonard's *A Guide to the History of Physical Education*
(1927), and Georgia Borg Johnson's *Organization of the Required
Physical Education for Women in State Universities* (1927) are
examples of the kinds of research and historical narrative produced in the 1920s. They focus on the European origins of
the physical-education systems adopted in nineteenth-century
America, and tend to justify a national commitment to physical
exercise through the school system in terms of its relationship to health, rather than through a return to Greek educational ideals on the importance of athletics in moral development.

Dorothy S. Ainsworth's *The History of Physical Education
in Colleges for Women* (1930) traces the movement for physical
education for women through three periods, the first from
1860 to the 1880s motivated by the desire to use exercise to
cure deformities brought about by customs in dress, the second

informed by the value of exercise as a preventive measure
against ill health, and the third inspired by the influence
of John Dewey and Progressive education directed toward ethical and social development as well as to the goal of health
and fitness. Mary Taylor Bissell's *Physical Development and
Exercise for Women* (1891) is one of the best examples of the
view of exercise as a preventive measure forestalling the
usual dangers of female ill health. By contrast Thomas Denison Wood and Rosalind Frances Cassidy's *The New Physical Education: A Program of Naturalized Activities for Education
Toward Citizenship* (1927) is the classic statement of the use
of physical education programs in social development. It is
noteworthy for its hostility to competition for either males
or females and for its deliberate blurring of the line between exercise and recreation.

Two pieces of biographical and autobiographical writing
capture the mood and social values of the period. Mary F.
Eastman and Ceilia Clark Lewis's *The Biography of Dio Lewis*
(1891) conveys the missionary zeal of those wishing to educate women for health. Dudley A. Sargent's *Autobiography*
(1927) contains a charming account of his discoveries about
women's athletic prowess as supervisor of physical education
programs at the Annex, shortly to become Radcliffe College.
These may be supplemented by Lucille Eaton Hill et al.,
Athletics and Outdoor Sports for Women (1903), Harriet Isabel
Ballantine's "Out-of-Door Sports for College Women" (1898)
and Ray Greene Huling, "College Women and Physical Training"
(1894). A noteworthy piece of early research is reported in
Sophia Foster Richardson, "Tendencies in Athletics for Women
in Colleges and Universities," *Popular Science Monthly*
(February 1897). Senda Berenson's *Basketball for Women*
(1901) contains the rationale for Berenson's decision to
introduce new rules for the game to suit the supposed needs
of women players and in so doing provides valuable evidence
about assumptions concerning women's physical endurance and
athletic abilities.

The most useful source of information on the popularity
of water therapy for nervous and physical ailments is Harry B.
Weiss and Howard R. Kemble, *The Great American Water-Cure
Craze* (1967). Weiss and Kemble attempt to explain the fashion
for hydrotherapy in terms of rebellion against standard medical treatments which relied heavily on opium as a painkiller
and on leeching and bleeding as a cure for fevers and inflam-
mations. A broader cultural view of the new significance of
hydrotherapy may be found in Siegfried Giedion's *Mechanization Takes Command* (1948) in which Giedion reviews the reasons
for the selection of the shower bath as the most healthful
form of bathing between 1840 and 1870 and the reasons for the

American concern with the bathroom as an adjunct to the bedroom providing a place of rest and renewal through the assumed regenerative qualities of water. Kathryn Kish Sklar,
in her *Catharine Beecher: A Study in American Domesticity*
(1973), points out that water-cure spas could be valuable for
women's health simply by bringing women together in a climate
which encouraged free discussion of the female body and its
functions and enabled women to teach one another about folk
medicine.

Thus we can see many positive results of the new biological
definition of the female and the new focus on her contribution to evolutionary progress. This definition was responsible for a new openness in writing and speaking about women's
diseases and about patterns of dress, diet, and exercise that
would promote women's health. However, it is important to
read the medical manuals and the health reformer's argument
alongside the marriage manuals of the period. Marriage manuals of necessity address the question of women's status
within the family and the nature of her relationships with men.
They thus state directly or imply what the new interest in
women's health was for and how it related to her position in
society.

BIBLIOGRAPHY

Ainsworth, Dorothy S. *The History of Physical Education in
    Colleges for Women*. New York: A.S. Barnes and Co., 1930.

Ballantine, Harriet I. "Out-of-Door Sports for College
    Women." *American Physical Education Review* 3 (1898):
    38-43.

Berenson, Senda, ed. *Line Basketball, or Basketball for
    Women*. New York: American Sports Publishing Co., 1901.

Bissell, Mary T. *Physical Development and Exercise for
    Women*. New York: Dodd, Mead & Co., 1891.

"[The] Bloomer Costume." *The Water Cure Journal*, May 1853:
    106.

Cassidy, Rosalind Frances. "Trends in Women's Athletics."
    The Woman's Press, November 1939:451-452.

Conn, Mrs. Josef. "Physical Regeneration of Women." *The
    Humanitarian*, February 1899:116-120.

Dallenbach, Karl M. "Phrenology versus Psychoanalysis."
    American Journal of Psychology 68 (1955):511-525.

Davies, John D. Phrenology: Fad and Science; a Nineteenth-
    Century American Crusade. New Haven: Yale University
    Press, 1955.

Eastman, Mary F., and Lewis, Ceilia Clark. The Biography of
    Dio Lewis. New York: Fowler & Wells Co., 1891.

Fletcher, J. Hamilton. "Feminine Athletics." Good Words 20
    (1879):533-536.

Garrignes, Henry J. "Woman and the Bicycle." The Forum,
    January 1896:579-587.

Giedion, Siegfried. Mechanization Takes Command, a Contribu-
    tion to Anonymous History. New York: Oxford University
    Press, 1948.

Greenhow, Thomas. Medical Report on the Case of Miss H- M-.
    London: S. Highley, 1945.

Hill, Lucille Eaton, et al. Athletics and Outdoor Sports for
    Women. New York: Macmillan Co., 1903.

Huling, Ray Greene. "College Women and Physical Training."
    Educational Review 7 (1894):78-80.

Johnson, Georgia Borg. Organization of the Required Physical
    Education for Women in State Universities. New York:
    Columbia University, 1927.

LeGarde, Ellen. "Physical Training at Bryn Mawr and Welles-
    ley." The Woman's Journal, July 1890:214.

Leiter, Frances W. "Physical Education for Women." World's
    Congress of Representative Women (1893):877-879.

Leonard, Fred Eugene. A Guide to the History of Physical
    Education. Philadelphia: Lea & Febiger, 1927.

Martineau, Harriet. Letters on Mesmerism. London: E. Moxon,
    1845.

Mortimer, Geoffrey. "The Physical Development of Women."
    The Humanitarian, August 1901:111-118.

Napheys, George H. *The Physical Life of Woman: Advice to the Maiden, Wife, and Mother.* Philadelphia: G. Maclean, 1869.

Pichanick, Valerie K. *Harriet Martineau: The Woman and Her Work, 1802-1876.* Ann Arbor: University of Michigan Press, 1980.

Powell, Lillian. "The Physical Culture of Girls." *The Humanitarian,* August 1901:111-118.

Putnam, Granville B. "The Introduction of Gymnastics in New England." *The New England Magazine,* September 1980: 110-113.

Rice, Emmett A. *A Brief History of Physical Education.* New York: A.S. Barnes & Co., 1926.

Richardson, Sophia Foster. "Tendencies in Athletics for Women in Colleges and Universities." *Popular Science Monthly,* February 1897.

Riegel, Robert. "Early Phrenology in the United States." *Medical Life* 35 (1930):361-376.

Riegel, Robert E. "The Introduction of Phrenology to the United States." *American Historical Review* 39 (1933): 73-78.

Sargent, Dudley A. *Autobiography.* Philadelphia: Lea & Febiger, 1927.

Shryock, Richard H. "Sylvester Graham and the Popular Health Movement, 1830-1870." *Mississippi Valley Historical Review* 18 (1931):172-183.

Sklar, Kathryn Kish. *Catharine Beecher: A Study in American Domesticity.* New Haven: Yale University Press, 1973.

Stern, Madeleine B. *Heads and Headlines: The Phrenological Fowlers.* Norman: University of Oklahoma Press, 1971.

Waite, Frederick C. "Dr. Lydia Folger Fowler." *Annals of Medical History* 4 (1932):290-297.

Walker, Gertrude. "Physical Education in Women's Colleges." *The Woman's Journal,* March 1885:90.

Walker, William B. "The Health Reform Movement in the U.S., 1830-1870." Ph.D. dissertation, Johns Hopkins University, 1955.

Weiss, Harry B., and Kemble, Howard R. *The Great American
    Water-Cure Craze, a History of Hydropathy in the United
    States.* Trenton, N.J.: Past Times Press, 1967.

Wood, Thomas Denison, and Cassidy, Rosalind Frances. *The New
    Physical Education: A Program of Naturalized Activities
    for Education Toward Citizenship.* New York: Macmillan
    Co., 1927.

Woolson, Abba Louisa. *Dress-Reform: A Series of Lectures
    Delivered in Boston, on Dress as It Affects the Health
    of Women.* Boston: Roberts Brothers, 1874.

Ziegler, Earle F., ed. *A History of Physical Education and
    Sport in the United States and Canada.* Champaign, Ill.:
    Stipes, 1975.

C. Marriage Manuals and
Advice About Sex Roles

A chronological study of books of advice about the marriage relationship and the appropriate roles for husband and
wife demonstrates a clear pattern of change from the evangelical emphasis on the sacramental nature of the home and parent-
hood, seen as stages in the pursuit of heavenly happiness, to
an evolutionary concern with sound mate selection, healthy
reproduction and the pursuit of legitimate sexual pleasure
within the marriage union. The major points of transition
occur during the early 1850s when a significant body of writing on marriage was produced by disciples of phrenology or
mesmerism, in the 1860s when the emergence of the medical
specialty of gynecology prompted physicians to offer expert
advice on the marriage relationship, and in the 1890s when
moralists began to express concern about the durability of
marriage, perceived declines in fertility and the appropriate
patterning of roles within marriage.
The evangelical view of marriage is admirably conveyed by
James Bean's *The Christian Minister's Affectionate Advice to
a New Married Couple* (1814). William Thayer's *Pastor's
Wedding Gift* (1854) is a later variant of this genre which is
already influenced by ideas drawn from popular science and
mingles advice on healthy patterns of life with moral instruction. In these works marriage is seen as a union designed to
ensure the salvation of both spouses and their offspring.
Because of the necessity of securing the conversion of children and the perfection of their spiritual development, the
role of the wife is seen as one which is spiritually the equal

of her spouse, though her complete subordination in economic
and social terms is taken as given.

By the 1850s works like George W. Quinby's *Marriage and
the Duties of the Marriage Relations* (1852) and Lorenzo
Fowler's *Marriage; Its History and Ceremonies* (1847) began to
display an historical sense that the institution of marriage
was a product of social evolution. Nelson Sizer's *Thoughts
on Domestic Life* (1850) is also evidence of the tendency to
view the family and domesticity as subject to changes in
function though Sizer is clear that women's role within the
family must be preserved. Thus we see popular science prompting an historical and comparative view of marriage and encouraging speculation about sex roles. This is certainly most
evident in Lorenzo Fowler's writing which is the most sweeping
in its readiness to apply his ideas about mental health and
sexual adjustment to a broad range of social institutions.

The free-wheeling speculation unleashed by phrenology and
the mesmerists' concern with mental health is reined in in
the new school of medical writing about marriage. Edward
Bliss Foote's *Medical Common Sense; Applied to the Causes,
Prevention and Cure of Chronic Diseases and Unhappiness in
Marriage* (1858) takes the existing institution and its pattern
of relationships for granted and adopts a common sense attitude toward the care and prevention of so-called "women's
diseases." George Napheys, the most widely read of the medical commentators, permits himself occasional asides about the
marriage relationship. Personal hygiene in women is essential to retain a spouse's affection. Her bodily makeup en-
sures that she will find happiness in marriage and frustration
in single life. His prose describing the afflictions of the
menopause is vivid, and his study of women's physical life
ends at the conclusion of the reproductive years, although
changing patterns of mortality might well have warranted some
discussion of life beyond the menopause. Naphey's tone is of
the expert offering information and assistance, throwing new
light in dark places. Thus he writes favorably of female
sexual pleasure, believes that conception is aided by orgasm,
and cautions against too frequent pregnancies. This positive
view is, however, modified by his view of the wife's responsibility to continue to interest her husband while the responsibility for controlling conception is firmly placed with
the male partner.

Uncertainty about the morality of controlling conception
or outright denunciation of family limitation can be docu-
mented in Augustus Gardner's *Conjugal Sins* (1870) and E.B.
Duffey's *The Relations of the Sexes* (1876). George McLean's
The Curtain Lifted (1887) and James R. Miller's *The Wedded
Life* (1886) are more popular versions of the medical writing

introduced by Foote and Napheys and are equally clear about
the responsibility of the female for retaining her physical
attractiveness and securing her spouse's faithfulness.

By 1888 we have a new set of concerns with the marital
relationship expressed in such works as H.S. Pomeroy's *The
Ethics of Marriage* (1888) which attempts to examine the ethical implications of female subordination, the control of
fertility, and the pursuit of sexual pleasure within the
marriage union. J.A. Houser's *Is Marriage a Failure, or,
Lessons of Life* (1892) and John L. Brandt's *Marriage and the
Home* (1892) both express ambiguity and uncertainty about the
relationship between the pursuit of sexual pleasure in marriage, the limitation of family size, and the early arguments
of divorce reformers that marriage unions that did not produce happiness and sexual adjustment should be terminated.
George Shinn's *Friendly Talks about Marriage* (1897) takes on
the tone of the modern sex counselor in its conversational
style but skirts the question of divorce, though Shinn, like
others of his generation, favors the controlling of conception if this is clearly understood to be a male responsibility.

In sum we may see in the books of advice about the marriage relationship a complex mixture of intellectual and
social forces at work. On the one hand, we may clearly trace
the decline of clerical guidance on marital matters and its
replacement by a scientific and secular culture. On the
other, it is clear that as learned or "official" science advanced during the nineteenth century, its publicists and
practitioners restricted the range of social issues to which
they would apply new knowledge of human physiology and sexuality and adopted a position firmly opposed to the liberation of female sensuality outside the marriage union. The
new knowledge of human physiology itself began to extend life
expectancy after the 1860s, though this did not prompt speculation about the female role beyond the reproductive years.
Much more important the definition of the marriage union as
one directed toward the pursuit of pleasure and only to a
limited extent toward reproduction placed a new responsibility on the female partner to preserve youth and to remain
sexually attractive. In the absence of any lively interaction between clerical culture and the institutions of learned
science, the field of speculation about the ethical aspects
of the marriage relationship was left open to secular moralists, while the early stages of the movement for easy access
to divorce began to focus attention on the family and domesticity seen in historically relative terms.

Scholarly comment on these trends is as yet limited to
periodical literature except for the full-length works treating the movement for divorce reform and the movement for

legalized access to birth-control information. Of these
William O'Neill's *Divorce in the Progressive Era* (1967) treats
this period in an admirable introductory section tracing the
intellectual antecedents of divorce reform. David M. Kennedy's
Birth Control in America (1970) devotes several chapters to
the nineteenth century and Linda Gordon's *Woman's Body,*
Woman's Right: A Social History of Birth Control in America
(1977) traces changes in attitudes to women's sexual pleasure.
Charles E. Rosenberg's "Sexuality, Class and Role in Nineteenth Century America" (1973) attempts an overview of the
forces dictating female subordination in the transition from
religious to secular culture. Carroll Smith-Rosenberg's
"Beauty, the Beast and the Militant Woman: A Case Study in
Sex Roles and Social Stress in Jacksonian America" (1971)
introduces the subject of emerging social pressures placing
the responsibility for sexual attractiveness on the female,
a response the author sees as related to unrecognized tensions arising from social change.

An important question which remains unanswered is why
the transition to secular culture took such a conservative
form with respect to female sexuality and women's social and
economic subordination. As yet no historical enquiry has
made clear precisely why the popular scientific culture was
so feminist and why the relationship between popular science
and social speculation was not preserved in the new discipline
of the social sciences. These are all questions related to
the social forces which produced professions in twentieth-
century America, and the new pattern of roles and power relationships which emerged as a result of the rationalizing
forces at work alike in economic, social and intellectual life.
While it has been customary to see the battle for easier divorce or for access to birth control information as "progressive" reforms, this particular focus on chronology obscures
the larger questions raised by examining the transition from
religious to secular culture in the nineteenth century. It
also obscures completely the convergence of forces which
linked the female to biological conditioning and defined her
in terms of reproductive functions. If we take the longer
view, we may see the acceptance of Freudian ideas as the
culmination of nineteenth-century thought about sexuality
rather than the supposed revolution in ideas historians have
associated with the 1920s.

BIBLIOGRAPHY

Bean, James. *The Christian Minister's Affectionate Advice*
 to a Married Couple. New York: American Tract Society,
 1814.

Brandt, John L. *Marriage and the Home*. Chicago: Laird & Lee, 1892.

Duffey, Eliza Bisbee. *The Relations of the Sexes*. New York: Estill & Co., 1876.

Eliot, William G. *Lectures to Young Women*. 3rd ed. Boston: Crosby, Nichols & Co., 1854.

Foote, Edward Bliss. *Medical Common Sense; Applied to the Causes, Prevention and Cure of Chronic Diseases and Unhappiness in Marriage*. Philadelphia: Duane, Rolison, 1858.

Fowler, Lorenzo Niles. *Marriage; Its History and Ceremonies with a Phrenological and Physiological Exposition*. New York: Fowler & Wells, 1847.

Gardner, Augustus K. *Conjugal Sins Against the Laws of Life and Health and Their Effect Upon the Father, Mother and Child*. New York: J.S. Redfield, 1870.

Gordon, Michael. "The Ideal Husband as Depicted in the Nineteenth Century Marriage Manual." *Family Coordinator* 18 (1969):226-231.

Holcombe, William H. *The Sexes, Here and Hereafter*. Philadelphia: Lippincott, 1862.

Houser, James Alfred. *Is Marriage a Failure, or, Lessons of Life*. c. 1892.

McLean, George N. *The Curtain Lifted: Hidden Secrets Revealed*. Chicago: Lewis Publishing Co., 1887.

Mantegazza, Paolo. *The Art of Taking a Wife*. New York: G.W. Dillingham, 1894.

Miller, James R. *The Wedded Life*. Philadelphia: Presbyterian Board of Publication, 1886.

Napheys, George. *The Physical Life of Woman: Advice to Maiden, Wife and Mother*. Philadelphia: G. Maclean, 1869.

Pomeroy, Hiram Sterling. *The Ethics of Marriage*. New York: Funk & Wagnalls, 1888.

Quinby, George W. *Marriage and the Duties of the Marriage Relations.* Cincinnati: J.A. & U.P. James, 1852.

Reed, James. *Man and Woman, Equal but Unlike.* Boston: Nichols & Noyes, 1870.

Saunders, Frederick. *About Woman, Love and Marriage.* New York: G.W. Carleton & Co., 1868.

Shinn, George. *Friendly Talks about Marriage.* Boston: J. Knight Co., 1897.

Sizer, Nelson. *Thoughts on Domestic Life, Its Concord and Discord.* New York: Fowler & Wells, 1850.

Stockham, Alice B. *Karezza: Ethics of Marriage.* Chicago: A.B. Stockham & Co., 1896.

Talmage, Thomas DeWitt. *The Marriage Ring.* New York: Funk & Wagnalls, 1886.

Thayer, William M. *Pastor's Wedding Gift.* Boston: John P. Jewett & Co., 1854.

Thorold, Anthony Wilson. *On Marriage.* New York: H.M. Caldwell Co., 1896.

Wells, Samuel R. *Wedlock; or, The Right Relations of the Sexes: Disclosing the Laws of Conjugal Selection, and Showing Who May, and Who May Not Marry.* New York: S.R. Wells, 1869.

The Young Husband's Book. Philadelphia: Carey, Lea & Blanchard, 1836.

Twentieth-Century Commentary

Benfield, Ben Barker. "The Spermatic Economy: A Nineteenth Century View of Sexuality." *Feminist Studies* 1 (1972): 49–64.

Collins, Randall. "A Conflict Theory of Sexual Stratification." *Social Problems* 19 (1971):3–21.

Gordon, Linda. *Woman's Body, Woman's Right: A Social History of Birth Control in America.* New York: Penguin Books, 1977.

Kennedy, David M. *Birth Control in America: The Career of Margaret Sanger*. New Haven: Yale University Press, 1970.

O'Neill, William. *Divorce in the Progressive Era*. New Haven: Yale University Press, 1967.

Rosenberg, Charles E. "Sexuality, Class and Role in Nineteenth Century America." *American Quarterly* 25 (1973): 131-153.

Sears, Hal D. "The Sex Radicals in High Victorian America." *Virginia Quarterly Review* 48 (1972):377-392.

Smith-Rosenberg, Carroll. "Beauty, the Beast and the Militant Woman: A Case Study in Sex Roles and Social Stress in Jacksonian America." *American Quarterly* 25 (1971): 562-584.

Strong, Floyd Bryan. "Sex, Character and Reform in America, 1830-1920." Ph.D. Dissertation, Stanford University, 1972.

AUTHOR INDEX

Abbott, Edith 57, 76, 94, 97, 229, 232
Abbott, John S.C. 33, 35
Abbott, Lyman 211, 212
Abrahall, Frances H. 112
Abrahams, Harold J. 92
Adams, Abigail 26
Adams, Charles Francis 194, 195
Adams, Hannah 47, 49
Adams, John 26
Addams, Jane 60, 99, 100, 102, 215, 216, 220, 221
Addison, Daniel Dulany 155, 159
Ahlstrom, Sydney E. 163, 165
Aiken, Conrad 124
Aikman, Louisa Susannah (Wells) 196
Ainsworth, Dorothy S. 265, 267
Albelda, Randy 228, 232
Alcott, Bronson 35
Alcott, William A. 35, 70, 254, 259
Aldrich, Mark 228, 232
Alexander, William 10
Allen, Grant (Rayner, Olive Pratt) 69
Allinson, William J. 53
Almgren, P.E. 22
Altbach, Edith 246, 247
American Academy of Political Science 221
Ames, Azel 63, 64
Amundsen, Kirsten 219, 221
Anderson, Mary 64

Andrews, Benjamin 79
Andrews, Edward Demira 50, 53, 179
Andrews, John B. 229, 232
Anthony, Katherine 194, 195, 201, 202
Anthony, Susan B. 199
Archorn, Erik 182
Aries, Philippe 6, 32, 38
Arndt, Karl J. 179
Arnold, Helen E. 124
Atkins, Gordon 76
Austin, Anne L. 106
Austin, Benjamin Fish 241, 243
Austin, George Lowell 259
Austin, Rev. Principal 70

Bailey, Florence A. (Merriam) 186
Bailey, Mrs. Abigail (Abbot) 28, 30
Bailey, Nettie F. 112
Bailyn, Bernard 83, 90
Baker, Elizabeth F. 73
Ballantine, Harriet Isabel 266, 267
Bancroft, Gertrude 57
Banner, Lois W. 168, 170
Bard, Samuel 9, 11
Barger, Harold 73, 77
Barnard, Hannah 53
Barnes, Gilbert H. 167, 170
Barnett, Ida Wells 111, 112
Barrett, John P. 73
Barry, Richard 211, 212